Lucky
Man

Lucky
Man

A Memoir

MICHAEL J. FOX

New York

ISBN: 0-7868-6764-7

Hyperion books are available for special promotions and premiums. For details, contact Hyperion Special Markets, 77 West 66th Street, 11th floor, New York, New York 10023-6298, or call 212-456-0100.

FIRST EDITION

10 9 8 7 6 5 4 3 2 1

In Memory Of
Dad & Nana

Dedicated with all of my love to Tracy, Sam, Aquinnah, Schuyler, Esmé
and of course,
Mom

In accumulating property for ourselves or our posterity, in founding a family or a state, or acquiring fame even, we are mortal; but in dealing with truth we are immortal, and need fear no change nor accident.
—Henry David Thoreau

Lucky
Man

CHAPTER ONE

A Wake-up Call

Gainesville, Florida — November 1990

> *I woke up to find the message in my left hand. It had me trembling. It wasn't a fax, telegram, memo, or the usual sort of missive bringing disturbing news. In fact, my hand held nothing at all. The trembling was the message.*

I was feeling a little disoriented. I'd only been shooting the movie in Florida for a week or so, and the massive, pink-lacquered, four-poster bed surrounded by the pastel hues of the University Center Hotel's Presidential Suite still came as a bit of a shock each morning. Oh yeah: and I had a ferocious hangover. That was less shocking.

It was a Tuesday morning, so while I couldn't recall the exact details of the previous night's debauchery, it was a pretty safe bet that it had something to do with Monday Night Football. In those first few seconds of consciousness, I didn't know what time it was, but I could be fairly certain that I hadn't overslept. If I was needed on set, there would have been a phone call from my assistant, Brigette. If I had to leave the hotel at 10:00 A.M., let's say, she would have called at 9:30, again at 9:40, then finally at 9:50 she would have taken the elevator from her floor up to mine, let herself into my room, propelled me to the shower, and slipped into the kitchen to brew a pot of coffee. None of that having transpired, I knew I had at least a few minutes.

Even with the lights off, blinds down, and drapes pulled, an offensive amount of light still filtered into the room. Eyes clenched shut, I placed the palm of my left hand across the bridge of my nose in a weak attempt to block the glare. A moth's wing—or so I thought—fluttered against my right cheek. I opened my eyes, keeping my hand suspended an inch or two in front of my face so I could finger-flick the little beastie across the room. That's when I noticed my pinkie. It was trembling, twitching, auto-animated. How long this had been going on I wasn't exactly sure. But now that I noticed it, I was surprised to discover that I couldn't stop it.

Weird—maybe I slept on it funny. Five or six times in rapid succession I pumped my left hand into a fist, followed by a vigorous shaking out. Interlocking the fingers of each hand steeple-style with their opposite number, I lifted them up and over behind my head and pinned them to the pillow.

Tap. Tap. Tap. Like a moisture-free Chinese water torture, I could feel a gentle drumming at the back of my skull. If it was trying to get my attention, it had succeeded. I withdrew my left hand from behind my head and held it in front of my face, steadily, with fingers splayed—

like the bespectacled X-ray glasses geek in the old comic book ad. I didn't have to see the underlying skeletal structure; the information I was looking for was right there in the flesh: a thumb, three stock-still fingers, and out there on the lunatic fringe, a spastic pinkie.

It occurred to me that this might have something to do with my hangover, or more precisely, with alcohol. I'd put away a lot of beers in my time, but had never woken up with the shakes; maybe this was what they called delirium tremens? I was pretty sure they would manifest themselves in a more impressive way—I mean, who gets the d.t.'s in one finger? Whatever this was, it wasn't alcoholic deterioration.

Now I did a little experimentation. I found that if I grabbed my finger with my right hand, it would stop moving. Released, it would keep still for four or five seconds, and then, like a cheap wind-up toy, it would whir back to life again. *Hmmm.* What had begun as curiosity was now blossoming into full-fledged worry. The trembling had been going on for a few minutes with no sign of quitting and my brain, fuzzy as it was, scrambled to come up with an explanation. Had I hit my head, injured myself in some way? The tape of the previous night's events was grainy at best. There were a lot of blank spots on it, but there were a couple of possibilities too.

Woody Harrelson was in Gainesville with me on this film, and he had been in the bar the night before—maybe we'd had one of our legendary drunken slap fights. Woody and I were (and remain) close friends, but for some reason after an indeterminable amount of alcohol consumption, we'd find some excuse to start kicking over chairs and stage elaborate mock brawls. No harm was intended, and the majority of punches were pulled, but Woody is a foot taller and fifty pounds heavier than me, which meant that whenever the game got out of hand, I was always the one that took the most serious asskicking. So maybe I'd caught a Harrelson haymaker to the side of the head.

But I couldn't recall any such melee. I did recall, however, a moment at the end of the night, when my bodyguard, Dennis, had had to prop me up against the door frame while he fumbled the key into the door of my suite. By the time he'd turned the knob, my weight had shifted onto the door itself; as he flung it open I'd careened into the room, barreling headfirst into the foyer table. But I didn't feel any bumps, so that couldn't have been it. Any pain in my head was from boozing, not bruising.

IRRECONCILABLE DIFFERENCES

Throughout the course of the morning, the twitching would intensify, as would my search for a cause—not just for the rest of that day, but for months to follow. The true answer was elusive, and in fact wouldn't reveal itself for another full year. The trembling was indeed the message, and this is what it was telling me:

> *That morning—November 13, 1990—my brain was serving notice: it had initiated a divorce from my mind. Efforts to contest or reconcile would be futile; eighty percent of the process, I would later learn, was already complete. No grounds were given, and the petition was irrevocable. Further, my brain was demanding, and incrementally seizing, custody of my body, beginning with the baby: the outermost finger of my left hand.*

Ten years later, knowing what I do now, this mind-body divorce strikes me as a serviceable metaphor—though at the time it was a concept well beyond my grasp. I had no idea there were even problems in the relationship—just assumed things were pretty good between the old gray matter and me. This was a false assumption. Unbeknownst to me, things had been deteriorating long before the morning of the pinkie rebellion. But by declaring its dysfunction in such an arresting fashion, my brain now had my mind's full attention.

It would be a year of questions and false answers that would satisfy me for a time, fueling my denial and forestalling the sort of determined investigation that would ultimately provide the answer. That answer came from a doctor who would inform me that I had a progressive, degenerative, and incurable neurological disorder; one that I may have been living with for as long as a decade before sus-pecting there might be anything wrong. This doctor would also tell me that I could probably continue acting for "another ten good years," and he would be right about that, almost to the day. What he did not tell me—what no one could—is that these last ten years of coming to terms with my disease would turn out to be the best ten years of my life—not in spite of my illness, but because of it.

I have referred to it in interviews as a *gift*—something for which others with this affliction have taken me to task. I was only speaking from my own experience, of course, but I stand partially corrected: if it is a gift, it's the gift that just keeps on taking.

Coping with the relentless assault and the accumulating damage is not easy. Nobody would ever choose to have this visited upon them. Still, this unexpected crisis forced a fundamental life decision: adopt a siege mentality—or embark upon a journey. Whatever it was—courage? acceptance? wisdom?—that finally allowed me to go down the second road (after spending a few disastrous years on the first) was unquestionably a gift—and absent this neurophysiological catastro-phe, I would never have opened it, or been so profoundly enriched. That's why I consider myself a lucky man.

PERVERSITY OF FATE

Recognizing just how much irony figures in my story, I recently looked the word up in the dictionary:

> irony *n.* expression of meaning by use of words normally convey-ing opposite meaning; *apparent perversity of fate or circumstances.*

The definition floored me, particularly the second part, in italics. Now I looked up the word *perverse*: *"directed away from what is right or good . . ."* and realized that here was yet another rich irony. Despite *ap-pearances*, this disease has unquestionably *directed me* toward *what is right or good.* I went back to the first definition—*expression of meaning by use of words normally conveying opposite meaning; apparent perversity of fate or circumstances*—and smiled. How ironic.

Here's one more "apparent perversity": If you were to rush into this room right now and announce that you had struck a deal—with God, Allah, Buddha, Christ, Krishna, Bill Gates, whomever—in which the ten years since my diagnosis could be magically taken away, traded in for ten more years as the person I was before—I would, without a moment's hesitation, tell you to take a hike.

I am no longer the person described in the first few pages of this chapter, and I am forever grateful for that. I would never want to go back to that life—a sheltered, narrow existence fueled by fear and made liveable by insulation, isolation, and self-indulgence. It was a life lived in a bubble—but bubbles, being the most fragile constructions, are easily destroyed. All it takes is a little finger.

BUBBLE BOY

New York—July 1990

> *In order to illustrate the full dimensions of the bubble in which I lived and to trace the events leading up to that fateful morning in Gainesville, I need to go back a few months, and then back a few months more. The story would start, not in a hotel room in Florida, but inside my dressing room–trailer, parked in the Lower East Side. Anyone who's ever come across a film crew shooting on the streets in Manhattan, Los Angeles, or any other American city has seen one of these motor mansions and wondered about the thespian holed up inside. You know we're in there, we know you're out there, and—to put the interests of candor over public relations—we like it that way. The trailer is one of the many bubbles within the bubble.*

On this particular early afternoon, I had a visitor to my trailer, a man I'd never met before. Michael Caton-Jones looked a mess, and that's meant as a compliment—believing, as I do, in a bit of wisdom gleaned from amongst the more scatological offerings scrawled on a toilet stall door in Vancouver's Arts Club Theatre, circa 1978: *A creative mess is better than an idle tidiness.* Shambling into my motor home, Caton-Jones was dripping sweat. His full, ruddy face unshaven, he wore the kind of loose-fitting, mismatched, thrift-store ensemble that was trendy in the summer of 1990, but that he would have worn regardless.

Handshakes, quick, friendly "Good-to-meet-you's" out of the way, he sprawled sideways across one of the Winnebago's two swivel chairs, threadbare from the asses of a thousand actors. "Have you got a beer?"—in a thick Scots burr, more of a mutter than a request. I liked this guy already.

Pulling a Molson's from the mini-fridge, I considered one myself, but instead grabbed a Diet Pepsi—which, contrary to popular belief, was my *second* favorite carbonated beverage. With several scenes remaining on the day's schedule, alcohol was not an option.

It was a blistering July day, the kind that feels especially oppressive in New York City. Heat like that, if you're angry, just makes you madder still, and from outside on the street, above the rattle and drone of traffic, I could hear voices pitched in fury. We were in the Alphabet City section of Manhattan, working on *The Hard Way.* We were technically on lunch break; shooting had been delayed much of the morning because a hastily organized act of civil disobedience blocked our access to the set. A homeless group was protesting outside, pissed off—justifiably—because the city had rousted them from the abandoned tenement they had been occupying. "Unsafe stairwells," the city had told them—then apparently turned around and sold Universal Pictures a film permit to haul thousands of pounds of lighting and camera equipment up those same stairs.

While producers, film commission reps, homeless activists, and city officials huddled in the production trailer trying to hammer out an accord, Mike and I enjoyed the sporadic bursts of air conditioning kicked out by the portable generator and talked movies. Warner Brothers wanted me for a project called *Doc Hollywood*, and with an eye toward green-lighting production that fall, they had flown a few potential directors out to New York to meet me, each pitching his particular take on the material. Caton-Jones was the latest candidate to pay a visit. Not knowing much about the guy—based in London, snooty sounding, *veddy* British hyphenated name—I was surprised and relieved to meet this working-class kid from Glasgow, early thirties at the oldest. His most recent work, *Memphis Belle*, a WWII drama about the final mission of the legendary bomber, was, I thought, a remarkably confident piece of work for such a young director. What he really wanted to do next, he announced, was make a Capra-esque American comedy.

Seated across from each other at the fold-down dinette table, I picked through an oily catering truck salad while he sipped his beer. We debated the best films of Frank Capra, the great populist director whose classics—*Mr. Smith Goes to Washington* and *It's a Wonderful Life*— had lightened the hearts of Depression-era audiences. These were among Michael's favorites, along with *Meet John Doe* starring Gary Cooper and Barbara Stanwyck. A romantic evening early in my relationship with Tracy had started out with a video of *It Happened One Night*—so I had to put that wry, sexy 1939 Clark Gable–Claudette Colbert comedy at the top of my list.

The mention of Colbert led us to 1942's *The Palm Beach Story*, directed not by Capra, but a director/screenwriter we agreed had had an even greater influence on us both: Preston Sturges. In tribute to Sturges, master of the American screwball comedy, Mike said he had named his production company "The Ale and Quail Club," after the train car full of rowdy, hilariously shit-faced millionaires in *Palm Beach Story*. For my part, I confessed that the movie I was working on owed a small debt to Sturges's masterpiece, *Sullivan's Travels*. In *The Hard Way*, I was playing a spoiled young Hollywood movie star who, after traveling incognito to New York, tags alongside a reluctant NYPD detective as research for a role that, he is convinced, will finally get him taken seriously as a dramatic actor—you can see how I could relate. In Sturges's film, Joel McCrea is a director who assumes the life of a hobo, an experience that, he is convinced, will prepare him to tell a cinematic story possessing much deeper social relevance than the silly but popular comedies that have brought him fame and riches. McCrea's character eventually discovers that the films he was already making had great meaning for his escape-hungry audiences. I discovered, in the end, that *The Hard Way* owed less to *Sullivan's Travels* than it did to *Beverly Hills Cop*, *Cobra*, or any of a number of other big-budget action movies.

Interrupted by a knock on the door, we looked up to see Charlie Croughwell enter, unbidden and apologetic. An inch or so shorter than me, ten pounds less body and twenty pounds more muscle, Charlie is even tougher than he looks—and he looks like George Raft.

"Sorry, Mike . . . but it doesn't look like we're getting inside that building today, so they're setting up to toss you through the barroom window in about a half an hour."

I had to laugh; it was typical of Charlie to phrase it that way. In truth, I wasn't being flung through any window—he was. Whatever hardships his diminutive stature may have presented in his life—and I could easily identify—it had been my good fortune that someone of his physical proportions, as well as skill, had chosen to become a stuntman. He had not only saved my ass on a number of jobs, but had accomplished the not-inconsiderable feat of actually making me look rugged.

"I've got the pads on now, but I'll give 'em to you for the roll-in." The roll-in: I lie down in roughly the same place my double made his nasty, bone-threatening landing. On "Action," I roll fully into the shot and, grimacing in shock and agony, expose my face to the camera's lens—as deliberately as Chuck had hidden his.

After I introduced Charlie to the visiting director, he left to prepare the stunt. Michael and I picked up the thread of our conversation, moving now to the Warner Brothers project, about which I felt lukewarm at best.

Based loosely on the book *What? Dead Again?*—the story of a surgeon who, waylaid in a small Southern town, grew to love it, and to establish a practice there—the *Doc Hollywood* script had been on my desk for months. It was funny, but more *Green Acres* than Frank Capra. Picaresque to a fault, it was a string of amusing anecdotal scenes with no cohesive arc or storyline to bind them. The secondary characters, stereotypical Southern rubes—Gomers and Aunt Beas—were as familiar as yesterday's reruns. The hero, the young doctor, was purely vain and avaricious; the script gave you no reason to root for him. But my reservations about the material paled in comparison to my reservations about taking on another film so soon after *The Hard Way*. There was a long list of excellent reasons to sit this one out, take a breather.

PERPETUAL MOTION

First of all, *The Hard Way* had been a trial. With a greater emphasis on pure action, and more spectacular stunts, than anything I'd ever done, I had taken a physical beating on this picture, the best efforts of Charlie notwithstanding. My co-star, James Woods, is a genius, an amazing actor, but to hold your half of the screen with someone of that intensity requires an energy, concentration, and vigilance that wore me out. Add in a tight schedule, a hyperkinetic character, and several reshoots of key scenes due to personnel hirings and firings, and I was left even more ragged than usual. I needed rest. A long rest.

Were I to sign on, assuming that their goal of an October start date was plausible, *Doc Hollywood* would be my fifth film in less than three years, during which I also taped the seventy-two episodes of *Family Ties*, including the series' emotionally draining last season and finale. A large part of this work had been on-location—film-speak for out-of-town ("town" in this case being either New York or Los Angeles). It was all but certain that a movie set in the South would be filmed, at least in part, on location.

Filming on location is not unusual, or even entirely unappealing. Many in the business consider the opportunity for travel a perk; a break from the structure of their established routines, the demands of their families, communities, schedules, and responsibilities. Many liken it to war—not in the sense of battle or danger, but in that they are thrown together with a group of people, many of them strangers, who have been charged with a single mission: get in, get it done on time, under budget, and get out. Oh yeah—and do your best work. The pressure, isolation, and narrow scope of our lives while at "movie camp" is known to promote prolonged and legendary drinking binges. Time not spent on the set is spent either in a bar or in a coma.

Life can get pretty crazy on a long shoot. *Casualties of War*, the 1988 Vietnam war epic I made with Sean Penn and Brian De Palma in Phuket, Thailand, was rife with some of the most outrageous examples of location fever I've ever witnessed. The stifling tropical heat, the culture shock, and the hurry-up-and-wait rhythm endemic to any film set was a potent combination. Waiting in this context meant waiting for Brian to finish cooking up one of his signature microchoreographed steadi-cam shots. Eager to do our scenes and be done for the day, we'd become restless and start pounding down the local beer. The stuff was rumored to be laced with formaldehyde, but we couldn't read the labels and the locals weren't talking. That's not quite true: they were talking incessantly, but we couldn't understand what they were saying. Formaldehyde, turpentine, Drāno, whatever . . . we'd swill it down and then—the big kick—drive out to the local snake farm and goad each other into drinking shots of a popular Thai cure-all: equal parts Thai whiskey and cobra blood.

Some members of the *C.O.W.* crew, many of whom were Aussies, had hired local prostitutes as companions for their entire stay in-country. One guy set up housekeeping with two women; an oddly civilized arrangement, they would accompany him into Phuket village to do his marketing. When finally asked, "Why two?" he answered, straight-faced, as if it was obvious: "So they can keep each other company while I read the paper in the morning." He obviously wanted to approximate the routines of his ordinary home life but kick it up a notch by including the fulfillment of his sexual fantasy. Location can be nuts.

NO PLACE LIKE HOME

My fantasy—at least it was beginning to seem like a fantasy—was not so much to escape a domestic routine as to establish one. I spent most of our brief engagement on location in Thailand.

Tracy made the marathon transpacific journey for an extended set visit. T never mentioned anything about having second thoughts, but she's a smart, observant woman and I can't imagine she wasn't horrified by the emaciated wreck of a fiancé she found in the jungle—her own personal *Heart of Darkness* featuring her future husband as Col. Kurtz. I'd contracted some nasty strain of exotic stomach rot; she nursed me through it, and as a reward had to battle it herself for the rest of her time in Southeast Asia.

Far more unnerving—hell, it was terrifying—was the weirdness she encountered upon her return to "civilization": waiting for her at home was a series of graphic and vitriolic letters, individually stamped and posted by a single troubled individual, threatening death to Tracy unless she called off the wedding. I remember the phone call. It must have been three or four A.M. Phuket time when I picked up the phone and heard Tracy weeping, spilling out the surreal details. I felt helpless and angry to be thousands of miles away from this woman who, simply by falling in love with me, had apparently placed herself in jeopardy. We decided to hire Gavin De Becker, a widely recognized expert in matters of threat assessment and personal security, to investigate the source of the letters and assign agents to ensure Tracy's safety in my absence. Some months later it was discovered by Gavin and the LAPD that the person responsible for what eventually amounted to more than 5,000 death threats was a lonely, disturbed young woman. After months in jail awaiting trial (at which Tracy and I both had to testify), she was convicted of making "terroristic threats" and ordered to undergo psychiatric treatment.

July 16, 1988: I'd been back from Southeast Asia a little over a week when we were married in a quiet ceremony at a small country inn in Vermont—or at least that had been the idea. In many ways it was the experience we had hoped for, an intimate celebration. Before our friends and family we affirmed our commitment to spend our lives together. But it was something else too, a kind of groundbreaking. My own bubble, the one that had sheltered me through the last seven years of public life, now had to be expanded, renovated into a duplex.

We had invited just seventy-odd guests, close friends and family only. As a precaution we hired Gavin's firm to provide security. This proved to be a wise move: dozens of tabloid reporters and paparazzi attempted to crash the party, deploying helicopters and even undercover spies disguised as llamas in order to blend in with the innkeeper's pet livestock. Locals and waitstaff were bribed and pumped for information, and a surreal siege began. It became a drama of spy vs. spy—and thanks to Gavin, our spies won. The paparazzi were unable to capture even a single photograph of the bride and groom, and the wedding went on exactly as we'd hoped, except maybe for the whir of helicopters overhead.

The honeymoon also had its share of gatecrashers. We island-hopped through the Caribbean, but at each step, we would find ourselves being tailed. Wherever we went, we'd look out our window to find boats anchored just offshore, bearing photographers with 500mm lenses aimed at our honeymoon suite. Finally we made our way to Martha's Vineyard, Massachusetts, where Tracy's family had vacationed during her childhood summers. Resigned to the fact that we were going to have to deal with these interlopers, we figured we might as well face them on our own home turf.

The rush that was my life then meant Tracy and I had no real opportunity to digest the strange twists and turns on the way to the altar, or the extended road comedy that had been our honeymoon. *Family Ties* started up again in August, *Back to the Future II* in the fall of that year (forcing me to moonlight again), segueing right into *Part III,* which wouldn't wrap until January 1990.

My bride, the one and only love of my life, was wondering what in the hell she'd gotten herself into. Pregnant one month after the wedding, Tracy found herself with a husband who, when he wasn't away on the job, was little more than a narcoleptic Lamaze partner. I did, however, negotiate time off to coincide with Sam's birth. A clause inserted into my deal—*labor plus three weeks*—had to be a first for a movie contract. But as soon as the three weeks were over, it was back to work again, leaving T nursing a baby and, no doubt, a few resentments.

Another issue for Tracy—one she rarely broached but that I wish

I'd been sensitive enough to acknowledge more often—was this: in-side of a year, a beautiful, exquisitely talented twenty-something ac-tress, career ascendant, had become a virtual single mother. Schlepping to and from the set, Sam in arms, was not only unfair and exhausting, but it underscored the notion that I was still free to work—that my creative identity was intact, while Tracy's was in limbo. Offers and opportunities were coming in for her; most, but not all, she had to turn down. In fact, as I was in New York shooting *The Hard Way*, Tracy was in San Francisco starring in a film-for-television. Sam, now fourteen months old, was with her, and I missed them both ter-ribly. We had a home in Manhattan, so I was not the one on location this time, she was. I was happy that she was working again. Still, here we were, thousands of miles apart once again.

Our marriage, and more important, our love and friendship, were surviving under the pressures, but the situation was not exactly the stuff of dreams. We were living a scattered, bi-coastal life—with sojourns to Vermont, where we'd bought a farm, in the naïve hope of living a more tranquil life there someday. We desperately longed to settle somewhere, sometime soon. But we'd both begun to wonder: was a normal life even possible?

So, only three months off between *The Hard Way* and *Doc Holly-wood*? No way. Well, at least New York was a fun city for a young di-rector on a studio expense account, I said to myself, because otherwise Caton-Jones was wasting his time. I wasn't doing *Doc Hollywood*. I was absolutely sure of that. . . .

Or was I?

Immensely charming, the sort of artist-as-human-train-wreck I seem drawn toward, Michael Caton-Jones was on his third Molson when I realized the son of a bitch was actually selling me on this project. His pitch put a completely fresh spin on the story. My *Green Acres* concerns vanished; half an hour in a motor home on Avenue B and Michael had convinced me that this movie could represent some-thing important to me—that it had personal significance. Young doc-tor, trained as a plastic surgeon, sets out across country in his Porsche Roadster, leaving the Washington, D.C., combat zone E.R. of his residency. He's Los Angeles–bound, boob jobs, butt tucks, and big money in his future. He cracks up the car in Grady, South Carolina, and the natives, in dire need of a local doctor, conspire to trap him there. A gentle life, the girl of his dreams, and the realization that the brass ring may not be worth reaching for convince him to stay.

My own knuckles white from hanging on to that goddamned brass ring, it sounded good to me.

SOUTHBOUND

Cut to an explosion of sugar-glass—followed by a glittery spray of shards from the nucleus of which emerged Charlie, completing at ferocious speed the exterior half-arc of his brief but turbulent flight through the window. From out on the street, it looked as though he was being propelled by the force of the shattering window, rather than propelled through it. Charlie hit the pavement hard, executing a perfect shoulder roll, with his head tucked, more to avoid the lens than injury. Coming suddenly to a stop, he lay facedown, motionless. As soon as the director yelled cut, Charlie lifted his head and with a modest grin, indicated that he'd lived to be pummeled another day.

After a quick repositioning of the camera angle, I got into place, was sprinkled with pieces of broken sugar glass, and, on hearing "Action," did my roll-in. "Cut-print . . . one more please." As I reset for take two, I glanced up to see Michael Caton-Jones and Charlie Croughwell excitedly plotting the best way to crash Doc Hollywood's Porsche. They both knew I was in, and so did I.

So what had happened to my resolve to take an extended break? To the litany of reasons why my time would be better spent in the bosom of my family, to my understanding that so much time spent on location was taking a toll on me? All this had dissolved in an acid bath of fear and professional insecurity.

Actors don't become actors because they're brimming with self-confidence. Ross Jones, my junior high drama teacher, would, at a certain point in every school production, address the cast: "Remember," he'd say, "we are *all here* because we're not *all there*." An actor's burning ambition, when you think about it, is to spend as much time as possible pretending to be somebody else. For those of us lucky (or unstable) enough to become professional performers, the uncertainty about who we really are only increases. For many actors, this self-doubt is like a worm eating away at you and growing, incongruously, in direct proportion to your level of success. No matter how great the acceptance, adulation, and accumulation of wealth, gnawing at you always is the deep-seated belief that you're a fake, a phony. Even if you can bullshit your way through whatever job you're working on now, you'd better prepare for the likelihood that you're never going to get another one.

In the face of all evidence to the contrary, this is exactly how I felt about my own career in 1990. Throughout the eighties I had worked incessantly, and the rewards had been enormous. Achieving that level of acceptance, getting to the top of the mountain, so to speak, had been arduous, but there were so many new highs on the way up that it felt more like celebration than sweat. Staying there, however, maintaining that foothold, was an ordeal.

A large part of my success was a result of the two "franchises" I had stumbled into—the twin phenomena of *Family Ties* and the *Back to the Future* series. They offered me financial security and the guarantee I could reprise the roles of both Alex Keaton and Marty McFly more or less indefinitely.

This left me free to experiment and accept riskier roles for less money. So when *Light of Day*; *Bright Lights, Big City*; or *Casualties of War* failed to perform at the box office, it was hardly the end of the world. I'd go back to my television series in the fall, and at some point be able to climb back into the DeLorean. But by the summer of 1990, all that had changed. The TV series had wrapped for good, the *Back to the Future* sequels had been released and were already on their way to video. My cockiness had morphed into caution. I just didn't feel comfortable finishing any job without a contract for another in hand. Without the safety net of *Family Ties* and *Back to the Future,* the stakes were greater now than they'd ever been.

If the new project meant time away from my family, that had to be weighed against the reality that I now *had* a family. That hoary old phrase "the lifestyle to which they have become accustomed" suddenly had meaning for me. This wasn't a time for resting on my laurels or sitting on my ass. This was a time to get while the getting was good.

Who knows, maybe I sensed it wouldn't last forever, that the other shoe was about to drop. Could it be possible that I had somehow intuited that my career clock was ticking?

Unlikely. This keep-your-head-down-and-keep-moving mentality had always been, as far back as I could remember, a major part of my personality, my modus operandi. Even as a kid, I lacked the faith required to be still. Maybe it was because I was undersized or because my dreams were oversized, but I'd always relied on my ability to elude, evade, and anticipate any obstacle or potential bully. It is one of the great ironies of my life that only when it became virtually impossible for me to keep my body from moving would I find the peace, security, and spiritual strength to stand in one place. I couldn't be still until I could—literally—no longer keep still.

THE PINKIE REBELLION

Gainesville, Florida—November 13, 1990
Fifteen minutes into that first morning of the custody battle for my pinkie, the tiny tremor simply would not stop. Maybe if I ignored it for a while . . . I went into the bathroom, pulled open the mirrored door of the medicine cabinet, found a bottle of Tylenol, and dry-swallowed two. Standing in front of the larger vanity mirror, I held up my left hand, as if by studying its reflection I might gain a little objectivity. No such luck. Now there were two twitching pinkies. But wait, the medicine cabinet's mirrored door was ajar, creating a reflection within a reflection, *ad infinitum*; now there weren't just two—there were too many to count. It was a chorus line of dancing pinkies—it was the freakin' Pinkettes.

The pills weren't going down. I padded out to the kitchen, pulled a ginger ale from the refrigerator, and wandered into the sitting room. Hair in revolt, eyes at half mast, I stood buck naked in the center of the pseudo-luxurious Presidential Suite doing everything short of talking to my hand like Señor Wences. Hell, forget Señor Wences, I was about five pounds of fingernail short of an end-stage Howard Hughes.

I continued wandering from room to room, as if a solution might appear around the next corner, all the while trying a variety of strategies to impose my dominion over this digit. I pinched and pulled it. I pinned it to the nightstand with the Gideon's Bible. I folded it into a fist and held it flat against my chest, and always the result was the same. It would submit to whatever hold I applied, but four or five seconds after I let up, away it would go again. Frustrated to the point of wanting to amputate, I was convinced that would only mean having to watch the little bugger skitter across the carpet like an extra from a Roger Corman movie.

"For Christ's sake, Mike," I tried to tell myself. "It's just your freaking finger." But that was just the point: it wasn't *mine*, it was somebody else's. My pinkie was possessed.

Perspective was key, though, and since I'd clearly lost mine, it was time to avail myself of someone else's. I called Brigette, my assistant. Brig did a fantastic job running my office, but out on location, on nonindustry soil, she was a godsend. Her job, as she saw it, was to make my job as easy as possible. To that end, she'd keep track of my schedule, anticipate my needs and concerns, act as point person with the production company, and generally run interference with the whole outside world. In short, her mission was to protect and polish the bubble.

Trying my best not to sound panicky, I casually mentioned that I might be having a minor physiological reaction to something. I described what was happening to my finger. She scared the hell out of me by suggesting that it sounded to her like a neurological problem, and did I want to speak to her brother, who happened to be a brain surgeon up in Boston? "No, that's okay. I really don't think it's that big a deal," I said, trying to convince myself as much as her. "I'll just give Tracy a call."

Before hanging up, Brig reminded me I was on a "will notify," which meant my call time had yet to be determined—I'd probably be needed on set later in the afternoon.

Brigette may have had a doctor in the family but, in Tracy, I had the next best thing: a hypochondriac. By that I don't mean she's an obsessive-compulsive, doom-and-gloom, stay-in-bed-with-the-covers-pulled-over-her-head neurotic who spends her spare time taking her own blood pressure. She's not crazy, just a little sensitive to the subtlest fluctuation in her health, not to mention the health of all those around her. As long as I've known her, she's owned the latest edition of the *Columbia School of Medicine Encyclopedia of Health*, and has an uncanny knack for matching symptoms with life-threatening diseases. While I was in Florida, Tracy had remained in Manhattan with Sam. I reached her by telephone that morning at the gym. Tracy was just about to start her workout, but she encouraged me to take my time and explain in complete detail exactly what I was experiencing. Without sounding at all patronizing, she promised me that what I was describing didn't fit the profile of any disease, affliction, or injury that she was familiar with. I was relieved to hear this, and clung to her assurance that the episode would almost certainly pass and be forgotten by the end of the day. Had I ever been this patient and empathetic with her? So many times I'd dismissed her fears: "That's a freckle, Tracy, not a malignant melanoma." "No, you're not going deaf, it's called swimmer's ear." I felt guilty, but I felt better. She was right. This was nothing. It would blow over. I was fine. We traded "I love you and miss you's," but just as I was about to hang up, as an afterthought she quickly added, "You know, Brigette's brother is a brain surgeon. Why don't you give him a call just for the hell of it?"

Shit.

Ten minutes after I'd spoken to Tracy, Brigette was in my room with her brother on the line. "Just a second, Phillip, here he is." Brigette handed me the phone. And so I went through the whole pinkie deal one more time. Brigette's brother, Dr. Phillip Roux-Lough, very serious, very professional, came up with a host of possible explanations, each one more horrific than the last. I was amazed to learn that people my age actually had strokes and aneurysms—good God. The words *brain tumor* also surfaced, but this was not an area I wanted to explore too deeply. He asked if I'd had any recent episodes of physical trauma. With so many to choose from, I ran through a few of my greatest hits, so to speak, and one incident in particular intrigued him.

While making *Back to the Future, Part III* in the winter of 1989, I had actually hanged myself during a botched film stunt. Marty McFly, stranded in 1885, finds himself at the mercy of a lynch mob. At the last moment before they string him up, he manages to insert his left hand between the rope and his neck. This shot was not designed to include my whole body, so for the first couple of takes, I stood on a small wooden box. While this was technically a stunt, it was also my close-up, so Charlie was on the sidelines. No matter how I shifted my weight, the swinging effect was not realistic, so I offered to try it without the support of the box. This worked well for the next couple of takes, but on the third I miscalculated the positioning of my hand. Noose around my neck, dangling from the gallows pole, my carotid artery was blocked, causing me briefly to pass out. I swung, unconscious, at the end of the rope for several seconds before Bob Zemeckis, fan of mine though he was, realized even I wasn't that good an actor.

Dr. Lough suspected a connection between the events of that morning in Gainesville and the unintended drama on a film set ten months or so before. He suggested I consult a local neurologist.

As it happens, the University of Florida in Gainesville is home to a world-renowned neurology department. That afternoon, the *Doc Hollywood* producers arranged for the doctor in charge to give me a checkup. I was greeted at the front door by the neurologist, a few of his associates, and perhaps a favored student or two, as though I was some sort of visiting dignitary. Didn't they know that this was a patient visit, not some sort of celebrity meet-and-greet?

That question was answered when I was shown into an examination room, handed a robe, and instructed to strip down to my underwear. For the next twenty minutes or so I was put through what resembled a battery of highway patrol sobriety tests: walking a straight line one foot in front of the other, extending my arms and bringing each forefinger to the tip of my nose, closing my eyes and walking forward, backward, sideways, and hopping up and down on each foot. The exercises most relevant to my particular complaint involved an intense exploration of the wonders of the opposable thumb. The doctor asked me to touch the tip of each finger to the tip of my thumb, one after the other, again and again, each time more rapidly than the last. I was quickly reminded of why humans wear the pants in the primate family. I could do whatever they asked, which was reassuring. What was even more reassuring was the attitude of the doctors after observing me. They didn't seem at all worried. After I had dressed and taken a seat in the doctor's office, he informed me that not only was I fine, but that he wished he had videotaped my examination for his students as an example of what a completely normal and healthy neurological specimen looked like. In his opinion, the source of the finger spasms was most likely a minor injury to my ulna. "You mean my funny bone?" With a confirming nod, the doc joked that wasn't it appropriate, given what I did for a living. We had a nice little chuckle over that one.

So did these doctors screw up? I honestly don't think so. Neurological disorders like mine are so rare in people my age that the symptoms would have to be blatant before any responsible physician could confirm so serious a diagnosis. In retrospect, though, I like to joke that what else should I have expected from the University of Florida, home of the football Gators, than for the team doctor to tell the quarterback he was okay to go back into the game?

So back into the game I went. I finished filming *Doc Hollywood* in February 1991. For the final two months, production had moved from Florida to Los Angeles. Once again, ever restless, always on the search for my next opportunity, I launched myself headlong into another job. Bob Zemeckis was producing *Tales from the Crypt*, an anthology series for HBO based on the gruesome blood-soaked EC comic books of the same name, and he'd offered me an episode to direct. Eager to develop my directing skills as a backup to my acting career, I threw myself into the project with high enthusiasm—but flagging energy.

The twitching in my pinkie persisted, but now my ring and middle finger occasionally joined in on the act. I was experiencing weakness in my left hand, stiffness in my shoulder, and achiness in the muscles on the left side of my chest. I was convinced now that my problem was physiological and not neurological, probably related to the *Back to the Future* hanging. I assumed it was something I could take care of with physical therapy, and that could wait until after I finished working. As a matter of fact, I decided it might as well wait until after my summer vacation. Maybe it was out of embarrassment for being so uncharacteristically panicked in the first place, but I retreated into my inherited Anglo-Irish predisposition toward stoicism. Finishing up my directing chores on *Crypt,* I resolved not to accept any film offers until after a good long break with my family. I owed that much to Tracy and to Sam. Hell, I owed that much to myself.

I was in New York when *The Hard Way* opened in March of 1991. I received some of the better reviews of my career, but for the most part, the film was met with critical scorn and audience indifference; in plain terms it was a very expensive, very damaging bomb. Universal had been making overtures about a multi-picture long-term contract; now they were having second thoughts, though they assured my agent that this was not the case. We both knew better. The executives at Universal were going to sit back and watch to see if Warner Brothers had the same problem with *Doc Hollywood* before they bet any more money on my career. Everything was riding on *Doc Hollywood.* Or more precisely, the opening weekend of *Doc Hollywood.*

An actor's bankability is determined by his power to draw an audience to those all-important first three days of a film's release. After all, attracting an audience to sample a picture is the reason the studios pay all that money for a big-name star. The pressure to ensure that the film continues to do strong business (has "legs," in industry parlance) then shifts to the marketing and publicity departments and away from the actor. All I needed was three days of solid box office, and I was out from under the failure of *The Hard Way.*

BEFORE THE FALL

Martha's Vineyard — August 1991

Most people who consider themselves lucky are also plagued by superstition, and I had developed a ritual around the opening of any movie I appeared in. I was in London during the openings of *Back to the Future* and *Teen Wolf*, both of which had huge first weekend grosses. Ever since, I had made an effort to be, if not out of the country, then at least out of any major city when my movies hit the theaters. *The Hard Way* had been the exception—and look how that had turned out.

I wasn't going to make the same mistake with *Doc Hollywood*. Obviously there was no rational point to this ritual, but I was looking for every possible edge. There was cause for worry. Audience tracking— exit polling of moviegoers to assess their likelihood of electing to see a new film—indicated that not many were likely to go see *Doc Hollywood*. There's always a target number for the gross ticket sales a new movie should meet or surpass on its first weekend: a figure based on a variety of factors, including the number of screens on which it is shown. In 1991, $6 million was the consensus number below which we'd be in trouble. It didn't help that we were an August release, since late summer is the dumping ground for a less-than-promising product. If ever there was a time to get the hell out of town, this was it.

Tracy, Sam, and I had plans to spend the month of August at her parents' place on Martha's Vineyard. On the Thursday before Friday's release, I flew there myself; my family would join me on Saturday. Tracy and I agreed that it would be a lot easier for me to sweat out opening night solo.

Coincidentally, and unfortunately for him, my agent Peter Benedek was also vacationing on Martha's Vineyard with his family. They had rented an elegant Victorian house in Edgartown with a view looking across the bay toward Chappaquiddick, site of Teddy Kennedy's date with infamy. Pete extended a gracious but ill-advised invitation for me to join his family and friends for dinner that Friday night. On edge and looking forward to nothing less than the complete collapse of my career, I made a poor dinner guest, to put it mildly. I skipped the appetizers and went straight from an extended cocktail hour into several bottles of wine for dinner. By the time the entrée was served, I was completely blotto. It wasn't a fun evening.

Traditionally a charming, mushy kind of drunk (I'm told), my fear and anxiety mixed with all that alcohol made me belligerent. I was staggered not only by the effect of the drinks, but by the reality that at that very moment, in cineplexes across the country, my fate was being decided by strangers. Moviegoers were either buying or not buying a ticket for my film—and my gut told me it was the latter. Unable to vent my spleen on each one of the non–ticket-buyers, I turned on my agent.

"You're going to fucking call me tomorrow morning, Pete, and you know what you're gonna fucking say? You're gonna fucking say, 'I'm fucking sorry, man.' And then what? I'll tell you what. I fucking quit. I can't take this shit anymore." Pete, one of the gentlest, sweetest, kindest people in the business, never mind agent-ry, really had no counter. He knew I was right, although he probably doubted the sincerity of my threats to retire. He promised me that whatever happened, we'd ride it out. And then he offered me a ride home. Fortunately the way home didn't pass over the Chappaquiddick bridge.

When the phone rang at about 9:00 the next morning, I let it go for a while. Hung over, I was worried that the news I might be about to hear would make me puke my guts out. After a half-dozen rings, I picked up the phone without saying anything. Pete broke the silence. "Mike? . . ." he said tentatively. I winced. His tone brightened. "We did it, man. We opened this motherfucker! They think it's going to do eight to nine for the weekend. It's killing in the secondary markets— Saint Louis, Chicago, Atlanta." I thanked him and apologized profusely for my behavior the night before. I hung up the phone and smiled. *Doc Hollywood* was a hit. Not a gigantic hit, not a blockbuster, but an undeniable, guaranteed-to-make-a-profit box office success. I was still in showbiz—had earned a couple more at-bats. My hangover was gone.

It seems to me that the quality of a moment in time is not always a reflection of the moment in and of itself—what happens before and what happens after are often what give it its savor. Having forestalled a professional crisis, that monkey was, at least for now, off my back— and with no way of anticipating the gorilla that was waiting for me in the fall, the rest of that summer was a parenthesis of bliss.

The Pollans' Vineyard home, a tiny but sweet reconfigured fishing shack nestled in the dunes overlooking Menemsha Sound, was for Tracy, Sam, and me as cozy as a hug. Our days were spent at the beach or riding our bikes along Lobsterville Road. Two-year-old Sam was in his glory. A curious tidepool detective, he'd spend hours chasing horseshoe crabs along the muddy banks of Menemsha Pond. One day Tracy and I introduced him to The Flying Horses, an antique carousel in Oak Bluffs complete with calliope music and brass rings. We followed that up by treating him to a dish of ice cream from Mad Martha's, which he greedily consumed. We plugged some quarters into the ice cream parlor's fifties-style jukebox, and fueled by the sugar, he threw himself into a dance of toddler joy.

We laughed about it all the way home and somehow even managed to giggle, if somewhat guiltily, when he threw up the sticky-pink ice cream all over his crib.

Tracy and I sipped wine on the veranda and watched the sun set each night. On mornings when Sam was restless and I wanted Tracy to enjoy the rare luxury of sleeping late, I'd scoop him up and, sitting on the porch, we'd watch that same sun rise up to greet another perfect summer day. I remember the warm paternal satisfaction I'd felt pointing out to Sam the various wonders of a Vineyard morning. There was an osprey, for example, who would glide back and forth across the surface of the sound in competition with the many anglers who rose early to line the shore and fish for stripers.

Energized by the success of the movie, which continued to play strongly through the rest of the summer, I resolved to get myself in shape—cut back on the beers, lose a few pounds. There's no more beautiful place to jog than Martha's Vineyard, particularly along the winding beach roads of Gay Head. I designed my runs so that in the beginning the ocean breezes would cool me down, and on the second half, gently push me toward home. Near the end of our stay, I decided to go for it and do the entire five-mile loop along Moshup Trail. It was late afternoon on a particularly gorgeous day. A cyclist passed by and offered me a friendly tip of his bike helmet; I was pretty sure it was James Taylor, and I considered that a good sign.

After a strong start, I began to falter in the home stretch. It was taking longer than I'd expected, but I wasn't worried, just spent. About a half mile from the turn down the dirt driveway to the house, I saw Tracy driving toward me. She pulled over, got out of the car, and waved me to stop. She appeared slightly stricken. "Are you okay?" she asked. I assured her that I was, but that I may have overestimated my stamina; after all, I was almost thirty now. This was meant as a joke, but it did little to alter the expression on her face.

"You look like hell," she said. "The left side of your body is barely moving. Your arm isn't swinging at all. I don't think you should run anymore until you get a chance to see a doctor. I think you should make an appointment as soon as we get back to the city."

I promised that I would. Tracy gave me a ride the rest of the way home. *The Columbia School of Medicine Encyclopedia of Health* must weigh about five pounds; far too heavy to pack on vacations. Otherwise, it occurred to me as I took my shower, Tracy would be out there now, furiously flipping through pages.

New York City—Late Summer 1991
Upon returning to New York, I dutifully tracked down a respected sports medicine doctor and made an appointment. He was very thorough, and before prescribing a course of physical therapy to treat what I now assumed was extensive muscle and ligament damage from the long-ago date with the hangman, he ordered a series of X rays. The bones and musculature of my neck, shoulder, hand, arm, hip, and leg, the entire left hemisphere of my body, were photographed and examined. As a precaution, they also did a brain scan to rule out the possibility of stroke or a tumor. A routine formality, I reassured myself as I lay, my head encased in the strange tube that is the MRI machine, and listened for twenty minutes to its bizarre cacophony of knocks and pings.

The doctor assigned a physical therapist to go to work on my neck and shoulder, with attention also paid to the thoracic muscles on the left side of my chest. Finally I was taking care of this situation. While I resolved to be patient throughout the course of my treatment, I was eager to put this health crap behind me and get on with my now-resurgent career, with a renewed focus and commitment to my family. Those precious few weeks on the Vineyard had done much to reinforce how important Tracy and Sam were to me.

At the end of my second treatment, however, the doctor took me aside, handed me the business card of a neurologist friend of his, and strongly recommended that I see him as soon as possible. I'd already told him about the neurologist in Gainesville, and since we knew that there was no evidence of stroke or tumor, I didn't see the point. "I really think you should see him," he persisted. When I mentioned this later to Tracy, she was adamant that I make the appointment. Unbeknownst to me, the doctor had called her separately and put it very succinctly: "Just make sure he goes."

TWO WORDS

New York City—September 1991
Contrary to the happy-go-lucky image I cultivated, there were things that worried me more than I'd let on. My health, however, had never been one of them. But even if it had been, the most paranoid, hypochondriacal fantasy I could think of would not have prepared me for the two words the neurologist bludgeoned me with that day: Parkinson's disease.

Recollecting my exact response to this pronouncement is difficult; there are gaps. Dramatically, this scene would be served by the certainty that I broke down, kicked furniture, screamed "FUCK!," cursed God, or challenged this doctor, not much older than I was, maybe told him he was full of shit—and didn't he know who he was talking to? I might have charmed him—god knows I'd charmed my way out of some deep holes before. "Look . . ." one plausible in-character response might've been, "you've obviously screwed up here. But you've probably read in *People* magazine that I'm one of the nicer guys in showbiz, so I'm going to let this slide. Don't worry . . . this stays between us."

Didn't say any of that; I don't think I said anything. I don't think I felt anything. The doctor said some more words, like—*Young Onset, progressive, degenerative, incurable, very rare. At your age, new drugs, new hope. . . .* The air sucked from my lungs, my left arm was shaking clear up to the shoulder. My only clear memory is of wondering why the hell he was doing this to me, and what was I going to tell Tracy? There, on the bad news side of the doctor's desk, I sat listening quietly, nodding impassively—as if this man were my agent, telling me my last film had tanked. I wish.

He handed me a pamphlet: an elderly couple, on the beach, sunset. Which one had the incurable brain disease was not clear; they both looked happy, holding each other and beaming . . . a seagull overhead, he looked healthy too. I wanted to hit him with a rock. Something about a new drug. Maybe it was the nurse who slipped me the pamphlet, I don't know. I looked up at the doctor and stared; he was so composed. Tough for him, I bet, dropping this on a guy my age. He was really very good. I hated his guts.

As I stepped out the door of his office building and onto the rain-soaked streets of midtown Manhattan, it was as if I were entering a whole new world. In actuality, the world had changed little in the hour I had spent with the good doctor. True, the late afternoon rush-hour traffic, especially right there near the Fifty-ninth Street bridge, had intensified, but the only profound change was not around me, but within me. Dazed and confused, I could have easily stood in the rain for hours until the late afternoon gloom turned to night and the blare of car horns faded away. I had to get home, though. Hailing a cab wouldn't be easy in this weather, at this time of day, and the ride itself would be slow going. That was okay—I needed every second of that time to sort out what had just happened and how I was going to translate it into an explanation for Tracy, and for that matter my mother and the rest of my family and friends. However long it took, it wouldn't be nearly enough time.

I let myself into the apartment. I could smell dinner cooking in the kitchen and hear Sam giggling with Iwalani, our friend and Sam's nanny. I couldn't go in there and face him right at that moment. Tracy entered from the kitchen and I met her in the foyer and silently motioned her toward our bedroom. It is seldom that my face was set in so serious an expression, and she sensed immediately that the news was not good. As she followed behind me, I could feel her curiosity escalating toward panic.

There's an odd little hallway, shaped like a **7**, leading to the master bedroom in our old West Side apartment. The bottom of the **7** opened onto the bedroom where I told Tracy. We cried, we held each other. I remember thinking the scene was a very strange, sad, upside-down, version of the pamphlet I'd left in the cab—funny if it wasn't so . . . *happening to us.*

Having no real idea about what this monster was, vaguely understanding that it would be years before we would feel its teeth and claws, we exchanged assurances. Tracy, stunned and frightened, was at the same time so present, and loving . . . *in sickness and in health,* I remember her whispering, arms around me, her wet cheek against mine. Typically, my first instinct was: *There's an angle here, there's got to be a way out of this, just keep moving.* To Tracy: *It'll be okay* . . . To myself: What *will be okay?*

Only a few of us will admit it, but actors will sometimes read a script like this: *bullshit . . . bullshit . . . my part . . . blah, blah, blah . . . my part . . . bullshit . . .* I loved it /I hated it really depends on the *bullshit* to *my part* ratio. Days, maybe weeks into it, I transitioned into high bullshit mode: *not my script, hate it, not doing it.* I went through the motions, sought second opinions; the opinions were unanimous. I had Parkinson's disease. Resolving never to see the neurologist again unless a hurricane blew him through my living room window, I had my internist prescribe P.D. meds. I'd carry these around with me, loose and broken in the pockets of my trousers, like Halloween smarties. Therapeutic value, treatment, even comfort—none of these was the reason I took these pills. There was only one reason: to hide. No one, outside of family and the very closest of friends and associates, could know. And that is how matters stood for seven years.

CHAPTER TWO

The Escape Artist

Chilliwack Army Base, British Columbia—1963

> *The boy was gone . . . vanished. I had slipped away while my mother was occupied with that thankless task familiar to any career military wife: unpacking the family's possessions and setting up yet another new household.*

My mom, Phyllis, and dad, Sgt. William Fox, Royal Canadian Army Signal Corps, had become experts at relocation. Between their wedding day in 1950 and that afternoon Mom spent uncrating the effects of thirteen years of family life, Dad had been stationed at six different army bases.

My father's job involved encryption and decoding—his skill at these arcane arts is the reason the army required him at postings all across Canada. (We could never visit him at his office, which was always sealed off.) There had been a previous stint in Chilliwack from 1955 to 1958. The family was returning there from the province of Alberta, where Dad had spent the intervening years at bases in both Calgary and Edmonton. (I was born in Edmonton in June of 1961.) This was life in the military, and if it was inconvenient, or even traumatic for a serviceman's family—*well, tough*. Dad knew the reply he'd get from the brass should he ever complain, and with a rueful half smile he'd often remind us, "If the army wanted me to have a family, they would have issued me one."

Dad had actually put in for this latest transfer, though, and it was no hardship saying good-bye to the flat, featureless landscape and insultingly cold winters of the Canadian prairie. Mom and Dad still had many friends in Chilliwack and both had grown up in British Columbia. Driving westward from Alberta, Mom remembers crying all the way across the Rockies, so thrilled was she to be traveling toward home. The Chilliwack base sat right at the spot where the rugged mountains settled into miles and miles of rich Fraser River Valley farmland. If you followed the Fraser eighty winding miles or so from Chilliwack, toward the delta where it empties into the Pacific, you'd come to the small community of Ladner. The daughter of one of that area's many Depression-era tenant farmers, Mom considered Ladner the home she always carried with her in her heart. So, if the Fox family had to load into the Chevy and hit the Trans-Canada Highway once again, at least they were moving in the right direction.

Unpacking was tedious work and having a toddler underfoot couldn't have made it any easier. I was a handful, a whirlwind—

cheerful, bright, and precociously funny in a what-spaceship-dropped-off-this-alien kind of way. But I'm sure that I was testing her limits, chattering, digging into boxes, making nests in the piles of clothes she had unpacked, unfolded, refolded, and set aside to be carried upstairs to each of the three cramped bedrooms.

Cramped was the operative word for army housing. PMQs—Permanent Married Quarters—did not provide generous living space, but situated as they were on well-guarded government real estate, you couldn't ask for a safer environment in which to raise children. Sprawling grids of identical row housing, PMQs were tidy neighborhoods where folks quickly forged new friendships or reestablished old ones. Everybody looked out for everybody else and everybody was in exactly the same socioeconomic boat. If another family owned something yours didn't—a color TV, say, or a fancy car—all you had to do was count the kids: chances are they had one or two fewer than you did. In 1963 we had four: Karen, Steven, Jacqueline, and me. In 1964 our baby sister Kelli showed up—effectively postponing the purchase of a color TV until the early seventies.

As Mom counted casualties among the stacks of mismatched dishes wrapped in crumpled sheets of old Edmonton newspaper, it's not hard to imagine how I might have escaped unnoticed. If she could no longer hear me, she'd have assumed I'd curled up for a nap somewhere, and would have been grateful for the respite. If she didn't see me, well, that was even easier to explain. It might sound redundant to say "tiny for a two-year-old," but that's exactly what I was—knee-high, weighing little more than a wet beach towel, and slippery-quick. Several minutes would pass before Mom realized I was missing.

Ladner, British Columbia — 1942

> *Every family has its stories, its formative legends. In mine, they tend to revolve around the figure of Nana, my grandmother. It was accepted as fact in our family that Nana had a gift for prophecy; whether literally true or not, what matters most here is that those who believed, especially my mother, ordered their lives—and mine—accordingly.*

Two decades earlier, another mother discovered that her son was missing. In this particular story it was my mother's mother, Jenny Piper, and the son was my uncle Stuart. The year was 1942. Jenny—my "Nana"—and her husband Harry had been through this once before with their oldest boy Kenny: the telegram at the door, the brutal wording: "Missing and presumed dead"—shot down somewhere over Germany. Both Piper sons were serving in the Royal Canadian Air Force over the European theater of operations. Both had been declared missing and presumed dead.

When Nana had read that first telegram a year earlier, the words essentially the same, except for the names, she took it hard. Within weeks, she suffered a heart attack. Her health didn't rally until she received further word several weeks later that Kenneth was in fact alive—that he was a prisoner of war in a camp in Germany.

DREAMERS

So when word of Stuart's disappearance reached Nana's relatives in Winnipeg (in search of better work prospects, Henry and Jenny had relocated from Manitoba to the West Coast at the outset of the Depression), they feared she would succumb to another heart attack, and pleaded with her to come back east for a rest. She wouldn't budge. "Not until I know for sure that Stuart's alive," she said. Then one day, several weeks into the nightmare of waiting for word about Stuart, Nana came downstairs into the kitchen and announced, "We can go to Winnipeg now. Stuart's okay. I had a dream."

There was a sudden and violent explosion. A fireball in the sky. From its center, she sees something small and white drift lazily toward the earth, toward the beach, in fact. She runs to it, recovering what now appears to be a small white envelope just before the lapping waves can claim it and take it out to sea. One word is typed on its white face: Stuart.

This collection of images, delivered to Nana from her unconscious, could be interpreted in any number of ways. But to Nana, the meaning was clear: just like Kenneth, Stuart had parachuted from a burning plane and survived. Her faith in this vision was unshakable. Two days after Nana's dream, a telegram arrived. It was just as she prophesied: the burning plane, the white parachute. Like Kenneth, Stuart had been taken POW and was very much alive.

So what does any of this have to do with my life? One thing about which I am absolutely sure is this: if Nana hadn't woken up with that dream, I never would have realized my own. For the unshakable confidence Nana had about Stuart's fate she would later have about me. He would escape what looked to every other member of the family like certain death. And I, she was equally sure, would escape the destiny everyone else in the family assumed was mine.

Chilliwack Army Base, British Columbia — 1963

I can't pretend to remember my two-year-old state of mind, but it's likely that my motive in wandering out the back door was not specifically to "escape." More likely, I simply failed to recognize boundaries; that the screened kitchen door represented a line beyond which an unsupervised toddler did not venture. The impulse to push against the limits of my world was something I would never grow out of, and it would by turns amuse, exasperate, frustrate, and terrify the adults in my life; all of them, that is, except for Nana.

I recently asked my mother about her reaction to my unscheduled field trip that afternoon in Chilliwack, an episode that, for her, set the pattern for her experience raising me. I was, she recalled, a mysterious, mercurial blur.

"I was unpacking and whatnot, getting things squared away, and all of a sudden I couldn't find you. This was a new neighborhood, of course, so I panicked. I went outside and I'm calling and calling for you, until finally this lady came out and asked, was I Mrs. Fox? When I said yes she said, 'You're looking for your little boy? Well, he was just here and what a charmer! He just talked and talked.'

"That's how it went: everybody in the neighborhood knew who

you were before we knew who *they* were. Over and over again I heard, 'Oh, that Michael. Are you Michael Fox's mother?' You know, after you became famous, everybody would say to me, 'You must get tired of being asked, "Are you Michael Fox's mother?" 'And I'd say, 'Not at all. I've been hearing it since he was a baby.' "

I turned up shortly after Mom's encounter with the new neighbor. Smiling, giggling, no idea I'd caused a stir—just doing a little reconnoitering of my new environs, which, I'd been happy to discover, included a candy store just across the grassy field behind our block. Dad got home from work, and while Mom was recounting my misadventure, I slipped out again. When the phone rang a few minutes later, the proprietor of the candy store tried to contain his amusement. "I've got your son here. He wants to buy something."

I can easily picture my mother, one hand gripping the phone, the other finding a handful of her thick red hair and giving it a tug, her pinkish Anglo-Irish complexion flushing crimson as she looked around in utter disbelief that I'd bolted once more. "Let him have a candy or something. My husband will be right there to pick him up and pay for it."

At this point, the store owner could no longer keep himself from laughing out loud. "Oh, he's got money. He's got quite a bit of money, as a matter of fact."

Thievery was not high on the list of my childhood quirks. I had simply made a two-year-old's connection between the pile of money my father had left on the counter—his entire transfer allowance—and the candy store, the coordinates of which I had already committed to memory. It was on days like this that I began to believe that nothing was impossible—and that my parents began to realize that when it came to their younger son, they would do well to expect the unexpected.

This was no small matter. Born into the uncertainty of the Great Depression and having come of age during World War II, Mom and Dad had carefully constructed a life together that avoided surprises. Dad's decision to embark on a career in the military must have been a calculated tradeoff—individuality for security—with no possibility for a windfall, but no nasty surprises either. If the powers that be saw fit to move you halfway across Canada, then at least you knew that waiting at the next destination was the same job, a similar neighborhood, and a nearly identical house.

Outside the lines, outside the experience of most of the adults in my life, and (according to my older siblings) completely out of my tiny mind—there's a brief but accurate sketch of what I was like in the first five years of my life. I'm constantly told what a friendly, curious, garrulous child I was—hell-bent on all forms of self-expression, artistic and otherwise, with a pronounced attraction to new possibility and an equally pronounced indifference to expectation.

Naturally I developed an understanding of what was expected of me in terms of behavior—the basic rules of society. I only took my father's wallet to the corner store once. My mother describes me as more Tom Sawyer than Dennis the Menace. I just wasn't interested in people's expectations. Or perhaps I should say, I lost interest in them over time. I can recall two formative experiences that turn on the expectations of others and probably helped turn me away from caring one way or the other.

When my baby sister Kelli arrived in 1964, I wasn't jealous. She was cute and I liked kids and babies—and, what the hell, the more the merrier—but by the time I was five or six and she was two or three, we were the same size. I have a specific memory of trick-or-treating with Kelli and being asked at house after house if we were twins. My self-possession and verbal skills had always surpassed anything a grown-up would expect from one so small. But once told that my supposed "twin" was actually three years younger, people's reactions changed, giving me my first troubling experience with the flip side of that expectation. I was *expected* to be bigger. This was a new one on me. I could do all kinds of weird and wonderful things, but I couldn't do *bigger*. This infuriated me. I wanted to steal my sister's candy, bind her up in the pillowcase she was carrying, and stick her in a closet somewhere.

The other incident that prompted me to associate expectation with disappointment had to do with my father. Even as a kindergartener, I recognized that Dad was a no-nonsense kind of guy.

Though he delighted in the stories, pictures, and songs I would create, he inhabited a more orderly reality. While I was a dreamer, he was firmly anchored in the nuts and bolts of everyday existence. He never said it in so many words, but I had a strong feeling that someday he expected me to be more like him in this way. I remember one morning at preschool, on a day when my father was returning from an extended posting at a NATO listening post (euphemistically referred to as a "weather station") somewhere in the Arctic Circle; Dad would be picking me up at lunchtime and walking me home.

In place of the customary finger paints, construction paper, and crayons, the teachers had placed odd-sized scraps of wood, small hammers, and Campbell's soup cans full of nails at our work tables. I would rather have had the paints. But seeing the other boys apply themselves to this practical sort of project, I became fixed on the idea of building something for my dad. I was positive that was what he would like— what he would expect.

And so with mounting frustration I spent that whole morning laboring in vain to construct something, anything. I had it fixed in my mind that that would impress him in a way I never had. It was a disaster: I could not so much as attach one piece of wood to another. Dad finally arrived to find me inconsolable. He scooped me up, balancing my butt on the underside of his powerful forearm, and I buried my face in his uniform. I can still remember the coarseness of the wool and the tang of its smell when dampened by my tears. For once in my young life, I was at a loss for words. We walked home and on the way, I wet my pants. Even Tom Sawyer had bad days.

Whether it was that day or another, at some point in my childhood I simply stopped dealing with people's expectations and started going my own way.

BOX OF GHOSTS

Chilliwack, B.C.; North Bay, Ontario; Burnaby, B.C.— 1967–1972
Like a field researcher's string and twine grid laid over a fresh archeological dig, I've tried for the purposes of this book to organize the pe-

riods of my childhood into logically defined segments. If the first square on the grid outlined the murky, impressionistic soup of my toddlerhood up to the beginning of school, the second would frame the period of 1967–1972, ages six to eleven. As it happens, a few select scenes of this era are easy to recover.

For Christmas in 1989, my sister Jackie collected the remnants of Dad's old 8mm home movies. A sporadic family chronicler at best, Dad nevertheless had recorded enough fragments of our family's day-to-day existence to be compiled into a wordless, somewhat shaky and unfocused, but emotionally stirring family documentary. Jackie hired an editor to transfer the 8mm onto videotape, and filled him in on the chronology of the random snatches of footage.

Tracy, Sam, and I didn't make it back to Canada for the holidays that year, but when I received my tape via FedEx, I immediately fed it into the machine. I might have expected the flush of nostalgia, but the images of Nana, who'd been dead since I was eleven, blindsided me. I couldn't look at the tape very long, but promised myself that in a couple of weeks I'd watch it through. Before that happened, however, my father died in January of 1990. The last thing I wanted to do then was to see all those images of my father alive. So I put the tape away and didn't think about it for a very long time.

I didn't think of it again, in fact, until I began writing these pages. Finding it all these years later meant digging through countless sloppily labeled cassettes: children's birthday parties, leftover Super Bowls, prizefights, hockey games, and old Larry Sanders episodes. But to my surprise, it only took one trip to the tape shelves to uncover this treasure. A skewed label marked in Jackie's neat, if florid, hand, *Fox Family Home Movies: The Way We Were, 1967–1972.*

Weird, huh?

I removed it from its cardboard dustcover and made my way toward the VCR—not without some hesitation. Before that first viewing in 1989, I hadn't given much thought to what I was about to see, so the images of Nana surprised me. Now I knew that she was on there, as was Dad—walking and talking, smoking and joking—animate for the first time in more than a decade.

These two figures, my maternal grandmother and my father, represented two distinct poles of my childhood, two gravitational fields that helped form my character.

My father, the career military man, personified the boundaries of expectation and the acceptance of one's limitations, both external and self-imposed. He was a pragmatist, a realist, a sixth-grade dropout who called himself "a graduate of the school of hard knocks." He'd had dreams as a young boy and man, but they'd been effectively knocked out of him, and he'd felt the sting for the rest of his life. Fiercely loyal, his first commitment was to his family, whom he was determined to protect from any threat, including the disappointment that would inevitably result from the pursuit of romantic fantasy.

In comparison, Nana, the matriarch and wartime clairvoyant, possessed an essential nature that hinted at the possibility of escape, of transcending life's limits. She delighted in my accomplishments and eccentricities, always encouraging me to believe in the power of my dreams. When others in the family would express doubts about my direction, she was my staunchest defender and greatest champion. She'd laugh off their concerns with a wink at me, as if we both knew something that was beyond the understanding of others.

With the recovery of the videotape, I had the means to see the two of them again, a prospect that filled me with both curiosity and trepidation.

REELING IN THE YEARS

The opening frame features a medium shot of a black sheepdog, a small white blaze on his chest. The darkness of his coat is in sharp contrast to the bright green of the surrounding lawn. Dead for over a quarter century, he's alive again on my television screen, scratching furiously at a flea hiding in his shaggy coat. The dog's name was Bartholomew. He wasn't ours; he belonged to Ed, my older sister Karen's boyfriend. Dad hated the dog and he wasn't too crazy about Ed either, branding him a hippie, which in 1967

was the worst thing my father could think of to say about anybody. I don't remember the circumstances, but the dog disappeared after about a year or so; Ed, to my Dad's chagrin, stuck
around, for a time becoming my sister's husband.

Cut to my sister Kelli, three years old, adorable, towheaded,
scrunching her already twice-broken nose and smiling, her full attention focused on the lens. She puts on a sharp little red summer-
weight jacket and models it. It's an engaging performance, hinting
at a future on the stage.

An interior shot now; the camera is panning left and finds my
father. He looks great. Heavy, but not as heavy as I remember him.
More bulky than fat, he amply fills his plaid short-sleeved shirt. He
looks young, I think, and then realize that the man on the tape is
two years younger than I am at this writing. Beneath his crew
cut—his hair was never styled any other way during his entire career in the military—his eyes are bright, and he favors us with a
quick smile.

Outside again, a group shot with Mom in a sleeveless cotton
shirt and Capri pants, chatting with a group of neighbors. Kelli
dances in the foreground and a couple of the women observe her
through horn-rimmed, cat's-eye glasses.

Next sequence. From a distance, two figures are strolling
towards us through a heavily arbored, sun-dappled walkway. The
smaller of the pair has a distinctive bow-legged gait that I recognize
immediately. It's my grandmother. Closer to the camera now, her
features come into sharper relief. She's beautiful. On this particular
day, her unruly gray hair has been fashioned into tight little pincurls
and tamed with pomade and bobby pins. Her face is smiling—always
smiling—though it would be hard for a stranger to tell because the
left side droops from Bell's palsy. Round and comfy looking, Nana's
in a gingham housedress and black lace-up shoes; a comically oversized handbag dangles from her wrist. Grandmothers always used to
look like this. The slightly taller figure is my brother Steve, allowing
her to set the pace. More than anyone, she resembles the Queen
Mum; as a loyal British subject, she'd be tickled by the comparison.

And this: the six-year-old me pushing my bicycle. A couple of quick steps, and then with concentrated cool I quicken the pace, swing my leg, and I'm up on the bike, pedaling across vibrant green grass. My left hand grips the handlebars and from my right dangles a writhing garter snake.

We were still on the Chilliwack base, but out of the PMQs and into a duplex apartment on Nicomen Drive. Strictly speaking, these homes were reserved for servicemen of a higher rank than my father, but with five kids now he was entitled to a housing upgrade. Dad put in for the change in residence back in 1963 when Mom first found out she was pregnant with Kelli, but the army, remember, viewed families as "nonessential personnel" and were in no hurry to grant Dad's request. Their attitude was basically, "Show us the baby." In other words, only when the newest Fox child was an undeniable physical fact would they even consider his application. (My dad put up with twenty-five years of this shit.) Almost three years after Kelli's arrival, the papers finally went through and the duplex became available. Her birth may have cost us a color TV, but thanks to Dad's persistence, it did win us a little more elbow room.

Not that I required too much in the way of elbow room. On the tape, I am as tiny as advertised. In two-shots with my three-year-old sister, we do in fact look like twins; almost exactly the same size, except for our heads: mine is disproportionately huge, a major league pumpkin.

As I watch, I can't help but notice how self-contained I am as a six-year-old—not playing to the camera at all, wholly involved in whatever I'm doing at the moment. This comes as something of a personal revelation. Given my family reputation for childhood extroversion and relentless precocity at school, home, and in social situations, I'd always assumed that much of this was for effect—that I harbored an intense desire for attention and acceptance.

In searching through my own and my family's memories, hoping to understand who I am, I tend to view myself through the lens of who I have become. Those events and personal qualities that support the current version get singled out unconsciously, distorting memories in order to illuminate my path more brightly. But the tape short-circuits that process of subjective recall. To revisit the analogy of the archeologist's grid, viewing this thirty-odd minutes of videotape is like taking a core sample, reaching back to show me who I really was then.

I'd always bought into the notion that I became a performer because I craved love and attention; that approbation was, in my case, the mother of self-invention. At first glance, the tape supports this assessment. I mean, I'm very busy with all the activities I'd heard about: drawing, reading book after book, brandishing an oversized fishing net like a drum major's baton as I lead my parents on a bullfrog hunt around the reedy shoreline of a local pond, and—still my favorite—taking that snake on an involuntary bike tour of the backyard. On closer inspection, however, it's clear that all these antics were done for nobody's benefit but my own. First and foremost I am a boy out to entertain myself, completely undisturbed by the presence of the lens.

It is plain from these scenes that in many ways who I am is *who I always was*. So the question is then not "How did I get this way?," but "How did I *stay* this way?" The answer is, "I'm not sure that I did." Along the way came distractions and self-doubt, detours and adjustments, but the tape tells me that the adult I am today has more in common with the kid on the bike than with the person I was in between. It's gratifying to know that I somehow found my way back, and it's bracing to realize that my Parkinson's diagnosis played an important part in leading me there.

FAMILY TIES

The first time I saw *The Honeymooners* and Jackie Gleason blustered onto our old black-and-white TV screen, I thought, "Hey . . . that's my dad!" Aside from his striking physical resemblance to Gleason, Dad was Kramden-esque in many other ways: imposing, funny, passionate, capable of an exasperation at once comical and threatening. He, too, could swing in a blink of an eye from "How sweet it is" to "One of these days, Alice, *pow*, right to the moon!" Both men seemed to be at the mercy of forces beyond their control, but, unlike Ralph, Dad harbored no romantic notions about transcending his lot in life with a get-rich-quick scheme. Instead he relied on persistence, a solid work ethic, and his formidable intelligence. Besides, he had one very important thing that Ralph Kramden did not; the possession of which, I'm sure my father felt, made him wealthier than he ever dreamed he could be: a family.

There are a few key scenes on the tape that make me feel so close to my father, so overwhelmed by his presence, that I could cry. Each of these scenes takes place in a different year, but each is almost an identical replay of the one before. No one, not even my father himself, appears in the frame.

> This is the shot: a slow, loving, left-to-right pan of a lit Christmas tree in an otherwise darkened living room, with particular emphasis on the bounty that lies beneath the tinseled boughs. The quantity of the gifts seems to grow with each successive year.
>
> It's Christmas Eve and everybody else has gone to bed. The hand holding the camera is my father's. He's sitting in his favorite chair. A bottle of beer he'd convinced us to leave out for Santa in lieu of milk and cookies rests on the folding TV table beside him.

This was an annual and very private ritual. I know this because, on many a Christmas Eve, I'd creep down in my pajamas and stand on the landing at the bottom of the stairs quietly watching him. One year I fell asleep there, and when my father picked me up to carry me back to my bed, I stirred briefly. I asked him if he was waiting for Santa Claus. He smiled and said yes, "Just in case Saint Nick has to assemble something and he needs to borrow a wrench."

My father's tree-watching vigils continued well into my adulthood when, home from the States for the holidays, I'd stumble in from Christmas Eve reunions with my old high school buddies, sit down, and join him for a nightcap. He didn't say much, didn't share his thoughts. He didn't have to. I knew exactly what they were.

During the Depression, my father's father (also named Bill) struggled to provide for his family in the Vancouver suburb of Burnaby. It
was a losing battle. What little they had, they lost. By the outbreak of
the war, Bill Sr., desperate for work, turned to the military. The army
deemed him too old for active service and assigned him to guard duty
at a military prison in Alberta. This meant leaving my dad, his older
sister Edith, younger brother Doug, and little sister Lenore in the care
of their mother Dolly. But Dolly was a mother in name only. In her
husband's absence, Dolly could not handle the responsibilities of
being an impoverished single mother with four children. She sought
refuge in the beer halls along Hastings Street and the nightclubs of
East Vancouver.

Dad and Edie took on the role of raising their younger siblings.
They both left school early to find work; for a time Dad clerked at
Spencer's department store. Dad and Dougie, two years his junior, were
especially close, and they often wandered their down-on-its-luck,
working-class neighborhood in search of diversions to distract them
from their hunger. Half a mile from their home, west on Hastings
Street, North Burnaby's main drag, stood the fairground and Exhibition
Park, western Canada's largest, year-round horse racing venue. The boys
loved the track and spent hours peering through the slatted fence—not
only at post time, but in the mornings while the stable hands walked
and watered their horses and the trainers put them through their paces.
Growing bolder, the boys soon snuck in, and before long had insinuated
themselves into the exotic world of the racetrack.

Eventually the young brothers won low-paying jobs such as hot-
walking the horses. Dad, barely five feet six inches and thin as a rail in
those days, was considered "potential jockey material," my mother
tells me, and his apprenticeship began in earnest. By the time he was
sixteen, he was earning mounts in a few races. Giddy from this turn of
events, the Fox brothers got drunk one night and set out for the tat-
too parlors of Vancouver's rough waterfront district. Dad had his left
bicep permanently emblazoned with the profile of a thoroughbred, a
horseshoe-shaped laurel of roses draped around its neck.

The war ended, and with it Dad's short-lived dreams of a career
in horse racing. Servicemen returning from overseas flooded the job

market, and Dad soon found he had few options but to trade places with them. He had spent enough time around racing touts, punters, and pari-mutuel windows to know that a life in the military was his safest bet. Shortly after Dad enlisted, his kid brother Doug, his best friend, contracted spinal meningitis and died before reaching his seventeenth birthday. Bill Sr. returned from Alberta, but a year or so later Dolly drifted away for good. No one in the family ever heard from her again.

Something positive did come out of this period, however—a life-altering event that my father would credit as his salvation. As a new enlistee housed in Ladner's army barracks, he met a cute and spirited redhead at a local dance. In Phyllis Piper he found someone who made him feel needed. At the same time, she displayed a stubborn independent streak that he respected. He sensed, correctly, that if they married, settled down, and had kids, Phyllis was not someone who would ever drift away.

Christmas Eve after Christmas Eve, Dad sat there relishing the bounty of gifts spread out under the tree, thinking about how far he'd come. Certainly the presents symbolized material success, but beyond that they implied love and connection—a nuclear family, intact. For all his hardships, Bill Fox had managed to achieve something great. With my mom, he had helped to create a family, to care for and protect them, and at the end of another year they'd even managed to see to it that there was something left over. To ask for anything more would be asking for trouble. These, at least, are the thoughts I imagine going through his head those sweet evenings alone. Gaze never leaving the tree, he'd lean back in his chair, take a long pull on Santa's beer, *his beer*, and smile.

DON'T YOU WORRY ABOUT MICHAEL

Burnaby, British Columbia — 1971–1972

In 1968 we were transferred once more, to Dad's shock this time, clear across the country to North Bay, Ontario. Dad had been considering retiring in 1971 when his eligibility would come up, and the seeming capriciousness behind this latest transfer sealed the deal. After three years back east, Dad retired and moved the family back to B.C. for good. It was the start of a new life for us, a *civilian* life, with all of the freedom and uncertainty that implied.

We weren't the only ones making this change. Almost all of my adult male relatives had military careers, and the early seventies set off a wave of retirements. From every corner of Canada, all the branches of the Piper family tree returned to their roots in the west. Resettled into new homes in the greater Vancouver area, all within easy driving distance of one another, the progeny of Harry and Jenny Piper initiated a series of mini-reunion celebrations that would pick up where they left off virtually every weekend.

In the case of the large social gatherings I remember as a child— birthdays, backyard barbecues, holidays, and homecomings—the term "friends and family" is redundant. My parents' closest and dearest friends were almost all family. They needed very little excuse to get together, sit back, tip a few beers, cook up a big feed, and watch their offspring, a closely knit clutch of cousins, scramble in and out of whomever's home the tribe had assembled at that weekend. "In or out, kids, in or out—and close the door, *for chrissakes*, the neighbors are complaining about the *heat*"—that was a favorite of Dad's. Presiding over the festivities, and perhaps enjoying the warmth and camaraderie more than anyone, was the family's matriarch, Nana.

In those days, Nana split her time amongst the families of the children who lived in B.C., with extended tours across Canada to see the others. Always a welcome guest, she'd pitch in and help the adults, and always came bearing gifts for the kids. She'd pull us aside as we were running out to the candy store or local movie theater and discreetly tuck a dollar bill into our pockets.

I felt a very special bond with my grandmother. I'm sure my brother and sisters and cousins would share this sentiment, but mine goes back literally to the day of my birth. When the nurses came into that Edmonton hospital room to deliver me into my mother's arms for the first time, Nana was at her bedside.

"Do you and Bill have a name yet?"

"Well," my mom replied, pushing the blue bunting from around my pink and puckered face, "we've pretty much settled on Michael."

Nana was not pleased. "Michael's a fine name, but you know everyone will just call him Mike."

"Not necessarily," countered my mother.

"Yes they will," Nana promised. "But not me, I'm not crazy about the name 'Mike.' Don't like it. I'll never call him anything but Michael."

And she never did.

After Dad's retirement and our return to B.C., we settled into a three-bedroom flat in the Vancouver suburb of Burnaby. Situated across the street from a sprawling strip mall with an enormous parking lot perfect for endless hours of street hockey, the apartment complex also boasted a large if indifferently maintained outdoor swimming pool that was even cooler. The best feature of the neighborhood, though, was a block and a half away: the boxy, blue three-story walk-up where my Nana settled shortly after our arrival.

I'd gladly forsake slapping a hockey ball against the stucco wall of the liquor store or splashing around with my friends in the swimming pool to spend time visiting Nana in her new digs. We were an unlikely duo, a ten-year-old boy and a woman in her mid-seventies, but I liked nothing better than hanging out as she went through even the most mundane of her chores. Sitting in the kitchen, she'd tell me stories as she washed and sorted her collection of cups and saucers. Drying her hands on her housedress, Nana would fish into her gargantuan handbag for a candy bar or box of Chiclets she'd been saving for me.

"Now you tell *me* a story," she'd demand.

The shot starts with a wide pan of the room, which is thick with a blue haze of cigarette smoke. Everybody's there but Kenny, who survived WWII but succumbed to cancer in the mid-sixties at the age of forty-two. Moving in and out of the bottom of the frame are the tousled heads of various children, but the camera is concentrating on their parents. Smoking their smokes and quaffing their beers are Uncle Stuey, who, like Kenny, was released from

POW camp at war's end; my uncle Albert, who never saw combat duty; and Al's wife Marilyn, chatting with Stu's wife Flo. The pan continues and there's Mom's baby sister, Pat, standing with my parents and her husband Jake. The camera pulls back and we see that they're all grouped loosely around an overstuffed sofa upon which sits Nana, sipping from a beer mug that dwarfs her tiny hands. She lowers it, revealing a small wisp of foam painting her upper lip. She says something now, perhaps to herself, but more likely in response to a remark from off-camera.

There's no sound of course, so I have no idea what exactly the group has been laughing and gossiping about. But I do have personal knowledge of one frequent topic of conversation at many of these family gabfests: me.

Still tiny and decidedly hyper compared to the other kids in the family, I was considered something of an oddity. My parents would often share the latest twists and turns in the strange saga of their youngest son: a doctor's recommendation that I be administered growth hormone, a teacher's insistence that, as good as my grades were, my overwhelming appetite for stimulation needed to be tamped with a course of whatever the equivalent of Ritalin was in those days. (Dad nixed both suggestions.) Since the aptitude I demonstrated was for the arts, it was hard for anyone to imagine me holding a real paying job.

"You weren't going to be a laborer," my mother explains. "You weren't going to be a union guy. That wouldn't have suited your personality, never mind your physique. You were the dreamer and the artistic type. I mean, years later I see that, but at the time, I can't honestly say that I did because it was just something that had never been in either side of our family."

And so there was much chin-rubbing and worried conjecture about what would become of me. This is when Nana would always chime in.

"Don't you ever worry about Michael," she'd intone with a calming certainty. "He's going to be fine. He's going to do things you can't even imagine. And he'll probably be very famous one day."

And then with a smile, and no doubt a twinkle in her eye, she'd add, "And when he is, everyone will know him as Michael."

In most circumstances, this would be written off as the indulgence of a doting grandmother, but you have to remember Nana's position in our family. It was accepted, after all, that Nana was something of a psychic. She'd had The Dream. She'd come down the stairs that morning in Ladner thirty years earlier and announced that Stuart was alive. So, if Nana said it, who were they to argue? I mean, if they woke up in the morning and the sun was shining and Nana said "rain," believe me, they'd all spend the day packing umbrellas. Unlikely as it seemed to everyone else, maybe Bill and Phyl's boy Mike—*Michael* — was going to be okay after all.

SUDDENLY ONE SUMMER

Burnaby, British Columbia — 1972–1979
August 22, 1972: I was in the pool when I heard the sirens. My folks were both at work; Dad as a police dispatcher in Ladner (his post-retirement job) and Mom as a payroll clerk in a cold storage plant on the waterfront, so the summer day was like a blank check that I could fill in however I wanted. I might have gone to the movies, *Conquest of the Planet of the Apes* for the second or third time, then headed down to the lake on my new bike with its sleek banana seat and high-rise handlebars. It was a scorcher though, so I opted for the unheated waters of the swimming pool. Maybe I'd go over to Nana's later, I thought, scrounge some lunch.

It was around noon the sirens started; I remember being unsettled by the sound. I climbed out of the pool, grabbed my towel, pushed through the gate in the chain-link fence enclosure, and climbed the stairs to our second-floor apartment.

I barely had time to dry off and dress before the phone rang. Mom said she was leaving work early. Nana had had a heart attack.

Nana was the first real person I knew to die—not an actor or an American politician, but someone whom I loved, whose voice, touch, and laughter were as familiar as my own. Of my father's father I have the merest glint of remembrance—walking along a sidewalk with a thin, pleasant older man who held my hand—but I was three when he died. I was eleven now, and Nana's death was my first experience of loss. For a period of time afterwards—days? weeks? a month?—a door would open and I'd flush with the irrational expectation that Nana might walk in, or I'd daydream of going to see her in her apartment. The worst were the times I'd believe, for an instant, I did see her, at Woolworth's, or through the window of a passing bus. I would catch myself and simply feel sad.

In time, I absorbed the loss of Nana. I finished elementary school and prepared for junior high. My parents secured an economic foothold in the civilian world and began shopping for the first home of our own. Life moved on.

Over the years to come, though, Nana continued to figure in my life. I knew, in a general sense, that she thought I was a great kid; that she loved me and understood me better than any other adult in my world. I didn't, however, grasp the extent to which she'd been my pro-tector, my bridge to the world of other adults, including my father. And even after Nana was gone, her belief in me held sway. Her con-viction that I was somehow different, that special consideration was in order, became a posthumous gift, an emotional trust fund of which my parents were the dutiful, if sometimes dubious, executors.

ONE HAND CLAPPING

Nana wasn't the only one with a rock-solid belief that I was destined for a bright future. About this she and I were in complete accord. As a child I didn't define success in monetary or material terms, but I would tell my mom and dad that one day I'd buy them each a new car and a big house for us all to live in. They'd smile and shake their heads. Sometimes this wide-eyed hubris was not so charming. When Mom would tidy my room after endless demands that I do so myself, she'd ask, "You don't think someone's going to be doing this for you for the rest of your life, do you?" "Well, actually . . . yeah . . . I mean, I'll *pay* them for doing it." In my mind I was just being honest. So I'd be genuinely confused when she'd take her dusting rag in both hands and look as though she wanted to wrap it around my skinny neck.

How did I plan to achieve this life of leisure? Like most Canadian kids, I played hockey with religious devotion, and hockey represented our only realistic shot at fame and fortune. Being small, I regularly got my ass kicked (more than two dozen stitches in my face by the time I was a teenager and countless broken teeth). Still, I threw myself into the game. Realistically, the odds that I would be the next Bobby Orr (Wayne Gretzky was still a snot-nosed kid himself) were slim to none, but I could still dream.

Maybe my belief in myself sprang from a recognition that many things seemed to come easily to me. School was a snap, especially writing; that's what seemed to get the grown-ups (like Nana) the most excited. Even at five and six, I was writing long, multistanza, epic poems about my adventures, real and imagined, and later moved on to short stories, essays, and book reports that won praise.

But I had other passions too. When I was preschool age, my dad would return from his trips bearing gifts for all the kids; mine were often big picture books. Dad would later recount with amazement that I'd read a book, cover to cover, then find paper and pencil and, without tracing, replicate page after page of drawings in meticulous detail. This was the beginning of a lifelong love of cartooning, including caricatures that occasionally delighted but more often offended my friends and family.

Music was another obsession. I had to be one of very few eight-year-olds who got excited when Eric Clapton and Steve Winwood got together to form the supergroup Blind Faith. I bugged my parents for a guitar and one Christmas I found a shiny Fender knock-off, complete with amplifier, under the tree. Listening to my brother's LPs, I taught myself to play.

Maybe these proficiencies were what Nana had in mind when she'd preach her sermons of assurance; maybe not. For my own part, I never thought about success in terms of any one particular skill. I just knew there were a lot of fun things to do in the world, and a few of those things I was pretty good at.

I remember looking forward to junior high for two reasons above all others: the first being the hundreds of new kids who would soon be pouring into my little world from feeder schools across the district, and second, the elective class. Electives were opportunities for students to choose their subjects of study. Awesome responsibility. Serious implications. I weighed all this, and selected acting and guitar. My guidance counselors and parents were unenthusiastic, but that's where my interests lay and, just as important, that's where the girls were.

Guitar was a breeze, real basic stuff, finger picking "Alley Cat" from the Big Note Songbook. But it was in that class that I made a friend who would help me realize my musical ambitions. Andy Hill was a grade ahead of me and already the acknowledged king of Edmond's junior high school. A four-sport star athlete—hockey, basketball, rugby, and track—his athletic prowess paled in comparison to his self-taught proficiency in music. We'd swap Keith Richards guitar riffs, with me usually on the learning end of our jam sessions. By the end of the first semester, we'd formed a band, named Halex after the Ping-Pong balls of the same name. In our early teens we were already making the rounds—playing high schools, navy bases, and one or two places we weren't even old enough to enter legally. As I saw it, rock and roll offered a far more realistic shot at the big time than the NHL. Of course, to everyone else in my working-class Canadian world, a world with which I was beginning to feel increasingly out of sync, both fantasies were equally ridiculous.

Then there was drama class. Prior to junior high, I had appeared in a few school plays and discovered, if not a passion for acting, at least a mild affinity. Memorizing lines came easily. And I drank up the laughter and attention. At the secondary school level, with more challenging material and a greater focus on process, I felt myself being drawn deeper into the campus theatrical community.

And then I had what was for me a revelation: with a modicum of effort, I found I could effectively lose myself in whatever character I was called upon to play. At a time when I was increasingly finding myself at odds with various codes of conduct—school, family, social cliques—acting provided me with the freedom, in fact the imperative, that I follow my impulse, behave in any manner I saw fit, just so long as it served the role. Excellent!

I appeared in every new school production, eventually joining the school touring company, which meant spending a great deal of my time with Edmond's acting teacher, Ross Jones. One of those charismatic *anti*-teachers that artistic students tend to gravitate toward— long hair, droopy mustache, red-rimmed eyes—Mr. Jones was so subversive he actually let us call him Ross. Like most of the drama teachers I've known, Ross was a frustrated performer who was excited by students that showed a potential that in his own life he may have felt he hadn't taken full advantage of. He pressed me to take my theatrical studies as far as I could. "There could be a future in this for you, Mike." I'd laugh. "You're high, Ross. Acting isn't a job. You can't make a living at it . . . not like rock and roll."

For most of my secondary education, my head was in the clouds as I explored drama and music and art. Academically, however, it was somewhere else—up my ass, if you asked my father. My grades were slipping precipitously; the straight *A*s I brought home from grade school were a memory. If my junior high school career was any indication, I wasn't exactly poised to set the world on fire—not the *real* world, anyway.

Sure, in subjects that were outright creative, I excelled; drama, music, creative writing and various art electives, drawing, painting, printmaking, etc., consistently earned me *A*s. But in any subject that was based on fixed rules, like math or chemistry and physics, my grades tanked.

I can remember the exasperated look on my mother's face at report card time as I'd try to explain this to her. "These are absolutes, Mom. They're boring. Take math, two plus two equals four, I mean, that's already on the books, right? Somebody's already nailed that down. So what do they need me for?" Mom would sigh and make sure to sign the report card before Dad got home from work.

When red flags began to pop up on the school front, Dad, army signalman that he was, got right to work. A barely passing grade, or a call from school about a trip to the principal's office, meant a harsh reprimand from Dad, followed by probative questions about what the hell I was thinking and demands that I immediately cease and desist. My failure to comply wasn't rebellion, strictly speaking; it wasn't motivated by anger toward my parents, or anybody else for that matter. In fact, I shared their surprise I wasn't doing better in school. Yet, through junior high my academic grades continued to decline. The instant reprisals from Dad, once automatic, became more rare as he recognized their futility. Instead Dad resorted to curling his lip, throwing up his hands, and stalking off—that is, if I didn't slink off first.

I preferred to avoid confrontation. During my teenage years that meant avoiding my dad as much as possible. My essential approach to life, my predilection for winging it, was clearly antithetical to his. He just didn't get it. It's not that I consciously sought to flaunt my opposing point of view. To do that would be to provoke his anger, which was the last thing I wanted to do. But I could say things to Dad that seemed perfectly benign, yet in a flash our conversation would somehow shift into a one-sided recitation of the riot act.

With the benefit of hindsight, I can see that two powerful forces were at play here, the two gravitational fields I've already referred to: Dad's battle-tested pragmatism and Nana's idealistic belief in destiny. It seems obvious now that my reaction to her passing was to do whatever I could to bolster my detachment from the practical world. I instinctively resisted any effort to fit me into the work-a-day mold embraced by my parents and their parents before them.

So an uneasy standoff developed between Dad and me. When he eventually began simply to throw up his hands, this didn't mean I had worn him down—I was, after all, the fourth of five kids. No, I think the truth of the matter lies in Dad's own inner compass. What was most important to him was that his children be safe, and that meant developing a clear sense of what was expected of them in the world, preparing them to play contributing roles in a society that, if his experience was any indication, wasn't likely to cut them any slack. This was the test that I was failing, and he was at a loss about how to make me understand what was at stake.

It's not that Dad didn't take pride in my creative pursuits. He and Mom showed up for every dramatic production, and out of the corner of my eye I could always find them in the front row. And when I couldn't actually see his face beaming with enjoyment, I could always hear his laughter booming above everyone else's. He'd even brag about my musical exploits to his co-workers; I was surprised when I went with Mom to pick him up from work one day and all the cops were slapping me on the back, tousling my shoulder-length hair, and referring to me as "the Halex kid."

Rock and roll—loud, unintelligible, and antisocial—was anathema to Dad. Even so, he managed to show up at a couple of our band's gigs, though he'd always be standing at the back of the room, as far from the noise as he could get without stepping out the door. Once, sticking around after a show to watch us pack up, he asked about the massive PA speakers we were loading into the truck. I explained that they were rentals, $250 a night. "How much you getting paid?" he asked. "$100," I said with a flush of self-satisfaction. His face reddened, the lip curled, and I sensed him struggle to maintain composure. "Let me get this straight. You have to rent equipment to do a job that doesn't even pay you enough to cover the rental of the equipment that you need to do the job?" The arms went up and he stomped off. So much for détente.

I had a real job once. In the summer of 1976, when I was fifteen. My mom made an attempt to simultaneously ease my father's concerns and gently steer me toward a more responsible approach to my future. There was a summer opening for a low-level office clerk, gofer really, at the cold storage facility where she worked. I spent the summer in her office making coffee, doing odd bits of paperwork, and filing. Down on the docks, fresh fish was being unloaded from trawlers whose captains would fill out storage orders, which I would then run back upstairs and deliver to the main office.

I earned $600 for two months' work, an achievement my parents lavishly congratulated me on. Their delight quickly evaporated when I spent the $600 to replace my electric guitar, the Japanese copy, with the real thing: a 1967 wood-grained Fender Telecaster that I purchased from an old jazz musician through a classified ad.

My parents may have found my band's music (and economics) baffling, but there was an upside to my involvement with Halex, as they saw it, and that was Andy Hill. An honor student, star athlete, and respectful son of a prominent orthopedic surgeon, Andy was exactly the kind of kid you wanted your son to hang out with. Hell, he was exactly the kind of kid you wanted your son to *be*.

Not only was I in Andy's band, but I had been accepted into his social circle, an overachieving clique comprised of South Burnaby's best and brightest. Most of them were the sons and daughters of doctors, lawyers, and other professionals, and they lived in the pricey Buckingham section of town. To ride my bike from my apartment complex by the shopping mall, past the old elementary school, and then cross the tree-lined boulevard that marked the boundary of this enclave was to enter another universe. I hung out with my new friends in their homes, which seemed palatial, swam in their backyard swimming pools, and practiced my music in their basement recreation rooms. At Andy's house there was a room dedicated exclusively to Halex; its walls were soundproofed with four inches of cork.

In time, though, I came to resent the sense of freedom and opportunity these kids had inherited from their parents. By my sixteenth birthday I had already begun to drift away from Andy's crowd and eventually the band.

There were other kids at school with whom I had more in common, socioeconomically anyway, and I began to spend more and more of my time with them, both in school and out. This was an edgier group. Basically good kids (I still count many of them as friends) but more overtly rebellious—longer hair, louder music, and more dismissive of conformity. Where I might have spent a Friday night with Andy staying up late to learn all the songs from *Who's Next*, a night at my friend Bill's house would involve ritualistically smoking an entire pack of cigarettes and working our way through a case of beer.

Times had changed. I was no longer just moving away from accepted patterns of behavior as I followed my muse; now, perhaps emboldened by my newly acquired taste for beer, I was rejecting them outright. I picked up another habit in addition to smoking and drinking.

Having somehow obtained my driver's license, I became a serial fender-bender, inflicting varying degrees of damage to my parents' vehicles at every opportunity. I was exhibiting all the classic symptoms of a downward adolescent spiral—*teenage wasteland*—so what intervened to stop it?

PULLIN' OUT OF HERE TO WIN

Throughout my life, I've made a habit of somehow salvaging victory at the very threshold of ignominious failure. Now, as would happen many times in the future, just when the earth seemed to be sliding out from beneath me like loose scree on a mountainside, I somehow stumbled onto a foothold that would lead me to higher ground.

Why, for example, would my dad continue to let me drive his cars if I kept bringing them home with dents in the quarter panels and broken taillights? Well, for starters, I'd apologize profusely. And then I'd arrange for the damage to be repaired and pay for it promptly and in full. Because I was working again. Not at the cold storage plant, but in a new job—the one I'd continue to have off and on for the next quarter century.

One day in the summer of 1977, our acting troupe was packing up props and painted backdrops in preparation for a performance we'd be giving that afternoon for one of the local grade schools. Ross Jones was on the phone in his office, a converted broom closet at the back of the drama class. He called me over and thrust a newspaper clipping into my hands. It was a casting call for a new television show at the CBC—Canadian Broadcasting Corporation. "They're looking for a bright twelve-year-old kid," he said. "And I was thinking, 'Hell, you'd be the brightest twelve-year-old kid they're ever going to meet.'" Ross had always said my height and youthful looks would someday turn out to be a blessing. "I talked to them and they can see you later this week."

I was dumbstruck but intrigued and, odd as this might sound, immediately confident. Ross was right. I could nail this. "Oh, and Mike," he said as he sent me off, "you don't have to worry about my ten percent." I smiled. I had no fucking idea what he was talking about.

A massive open audition, "a cattle call," in showbiz parlance, the search for the kid co-star of the new CBC situation comedy *Leo & Me* offered a one in a thousand shot at the job. I wanted to do it even if it did mean playing a twelve-year-old. Ross was right: here was payback for all the years of short jokes. As the day of the tryout neared, my confidence grew. My mom gave me a ride to the CBC studios in downtown Vancouver. When we walked in the door, a receptionist handed me a script. Scanning the room, packed with young hopefuls and their doting mothers, I searched for a couple of chairs where we could sit down and I could study my lines. I read the words on the pages, quickly understood where the jokes were intended to be, and silently ran through them in my mind.

This is how my mom remembers it: "There were all these little kids in there and mothers were fussing with their hair, but you wouldn't let me touch yours. The kids were all practicing their lines with their mothers, so I asked, 'Do you want to go through the lines with me?' 'Nope. I'm okay. I'm okay.' You just took it all so in stride."

Leo & Me, explained the director, would be a half-hour comedy about a thirty-something gambler who lives on a run-down yacht won in a poker game. Leo's playboy lifestyle is cramped when he unexpectedly inherits guardianship of a twelve-year-old nephew, Jamie—the "me" of the show's title. I hadn't given any thought about how to tell the director, producers, and other network types present at the audition, that I was, in fact, sixteen and not twelve. Was this going to be a problem? It became a moot point during the small talk after my reading, which they liked. I let slip how pissed off I was after flunking my driver's test for the second time. "It's discrimination," I fumed. "The minute you lay a phonebook on the driver's seat, they just check the fail box." They kept asking me follow-up questions, and the more humiliating details I disclosed, the more flat-out hilarious they found the entire story. *Who cares how old the kid is*, they must have thought, *he's a riot*.

"When you got the callback, and then the part, well, it was just surreal," Mom marvels. "I couldn't believe it." She couldn't, but I could.

In addition to the lead in the series, which would begin filming later that summer, I was also offered the lead role in a separate project, a TV film that would begin production shortly after I got out of school. It was that easy. After making $600 for the entire summer the year before, I would now be getting a check for $600 every week. That summer, between the eight episodes of *Leo & Me* and the TV movie, I pulled in almost six grand.

I mention the money because when people ask how it was that, given my many interests, it was acting that I ultimately decided to pursue, I'll laugh and give the glib but essentially honest reply: "It was the first thing I got paid any real money for." In 1977, for a sixteen-year-old, working-class Canadian kid, an army brat, $6,000 was a *shit-load* of cash. But that's really only part of the answer.

I enjoyed the experience, the creative process, and as much as anything else, the working environment on the set. For the first time I was accepted as an equal among adults—people with far more experience than I had, who recognized in me abilities that I had not known I possessed and helped me to nurture them. This applied not only to my fellow actors, or the producers and directors, but to the seemingly endless numbers of people—gaffers, sound engineers, camera crew, hair and makeup people, and all the others—that it takes to make a TV show.

When the cameras weren't rolling it seemed as if we were always laughing, and the tone of the humor was often darker, more complicated and irreverent than anything I'd known. These artists and artisans occupied a world apart from the sober and serious sort of workplace most adults I knew had resigned themselves to. These were the people my father had warned me about. I was home.

In the fall of 1977, I entered high school (which in Canada begins in the eleventh grade) with a new confidence—not in my ability to meet a new level of academic challenge, but in the conviction that school was, more than ever, irrelevant to me. Throughout the eleventh grade, I continued to pick up acting jobs, commercials, radio work, and guest spots on other CBC television series. It became more and more difficult to reconcile my burgeoning acting career with what to my mind were the increasingly pointless demands of school. Somehow I muddled through, though by the end of the final semester, I was still technically a few credits short of completing the eleventh grade. If I wanted my high school diploma and hoped to graduate with the rest of the class of 1979, I'd have to repeat those courses in the fall. If eleventh grade was tough, twelfth was going to be killer.

But before that, taking what was left of the summer after *Leo & Me* wrapped, I decided to spend some of my fresh TV money on a trip to California, my first. I'd made a new friend during the previous school year, a senior named Chris Coady. As bright as Andy Hill but with more of an outlaw edge, Coady had an irreverence and a twisted sense of humor that made him my ideal running buddy. The Rolling Stones' *Some Girls* tour would be passing through California in August, and we made plans to go catch the band at Anaheim Stadium. Chris didn't have a lot of cash, so I paid for most of the trip—the plane tickets, the motel room near Disneyland—and we had a blast. Living it up in the Hotel California, we lounged by the pool, drank watery American beer, and chatted up girls who, like us, had come from various parts of the world to see the Stones. By the day of the concert, we'd run through most of our money and handed over what was left to ticket scalpers. By our last two days there we were completely broke, our only sustenance being the hot chocolate we'd get at a nearby Denny's with the free coupons we scrounged from the motel lobby. I had no idea, of course, that by the following summer I'd actually be living in California. Those few days of pseudo-poverty were a foreshadowing of the two or three years of very real economic hardship I would soon have to endure.

During much of that fall I was, at least ostensibly, going to school by day and performing at night in a long-running hit play at the Vancouver Arts Club, the most prestigious Equity theater company in town. This meant working until well after midnight every night. I would climb out of bed in the morning exhausted, go through the I'm-off-to-class motions, climb into my new pickup truck, and drive to the nearest park. I'd pull under the cool shade of a maple tree, fish a foam pad out of the cab, lay it down in the bed of the truck, and go back to sleep.

My first subject in the morning was drama, and having left the ever-supportive Ross Jones behind in junior high, I found myself in the strange position of receiving solid reviews for my professional acting at the same time I was flunking high school drama for too many absences. Naturally I pointed this irony out to my drama teacher, arguing that I should get credit for the work experience. She wouldn't budge.

By November it became clear that I was flunking just about every class I had. The whole high school thing had become a farce. I talked to my parents and told them I truly did want to graduate, but not at the price of throwing away the promising career I had embarked on. Mom urged me to hang in there, and made me promise that if she and Dad could work out a compromise with the school—credit for work experience combined with tutoring and makeup courses outside of the regular classroom—I would stick with it and do my very best. Surprisingly, my dad sympathized with my frustrations even more than Mom. I was making a living. Indeed, he'd be the first to admit that I was making more in a year than he was. So my parents agreed to fight for me and vowed that if no compromise could be worked out, they would support my decision to leave school and work full-time.

The school administration refused to bend, and to my relief and surprise, my parents held up their end of the bargain. They supported my decision to drop out, despite the fact it had always been their dream to see one of their children go to college.

Why did they let me do it? Well, some of the credit has to go to Nana. "We had no reason to doubt that these opportunities, the plays and the job at the CBC, were what Nana said was gonna happen," my mother says now. "Because Nana was so strong in her beliefs, if we hadn't followed through and supported your decision, I would have felt like we were letting her down, as well as you. So Dad and I said, 'Go for it.'"

With Mom and Dad's blessing I gave notice that I would not be returning for classes in the spring. I made the rounds at school, collecting my things and saying good-bye to friends and those teachers with whom I was still on speaking terms. Their doubt about the wisdom of my decision was nearly unanimous. I remember one exchange in particular, with a social studies teacher. "You're making a big mistake, Fox," he warned. "You're not going to be cute forever." I thought about this for a beat, and as I turned to make my escape from his classroom—from school and, soon enough, from my life in Canada—I shot him a smile and replied in a measured tone, "Maybe just long enough, sir. Maybe just long enough."

Courtesy of the Canadian Broadcasting Company

CHAPTER THREE

Hollywood High

U.S. Interstate 5—April 1979

Here's an unlikely concept for a buddy movie, a sort of late 1970s, cross-generational Farley-Spade road picture: my dad and I driving through the night to California, on our way to Hollywood for my shot at the big time. My sidekick lay stretched out in the rearview mirror, Dad's 250 pounds contorted into the backseat of our 1977

Dodge Aspen. He was catching a little shut-eye while I drove the night shift, following the treacherous twists of Interstate 5 through Oregon's Cascade mountain range. We'd meet the sun as it brimmed over the more hospitable hills of northern California. Now that he was asleep, I could tune out his twenty-four-hour-all-news radio station and tune in the only static-free music I could find—new Doobie Brothers. "What a fool believes, he sees," crooned Mike McDonald, "no wise man has the power to reason away."

I remember thinking that night just how far Dad and I had come over the past few weeks. The fact that he was accompanying me to Hollywood, after years of regarding my ambitions from beneath a skeptical brow, was a turn of events I never would have anticipated. Of course his decision to let me bail on school was a gesture that cut both ways: sure, it was a show of support, but it was also, I knew, a challenge—this was put-up-or-shut-up time. Still, he'd given my clichéd dream of escape—dropping out of school to chase fame and fortune in America—an interesting twist: if I was going to be a runaway, I was going to be a runaway with a chauffeur.

Deciding to make my move that April was the hard part. It meant passing on work I had already lined up for the spring and summer in Vancouver: a German television production of *Huckleberry Finn*. But Toni Howard, an L.A.-based casting director I'd met on an earlier job, had convinced me that the time to strike was now. She believed I held an advantage: American producers would be eager to hire an experienced actor who looked young enough to play a kid, since labor laws made it costly to use actors under eighteen. Spring was also the casting season for TV pilots. It didn't take much to convince me, so supremely confident was I that a Hollywood career was my destiny. But since I wouldn't turn eighteen till June, I'd need my parents to sign off on my plan—and that seemed inconceivable.

Mom: "Are you sure this is what you want to do?"

Me: "Absolutely."

Dad: "You realize what you'd be turning down, right? You're *that* confident?"

Me: "Absolutely."

And then Dad shocked me.

"Well if you're going to be a lumberjack, you might as well go to the goddamn forest."

Dad agreed not only to drive me down to L.A., but to underwrite the adventure, putting the whole trip on his Visa card.

"A down payment on my pension plan," he joked.

I couldn't have been more earnest in my reply: "It's a deal."

We were off to the goddamn forest.

Los Angeles—April 1979

As soon as we checked into our room at the Westwood Holiday Inn on Wilshire Boulevard, I hit the phone, confirming sit-downs with agents who said, yes, Toni had been in touch and they were expecting my call. Dad advised me that he'd just drive to the appointments and debrief me after each one—his way of signaling to me that this was my show, not his.

My composure was tested during one particularly memorable interview. The agent in the chair across from me seemed distinctly underwhelmed at the prospect of representing me. An awkwardness hung over the office like a methane cloud. For some reason, she couldn't look me in the eye—her gaze kept drifting down to my feet. Finally, she summoned up the nerve to say what was on her mind, in the process interrupting some of my wittiest patter.

"Listen, Michael, you've got a great look and you're very funny and charming. Toni had wonderful things to say about you, so you're obviously talented. It's just that I don't understand why she didn't mention . . . that is, I wasn't prepared . . . well, I wasn't aware that you had a disability." And with that her eyes went back down to my feet.

"I don't. At least I don't *think* I do."

"Then why are you wearing orthopedic shoes?"

Now we were both staring at my feet. Those weren't orthopedic shoes. They weren't shoes at all, in fact, they were boots—jet black, glam rock, platform boots with four-inch heels and two-inch soles—the very height of 1970s cool, in my considered opinion. Embarrassed, I managed to laugh it off while assuring her that my only

handicap was being a few inches too short—and, I realized in a sick-
ening flash, several years behind the California fashion curve. Anyway,
the cloud quickly evaporated and the rest of the meeting went well.

After rejoining Dad in the office waiting room, we went downstairs to a coffee shop and slipped into a booth. "Well, she wants to
sign me too," I reported. "By the way, can you lend me another fifty
bucks? I gotta get a new pair of shoes."

On the fourth day in Los Angeles, we packed to go home; not because anything had gone wrong—quite the contrary, everything had
gone preposterously right. Every agent I met had offered to take me
on. Most had sent me out on auditions in order to gauge reaction,
polling the casting directors for feedback. Every audition earned a
callback, and three of the callbacks produced solid offers. This Hollywood thing was beginning to look easy.

Deciding which role to take was straightforward. Only one movie
was scheduled to start production in June, after my eighteenth birthday—a Disney feature called *Midnight Madness*. The less said about the
script, the better, but *Midnight Madness* was my first real job in America, and I was thrilled to have it.

Now, all that was left to do was hire an agent. Dad and I had lunch
with the Gersh Agency's Bob Gersh, the agent who'd sent me out on
the Disney job. Bob was naturally solicitous of my father's approval,
and he asked Dad if he had any questions. My father just smiled, put
his big hand on my shoulder, and said, "I prefer to let him do all the
talking." You have no idea just how exotic those words sounded coming from my dad.

"Did you know," I asked Dad as we left the restaurant in Beverly
Hills, "that his father, Phil Gersh, was Bogart's agent?" Dad just
shook his head. *Too much.* We drove back to the Holiday Inn,
checked out, and loaded our bags into the trunk. One last stop, delivering a pot of flowers to Toni Howard, and we were on the I-5
again, heading north.

Queen Elizabeth Park, New Westminster, B.C.—June 9, 1979
It was my eighteenth birthday, and I celebrated it back in Vancouver. I
had a plane ticket to leave the next morning for Los Angeles and

begin work on the Disney picture. Plenty of congratulations and backslaps all around. Mom, Dad, and my sibs were there, of course, as were most of my extended family—everyone from the videotape, in fact, with the sad exception of Nana. Chris Coady was present, and so, too, was Diane, the girl I'd been seeing for the previous six months.

The colors in the park that afternoon were jaw dropping. A cobalt sky presided over early summer gardens of pastel pinks and purples. Elsewhere, a dozen different shades of green—from the pale streaks of lichen on streamside boulders to the deep jade of the Douglas firs. In the distance a white-capped mountain range crowned the treetops. This is why the license plates say *Beautiful British Columbia*, and I realized just how much I would miss it. But all this natural beauty exists only in response to rain, I reminded myself, and the occasional day of technicolor spectacle was bought and paid for with weeks and weeks of dull, damp gray. I wasn't going to miss the gray.

If they could have overheard my thoughts that afternoon, my friends and family probably would no doubt have found them silly and self-dramatizing. It was only one movie, after all—one job, six weeks. It's not like I was *moving* to California, they'd say. I'd be back. I knew otherwise, and so, in their hearts, did my mom and dad, especially Dad. He had made a point of telling me on the way back to Canada how well I'd handled myself and how proud he was. "You've got the world by the tail," he announced while driving north on I-5. "Just hold on." I realized that for me, the trip we made together to Los Angeles had been a rite of passage, a coming-of-age ceremony, like those in cultures the world over. But unlike many such rites, which often involve abandonment or even scarification—some physical evidence of a test or ordeal endured—mine was not a wounding ritual. Dad had found a way to get past his misgivings and make my rite a ceremony of healing.

Did this mean that on my eighteenth birthday, I had actually come of age? The events of the next fifteen years or so would lead one to a very different conclusion. But on that June ninth in the park, with friends, family, and other well-wishers gathered around, I felt as if I had reached a new level of maturity. There was no question in my mind that I was now indeed a *man*—as I leaned over and blew out the candles on a birthday cake decorated with an image of Mickey Mouse.

OPENING CREDITS

The Slums of Beverly Hills — 1979–1981

> *An inventory of my worldly possessions circa 1980: one duffel bag full of clothing (i.e., dirty laundry), one hot plate, some mismatched kitchenware, toiletries, blanket, bed sheets, and a wind-up alarm clock. Oh, and then there was the furniture: one mattress and one folding canvas director's chair.*

My studio apartment was seventeen by twelve feet with a microscopic bathroom—toilet, shower, no tub, and the domicile's one and only sink. The sink basin was too tiny to do dishes in, so I'd have to take them with me into the shower. More than once I washed my hair with Palmolive and my dishes with Head and Shoulders. A closet doubled as the kitchen.

Technically, my address was that of a small pink stucco apartment building on Shirley Place in Beverly Hills, although I rarely saw the building's peaceful, tree-lined street side—I came and went via the back alley. There was a tiny separate garage structure where tenants would park their cars. My unit was one of the three built into the space above it. My front window gazed across a six-foot-wide pathway at the pink backside of the mother building. Peering through the narrow transom window in the bathroom required standing on top of the toilet seat. With nothing out there but Dumpsters, parked cars, and oil-stained asphalt, the vista did not reward the effort. But for $225 a month with a six-month lease, this was paradise.

My alley marked the boundary between Beverly Hills and Century City, a tight cluster of soaring glass-and-steel office buildings constructed on land that was once the old Twentieth Century Fox back lot. Shirley Place was named for Shirley Temple, Fox's biggest star at the time the maps were redrawn. Sometimes referred to as "the slums of Beverly Hills," the ring of multi-unit dwellings that circle the more affluent residential areas are actually attractive and luxurious—by my standards, anyway. People can live in bigger apartments for less money elsewhere in the city, but they covet the 90210 zip code that Aaron Spelling's Beverly Hills High soap opera was going to make world famous. The school itself, which backed up against the end of my alley, reeks of privilege and exclusivity. Just to walk past it can be an intimidating experience, as I discovered the day I bought my folding canvas director's chair.

I'd picked up the chair—my first big purchase—for thirty bucks at Thrifty Drugs. Trekking back toward the apartment, *my home*, the chair slung over my shoulder, I must have looked like a complete rube, a total dink. Just as I was about to make the turn down my alley, a teenager from the high school drove by in a Porsche convertible. Slowing to a crawl, he considered me for a second and then, over the rumble of his turbo-charged engine, shouted, "Go back to the Valley!" I had no idea what he was talking about. *The Valley?* He meant the San Fernando, but for all I knew he was talking about the Fraser River Valley—Camp Chilliwack.

Life as a fish out of water in Beverly Hills didn't really faze me, though. I'd always been an outsider in one way or another, and L.A.—hell, America—seemed like outsider headquarters. As the number of days I spent there added up, so did the number of eccentrics, risk takers, and freethinkers I encountered. Equally captivating was the breathtaking racial and ethnic diversity. As I saw it, California was everything that Canada, with its polite provincialism and reverence for order, could never be. So, far from being alienated, I actually felt at home. The logic of this mecca of nonconformity was this: not fitting in meant that I truly belonged.

Along with a new country, new city, new job, new apartment, and new chair, I'd also picked up a new identity. The Screen Actors Guild prohibits any two members from working under the same stage name, and they already had a "Michael Fox" on the books. My middle name is Andrew, but "Andrew Fox" or "Andy Fox" didn't cut it for me.

"Michael A. Fox" was even worse, the word *fox* having recently come into use as a synonym for attractive. (Presumptuous?) It also sounded uncomfortably Canadian—Michael *Eh?* Fox—but maybe I was just being oversensitive. And then I remembered one of my favorite character actors, Michael J. Pollard, the guileless accomplice in *Bonnie and Clyde*. I stuck in the *J*, which I sometimes tell people stands for either *Jenuine* or *Jenius*, and resubmitted my forms.

So it said Michael J. Fox on the call sheet I picked up at wrap each night that summer, or more accurately, each morning. True to its title, *Midnight Madness* turned out to be an endless series of all-nighters: six weeks of almost exclusively night shoots. The mix of late nights and young actors gave the set a loose frat party ambience. At least we had a few laughs—several more, we correctly sensed, than the audience ever would. Personally, I was just happy to be there. So what if I was working all night on a lousy project?—it left my days free to audition for better ones.

Determined to stay in L.A., I hit the pavement looking for future employment. By autumn I'd landed my third post-*Madness* project. My only disappointment was not landing a feature film. I came close on a couple of movies, most notably *Ordinary People*, earning a callback to see the director. But Robert Redford seemed less than impressed by my reading; he spent the audition flossing his teeth. My next big screen role would not be until 1981, the then-futuristically titled *Class of 1984*, a teen exploitation flick that would make *Midnight Madness* look like *Casablanca*.

Instead, I appeared in episodes of *Family*, *Lou Grant*, and in September had begun work as a regular on *Palmerstown U.S.A.*, a CBS midseason pickup with an order for eight one-hour episodes. *Walton-esque* in tone, the drama chronicled a friendship between two families, one white, one black, in rural 1930s Tennessee. Reluctant at first, I committed to the show largely on the strength of its creator/producer team of Alex Haley and Norman Lear. As a bonus, the Southern twang I had to affect as the redneck but well-meaning son of the town grocer helped to flatten out the conspicuously rounded vowels of my Canadian accent.

With even more episodic TV work (*Trapper John, M.D.*; *Here's Boomer*); the odd industrial film and commercial (McDonald's, Tilex Foaming Tub and Tile Cleaner); as well as that previously mentioned cinema classic, *Class of 1984*, my first two-and-a-half years in Los Angeles had amounted to a reasonably successful run. Nothing spectacular, no redwoods were felled, but I had been able to find my way to a sufficient supply of nuts and berries.

So why then, as 1981 wound down and 1982 loomed through the trees, was I perilously near starvation?

Naïveté would be a generous explanation for the financial predicament I found myself in—abject stupidity, perhaps more honest. There's a cautionary lesson here. When I first arrived, the proverbial babe-in-the-woods, there were plenty of savvy forest denizens happy to offer guidance in exchange for a share of my earnings. I don't regard them as bad guys, but I don't think they woke up each morning wondering, "What can I do for Michael today?" The only true villain was a ravenous monster of my own creation, one I had unwittingly brought with me from Canada and kept locked in a kitchen cabinet.

NO ABSOLUTION

Those first days in L.A. were heady, but I was still only eighteen and a long way from home. I was always grateful whenever friends and family visited me in California. Coady came down for a week, and among other things, we hiked into the scrubby hills of the Cahuenga Pass in search of the Hollywood sign, where we shot a photo series of each of us dangling and lounging on its nine gigantic letters. My girlfriend Diane made a separate trip, and before leaving made plans to return, a pattern that would repeat itself until we were, for all intents and purposes, living together. All of my visitors expressed the same concern: while I'd taken great care of my career, I didn't seem to be taking very good care of myself.

It's true that I'd developed some unhealthy attitudes regarding food and shelter. Tired of wrangling with the hot plate and scrubbing pots and pans with a soap-on-a-rope, I enlisted Ronald McDonald as my exclusive nutritionist. For any sustenance not offered on the golden arches menu, I improvised—beer and cigarettes, I reasoned, must fit someplace within the four major food groups.

My casual approach to housekeeping made the one-room walk-up increasingly claustrophobic. A space that small simply couldn't withstand the accumulation of domestic debris that litters a bachelor's existence—Big Mac boxes, magazines, long-obsolete script pages, dirty laundry, dirty dishes, even dirty *dirt*. At one point, I adopted a cat for company. It turned out to be a tom who soon left for better prospects, but not before he'd permeated the apartment with an aroma well matched to its décor.

Bob Gersh picked me up for lunch one day. After getting a look at (and whiff of) my apartment, he realized that his newest client, while a decent earner, was no star in the self-maintenance depart-ment. It was time, he calculated, to call in reinforcements.

He introduced me to a husband and wife management team, who I'll refer to as B & S. Managers, they explained, do whatever agents cannot. Available at any hour, they'd devise the perfect career strategy, help me establish and meet goals, and so much more. With their vast network of contacts, they'd get me on a fast track to success. Bottom line: they'd be my new best friends in Hollywood.

For his part, Bob earned the standard ten percent of my paycheck off the top, and for holding my hand, my new managers took another twenty percent. (Who says you can't put a price on friendship?) Whenever I needed help they couldn't provide, B & S directed me to-ward the appropriate Hollywood professional: a photographer, publi-cist, or lawyer. In my teenaged, fresh-from-Canada cluelessness, this pattern of delegating any and everything that needed doing in my life produced what I thought of as an ever-widening circle of "allies." Only much later did I realize that "feeding frenzy" was probably a more apt description.

Halfway through the first season of *Palmerstown*, my lease was up. Diane was by now my roommate, and needing more space, we found a slightly larger but equally funky one-bedroom apartment in nearby Brentwood. The new rent was almost double, $425, but in addition to a bathtub, this place boasted an actual kitchen sink.

Above the kitchen sink there was a cupboard—just the right size for a monster. This was about the time that the mathematical "absolutes" I protested to my mother about during junior high school came back to bite me on the ass. You see, I had no patience for numbers, and therefore no facility for keeping track of my debts and expenditures.

I was earning SAG minimum rates, which, I came to learn, barely covered the basics—apartment, clothing, car rental, food—plus business expenses (all those percentages). Then there was Uncle Sam. I had overlooked a subtlety in my check stubs during that first year in L.A.: my employers hadn't been deducting any state or federal taxes from my payments, and it never occurred to me, or my high-priced handholders, that I should be putting any money away for that purpose.

Around this time I developed a habit of collecting all my bills, unpaid tax notices, and threatening missives from creditors into a loose, disorganized bundle and jamming them into that cupboard above the kitchen sink: a growing paper monster. Not wanting to think about it any more than I had to, never mind actually look at it, I'd open the cupboard only long enough to feed the beast more red ink, then quickly slam the door shut. Out of sight, out of mind, like a Fibber McGee closet full of daunting, implacable absolutes.

When I received my first tax bill from the IRS, I made a panicky call to B & S, and they recommended an accountant. This guy laid out an orderly method for applying all my present and future earnings toward achieving solvency, including paying off back taxes, for which services he would deduct from all present and future earnings five percent off the top. This brought my total up-front fees to a staggering thirty-five percent. "You also have to stop letting employers rent cars for you and deduct the charges from your paycheck," my new accountant advised. "Their rates are inflated." So, he generously leased me his Porsche.

My CPA's blueprint for financial recovery never made it off the drawing board. Unable to work during a prolonged SAG strike in 1980, I was nearly broke going into the second and last season of *Palmerstown*. After the series was canceled, there were a few jobs, but they barely earned me enough to live on—and nowhere near enough to begin seriously paying down my debts. While most out-of-work actors can supplement their income by boxing groceries or waiting tables, my alien status made this impossible. The only way I could work legally in the U.S. was as an actor. I was in a bind.

Buying into the time-honored Hollywood maxim that image is everything, I took some comfort in driving the Porsche—at least I didn't *look* unemployed.

Eventually the accountant deemed me more trouble than I was worth. I fell behind on his bills, too—not only for the lease of the car, but also for his bookkeeping services. He dumped me and repossessed the Porsche. Now he was just another name on my lengthening list of creditors.

"WHY DIDN'T ANYBODY TELL ME?"

A word about rejection. Auditions, most struggling actors will tell you, suck. You get a few pages of a script and read it over and over in hopes of picking up some clue to the character, some insight that will give you an edge in translating written words into a living, breathing, engaging, and profound approximation of human behavior. If you can do this better than any of the other actors in competition for the role, you get to eat; if you can't, you don't. At least, you delude yourself into thinking it's that simple. It's not.

You also have to be careful that you're not too skinny, fat, tall, short, blond, redheaded, dark, light, loud, quiet, young, or old, and that there isn't something about you that reminds the director of his or her girlfriend, boyfriend, father, mother, priest, therapist, or despised stepchild. You want to be familiar enough with the material to look up from the page every now and then, but for God's sake don't memorize it; you'll appear arrogant, like you already have the job. Above all else, no matter how badly you need work, no matter how hungry you are, how exhausted you've become from playing duck-the-landlord, never, ever show desperation. For me, that first rule of auditioning was getting harder and harder to pull off.

Back when I was the new kid in town, I didn't have to carry the burden of expectation with me into an interview. That is, the producer/director/casting director had no idea what to expect of me, no preconceived notion of who I was. So, I could do a halfway decent job with the material, dazzle them with a little small talk on either side of the reading, and be considered a *fresh* casting choice—new and different.

But by now I'd been on the scene for three years. I was a known quantity in every casting office in town, and I was all out of small talk. I began to long for the benign indifference of Robert Redford flossing his molars. That was like a standing ovation compared to some of the experiences I'd been having lately. Some were so humiliating they were almost comical, like the ad executive who screamed at me during a commercial audition. It seems I had not folded the stick of Wrigley's into my mouth as diagrammed on the instruction sheet posted in the waiting room, but instead had the audacity to jam it in sideways in a single indelicate motion. And I called myself an actor. *Next!*

The rejection can be so matter-of-fact, so impersonal, that there's a danger you'll get numbed by it. I still felt the pain, but it had less to do with what these strangers thought of me than what I was perilously close to thinking about myself. For so long, my actions had been instinctive, in confident defiance of the world around me. Without that faith in myself, I'd truly be lost. But until then, there was still a chance. Of course, more than anything, what I needed now, badly, was someone in a position to help me, who also shared in that faith.

Luckily, I was about to find that person, although—as he would recount to me many times later—it wasn't exactly faith-at-first-sight.

Paramount Studios, Hollywood—1982
"You gotta stop hocking me about this kid," writer/producer Gary David Goldberg pleaded with Judith Wiener, the casting director of his new sitcom pilot. "He's just not our guy." Gary was convinced that

in the month since Matthew Broderick, his first choice for the teenage-son role, declined, not one of the hundreds of young actors to audition was an acceptable alternative. Judith insisted Gary was making a big mistake by refusing to take another look at the very first actor she'd brought in to read. "Gary, you're forgetting how good he was. What's the harm of bringing him in for a callback?"

Goldberg bristled at having his instincts called into question. And why shouldn't he? They had served him well. A Brooklyn kid, high school all-city basketball star turned Berkeley dropout, Gary and his future wife, Diana, spent the late 1960s and early 1970s as counterculture nomads. With their black lab Ubu, they wandered the world, for a time living in a cave in Greece before a newborn daughter forced them to settle down and try adulthood. In his San Diego apartment watching a *Bob Newhart* rerun one day while Diana job hunted, Gary had a gut feeling he could write a *Newhart* script. So he did. He sent it off to the producers and in no time, the bearded former Berkeley radical was a rising star among MTM's stable of comedy writers.

Now, just a few short years since relying on food stamps to feed his family, Gary Goldberg was producing his own TV show. Grant Tinker, his old MTM boss and now the head of NBC, had a hunch that Gary and Diana's experience as ex-hippies raising a family made a great premise for a series. The young writer poured his heart into the pilot script, and he wasn't going to screw it up with bad casting. Judith was really driving him nuts though, so he agreed to see her candidate one more time, but not without a final protest. "It's a waste of time, Judith. There's no way I'm going to change my mind on this. I'm a grown man. I know what I want and I know what I don't want. And I'm telling you, I don't want Michael Fox playing Alex Keaton."

The Slums of Brentwood — 1982

If my first journey into the "forest" back in the spring of 1979 was like a Grimm brothers' fairy tale, by the spring of 1982, when I auditioned for Gary Goldberg, the scenario was just plain grim—no happily-ever-after in sight.

Now and then, I'd receive a residual check for an old commercial or TV episode—usually small amounts that passed first through the hands of my agent and managers, taxes paid up front, so the figure I actually netted would be pitifully small. Diane, while still nominally my girlfriend, had returned to Vancouver, this time staying there to find a full-time job. She liked California, but why live the life of the starving artist if she didn't have to? Whether or not I was an artist at all was debatable, as I had no opportunity to develop my craft and no offers to do so. The starving part fit, though. My diet had been reduced to cans and boxes with declarative, generic labels—like TUNA or MACARONI.

What few possessions I owned, like my furniture, I began to liquidate. Over a period of months, I sold off my sectional sofa section by section. The buyer was another young actor living in my building. Adding insult to indigence was the incremental nature of the transaction, emphasizing, as it did, the inverse trajectories of our respective careers.

My parents, and even Coady, God bless him, would send a few dollars when they had it to spare. Lately, however, my friends and family in Canada were urging me to quit and come home. Along with the last check my father sent to me, he included a particularly eloquent letter, which I no longer have, but the gist of it was this: In the three years since we'd first traveled together to Los Angeles, he was proud of what I'd accomplished and I had every reason to be, too. Given my present situation, though, he suggested that it might be wise to pull the curtain, at least for now. There would be no shame in returning to Canada and rethinking my options.

Options? These were my options as I saw them: My brother would no doubt be good enough to hire me as a laborer on one of the construction sites he supervised. Given my size and experience, that would amount to picking up nails until a clerking job opened up. Coady could find work for me at the railroad, probably on the night shift patrolling the yards with a flashlight, chasing bums out of boxcars. Or maybe I'd make a less-than-triumphant return to the cold storage plant where my mother worked. Then there was my debt to the IRS to consider. If I ran out on that, it'd be good-bye to the United States forever.

My folks had one thing figured correctly: whether it would be an ignominious slouch homeward or a miraculous reversal of fortune, something had to give, and soon. I was down to days.

Paramount Studios, Hollywood — 1982

Judith Wiener met me in the reception area. It was empty, the door to the inner office closed. The callback had surprised me. It had been, what—a month since I first read for *Family Ties*? I tried to affect an air of confidence, though I'm sure I reeked of desperation. Judith prepped me. "You'll be meeting the same people: three of the writers and Gary Goldberg, the creator/producer. Everybody thought your first audition was great." This was a fudge. It was true, I'd find out, that the other writers had been as vocal as Judith in their support for my casting, but Gary remained skeptical.

"One suggestion . . . Do what you can to make the character a little more lovable."

Lovable? The guy was a know-it-all, tie-wearing, Nixon-worshipping teenager who valued money above all else. You'd think they would have addressed the whole "lovable" thing in the writing.

"You got it," I promised. I had to land this job. Whatever happened in the next ten minutes was going to decide my fate one way or the other.

Judith showed me in. Gary recited a rambling monologue about what made Alex tick. I nodded. And then I read. Right away I could feel I was in *the zone*. The laughter was huge, and it wasn't just "writers laughing at their own jokes" laughter, they were laughing at what I was bringing to it.

Gary offered a few brief notes and I went through it again. Now I was feeling, if not cockiness, then something akin to joy. I even ad-libbed a little—sometimes a risky play, but I was scoring with every single line. After I finished, the laughter rolled on, but it had a different quality now; something I'd later understand to be relief. Gary David Goldberg, a dark, bearded, thick-set bear of a man, leaned back in his leather chair and tried in vain to cover his delight with a mask of mock outrage.

"Judith," he bellowed, "why didn't anybody tell me about this kid?"

ROLE REVERSAL

NBC Studios, Burbank, California—March 1982
The casting of *Family Ties*, as with any TV pilot episode, would never be a done deal until the prospective cast members—the producers' final choices—had "gone to the network." The Keaton family, as selected by Gary Goldberg, consisted of Michael Gross and Meredith Baxter Birney as the hippie parents, and myself, Justine Bateman, and Tina Yothers as the yuppie-era kids. This roster could not be officially locked in, however, until the NBC brass—specifically Brandon Tartikoff, the new *wunderkind* head of programming—gave the official seal of approval. Given Gary's desire to cast me in the role—he now had the unmistakable zeal of a convert—I naïvely viewed this last round of auditions as a formality. I was not only positive that I would be cast, but was even looking past the fact that this was only a pilot, its future as an actual series not yet assured. No, this was my ticket out of impoverished oblivion, that foothold I'd always managed to find that would lead me to higher ground.

It's a SAG requirement that, even before a performer "goes to network" on a series, a contract be negotiated and in place, effective immediately upon network casting approval. So, as I saw it, I already had a six-year deal.

Bob Gersh, B & S, and I had hammered out the details that morning on a conference call. What made the scene particularly memorable was where I stood, quite literally, during this conversation. Pacific Bell had long since cut off service to my apartment, and as I spelled out my contract demands—modest by today's standards, but inconceivably lucrative given my financial straits—I was standing at a pay phone outside of a Pioneer Chicken franchise. While my agent was talking about a seven-figure salary should the series go six years, I stared at the menu

through the restaurant's window, wishing I had $1.99 to buy the buf-
falo wing–mashed potato combo.

There was plenty of laughter during my audition before the Ar-
mani-suited NBC executives in Burbank, although I couldn't help
noticing that Gary's was the loudest—certainly much more enthusi-
astic than Brandon Tartikoff's. Brandon asked me to fill him in on my
prior television experience, and I figured I should list my appearances
on NBC programs—an unbelievably dumb idea. At that time, NBC
was in a hopeless ratings slump, and my litany of the network's bombs
did nothing to endear me to Brandon; it only made him wince.
Thankfully, Gary came to my rescue, generating a gigantic laugh
with his shout from the back of the room—"Get to the hits, Fox, get
to the hits."

As I left the NBC offices, I had an inkling of the power struggle
under way, but only later would I understand the big picture. I was
back in the same limbo I'd been in for the last month, only now Gary
had taken over Judith's role as president of the Michael J. Fox Fan
Club, and Brandon was the adamant skeptic. He was absolutely against
giving me the role of Alex Keaton.

"We weren't bothered by (Fox's) comedy skills," he wrote later in
his book, *The Last Great Ride*, "but by his height. How could someone that short have Michael Gross and Meredith Baxter Birney as his
parents?"

He laid out his case to Gary: "It always annoyed me as a kid
watching *Father Knows Best* that Bud Anderson was so much shorter
than his parents. To me, that undercut the credibility of the whole
show. Let's not make that same mistake here."

Unbeknownst to me, the argument raged on, right up to the day
we began rehearsal for the *Family Ties* pilot. Gary Goldberg stood his
ground. "Goldberg is not a person who changes his mind easily,"
Brandon wrote, "so I relented. 'Go ahead if you insist.'"

Throughout the eight days of rehearsal, I experienced a dizzying
mix of feelings; day by day I developed a strong affinity for the character and the material, discovering and flexing comedic muscles I
never knew I had. At the same time, with victory in my grasp, I felt

terror at the thought it might slip away. Although oblivious of Gary and Brandon's tug-of-war, I understood that until the moment we began rolling videotape, it would be a relatively simple matter for me to be fired and replaced. This had already happened to a guest actor on the fourth day. We broke for lunch and when we came back, someone else was reading her lines. My overriding emotion, though, was relief and joy at being given this opportunity. And as I rode the bus down Sunset Boulevard toward the studio each morning, I felt like the luckiest guy on the planet.

Alex Keaton was never meant to be *Family Ties*' featured character. The original plan was for the sitcom to revolve around the experience of the parents, especially its only established star, Meredith Baxter Birney. It was just a quirk of fate that the story told in the pilot episode happened to be centered on Alex's desire to date the daughter of a wealthy Republican country club family. The writers clearly enjoyed the character they'd created as much as I enjoyed playing him. From the moment I ad-libbed the initial "P" during a scene when Alex answered the phone, as in "Alex P. Keaton here," the writing staff and I became de facto partners, together creating a benevolent monster.

The night we taped the pilot was an unqualified triumph. The audience's appreciation was deafening, and it was obvious and especially gratifying, given my recent tribulations, that I was being singled out for my performance. During my curtain call, a slow trot out to the duct-tape line that marked the edge of the proscenium, the audience's applause meant more to me than anyone could realize. I felt as though they were aware of my full history—the years, months, and desperate days—leading up to that moment, and this was a salute: "Way to go, Mike, you gritty little son of a bitch. You made it."

NBC loved the pilot, ordering thirteen episodes for the fall season and also singling me out—but not for approval. Brandon took one more run at Gary in an attempt to have me fired. But Gary, now more than ever, would not be swayed. "Brandon, I'm telling you, this guy is amazing."

"Maybe," Brandon countered. "But I'm telling *you*, this is not the kind of face you'll ever see on a lunchbox."

Gary was dumbfounded that this should be the criteria for select-ing an actor. "Look, all I know is this," he said finally in exasperation. "I send the kid out with two jokes, and he brings me back five laughs." And those, gratefully, were the closing salvos in Brandon's Dump Fox campaign. The war was over, and Gary David Goldberg had prevailed.

I heard about these exchanges, not from Gary, as you might ex-pect, but from Brandon himself. It is a credit to his humility and fa-mously self-effacing sense of humor that he spoke publicly about them three years later, at the height of my success in *Back to the Future*, as if to point out what a fool he'd been. By that time, Brandon and I were good friends, regularly meeting to have lunch and pick each other's brains about the state of television comedy. It was at one of these luncheons when I presented him with a custom-made lunchbox I'd commissioned, emblazoned with my smiling and by now very fa-mous face. There was an inscription: "To Brandon: This is for you to put your crow in. Love and Kisses, Michael J. Fox."

In 1997, Brandon lost the battle with brain cancer he had been se-cretly waging for over a decade. In his brief but brilliant career, Bran-don brought a contemporary sense of humanity to television, inspiring innovations in programming that still resonate today. I'm proud that, however reluctant he may have been at first, he allowed me to come along for the ride. And I am flattered that right up until the last day of his life, he kept my lunchbox on a shelf behind his office desk.

Diane was in the studio the fateful night of the pilot taping. Al-though we hadn't formally let go of the relationship, by now she was settling into her new/old life in Vancouver. She had come down to L.A. during the week of rehearsal, accompanied me to the post-show celebration, and was at my side as one well-wisher after another— from the families of cast members and writers to network executives, to members of the crew—approached me with congratulations and compliments. My adrenaline was running so high, I couldn't imagine ever finding an outlet to release it. Diane had an idea though, and we quickly said good-bye to everybody and returned to the apartment.

We lay on the floor at the foot of the bed, tangled in bedsheets and passing between us a bottle of champagne I had boosted from the wrap party. By now it was 4:00 A.M. and the mood was bittersweet.

Although we had only begun seeing each other in the months prior to my moving to Los Angeles, I had known Diane since the first week of junior high. Part of the Andy Hill crowd, she was one of the pretty, smart, athletic girls I could never imagine having any interest in me. Now, looking into her brown eyes that night, I could see that she understood the impact of the evening's events and the direction that they would soon take me. Sweetly, generously, she said as much that night.

"This is what you've always wanted and I'm happy for you," she began. "Your life is going to be so different from now on, and I'm not going to be a part of it. I just want you to know that I understand— it's okay. This is not the kind of life I'm looking for. But you have to promise me you'll be careful. I'll be very upset if anything bad happens to you."

She was right, of course. From that evening on, my life would never again be the same. The next morning, Diane returned to Vancouver, and although we continued seeing each other sporadically for a while, we soon drifted apart. A few years later I heard from Diane again. She'd married an airline pilot, settled down in the suburbs of Vancouver, and was raising a family.

The Rolling Stones' *Exile on Main Street* album cover included a detachable insert—a perforated sheet of postcards. A couple days after the taping, I pulled one out, affixed a stamp on it, and jotted down a message to Coady.

"Just did a pilot for a sitcom called *Family Ties*," I scribbled. "Pretty damn funny."

Did I dare put it in writing?—I could, and did:

"Think I may finally be about to go large."

LONDON CALLING

Churchill Hotel, London—June 1985, 3:30 A.M. BST
Ring . . . rrring . . . Ring . . . rrring . . .
   "Aaaarrgh!"
Not a purring twenty-first-century American slimline, but an

old-style, Brit double ringer—the phone clanged like Big Ben on my nightstand. It woke me with all the subtlety of a cleaver slicing through my beer-and-wine-soaked brain. *Jesus, my head . . . Where the hell am I?*

Still in London was the answer that came slowly into focus, shooting the never-to-be-a-classic television movie, *Family Ties Goes to London.* This was our third season, and after a steady climb, and blessed with the juggernaut of the new *Cosby Show* for a lead-in, *Family Ties* finished number two in the Nielsen ratings. We were a hit.

The cast genuinely liked being with one another, and all were in good spirits as we landed at Gatwick, many of us with family in tow. Plans to explore, shop, and sightsee were soon crushed, however, by the logistical reality of shooting a TV movie on a tight schedule in a foreign country. Making matters worse was the material—a contrived story and slapdash script—not up to the show's usual standard.

The writers were apologetic. They'd burnt themselves out over the course of the previous season, rising to the challenge of pleasing an audience suddenly doubled in size and churning out one outstanding episode after another. They'd also had to deal that season with Meredith Baxter Birney's pregnancy. Expecting twins, she was put on bed rest, which meant Gary and the staff would have to write around her for several episodes and then write her out of several more. On top of that, we had to shut down for a month right in the middle of our season.

Another complication that season was entirely my fault and was, in fact, the reason I was now being terrorized by the telephone at such an ungodly hour.

"Hello," I croaked. In the half-second, transatlantic delay before my caller's words reached me, I peered through slitted eyes at my disaster area of a hotel room. Assessing the damage wasn't difficult because all of the lights were burning. This indicated I hadn't fallen asleep so much as passed out. It would appear the party had ended here. Guinness bottles littered the suite. Plates of half-eaten room service desserts were scattered throughout, some spilled on the floor. On the nightstand next to the telephone was a shoe. Had it been on the near side of the nightstand, I'd be doing a Maxwell Smart imitation.

"Michael, it's Pete . . . Peter Benedek . . ." (Pause.) "Your lawyer?" (Pete would become an agent the following year. I'd be his first client.)

"Pete? You're in London?" My brain was on fire. The pain was so excruciating I felt nauseous.

"No. *You're* in London. I'm in Los Angeles."

"Right . . . I just woke up," I muttered. "I think it's really late here."

The evening had started out in low-key fashion over dinner at Tony Roma's with Mom and Dad, who'd been in London for the last week or so. Accompanying me to work every day, they even did a walk-through in one of the scenes. From the first days of *Family Ties*, they loved to come see me on the set at Paramount Studios. Perched in the otherwise empty audience bleachers for hours at a time, the two of them would intently watch me rehearse as if unable to believe what they were seeing. Gary told me that Dad would pull him aside at least once per visit and ask, "How's he doing, Gary, all right? Do you need me to talk to him about anything?"

"He's okay, Bill," Gary would laugh. "He's fine, believe me. He's doing great, no complaints."

Still a little dubious, Dad would say, "Well, fine . . . but just let me know."

At dinner we'd shared a couple bottles of wine and, a little tipsy, made our way back to the hotel. I walked them to their suite and said good night. I would have been better off if I'd just turned down the hallway to my own room and climbed into bed. Instead, I'd hooked up with a Cockney musician friend I knew from Los Angeles, and we set out on an extended pub crawl. (This was London, after all.) Exactly what transpired after that, I'm not entirely sure. I was partying fairly heavily in those days, in what had become a moveable celebration of my great good fortune. Though looking back on it now, there was a determined, even slightly desperate edge to my celebrating, as if the party could end at any moment.

The fact is, my life these past three years couldn't have been much sweeter. The first couple years of *Ties* had been pure bliss—a job I loved that gave me the perfect opportunity to develop my craft. Then, with the ratings explosion came a near guarantee of financial stability.

By the end of the season, just prior to leaving for England, I closed on my first house: a three-bedroom bungalow with swimming pool, tucked into the hills of Laurel Canyon. It hadn't been much of a negotiation. To protect his bargaining leverage, my accountant (a new one) had warned me not to look too eager while house hunting. I didn't help matters when, immediately upon entering the living room, I threw the keys to my new 300ZX in the middle of the floor and shouted, "This is it. This baby is *mine*." Heady stuff.

The monster in the cupboard had long since been vanquished, if not the impulse that had given it life in the first place: the denial of a more practical reality outside my own dreamscape. During those first years in California, the paperwork tiger growling in the cabinet above my kitchen sink served as a stand-in for my parents, teachers, and the others with their cautionary admonitions that I couldn't "get away with it," that there would be a day of reckoning.

Well, I *had* gotten away with it, there *had been* no day of reckoning. I had made believers out of all of them. Nana would be smiling her beautiful lopsided smile. And yet . . .

Pete again, "Mike, we just saw the movie. It was fantastic . . . amazing. It's gonna be huge."

"Great, Pete," I muttered. "That's cool . . . What movie?"

"Your movie. *Back to the Future.*"

"*Back to the Future.* Right." So that's why Peter was calling. He'd just come out of an industry screening of the movie, which was scheduled for release the following week. Now my mind was tracking backwards.

With a pregnant Meredith out of commission for much of the fall of 1984, I had decided to keep busy and so accepted an offer to star in *Teen Wolf*, a low-budget independent feature. Looking back, I have no idea what I was thinking. (It worked for Michael Landon?) One day on location, I entertained some lunchtime visitors to the set, receiving them in full wolf-boy mode. Several layers of form-fitted rubber foam, studded with yak hair and affixed to my face with airplane glue, made it impossible to eat properly, so I sipped my milkshake lunch through a straw. I begged my friends for reassurance that this choice of role wasn't a surefire career killer, and with kind hearts and straight faces, they lied, "Don't worry about it. It'll be great."

We were filming that day in old Pasadena, on a street lined on both sides with attractive split-level Arts-and-Crafts-style homes and shaded by oak trees so mature that their root systems buckle the sidewalks. The effect, at once exotic and familiar, made this area a favorite with filmmakers; and not surprisingly, while we exploited the neighborhood ambience for our little epic, an advance team from another production company was scouting the location.

"They're with a new Spielberg movie, *Back from the Future* or something like that," the assistant director told me later. "It's supposed to go in late October."

"Who's in it?" I inquired.

"Nobody I know," he answered. "Except for Crispin Glover."

Ouch. I knew Crispin too—an intense, eccentric, and brilliant young actor I'd worked with before—and while it was unusual for me to feel competitive with my peers, it did sting a little to know that crazy Crispin was gearing up to do a Spielberg film while I, layered in latex, toiled away on a B-grade, high school werewolf comedy. At least, I thought, fully surrendering now to my more covetous instincts, he hadn't landed the lead role. That, I had learned, went to an equally intense, equally brilliant, and only somewhat less eccentric actor named Eric Stoltz.

Oh well, even if *Teen Wolf* wound up destroying my feature film career before it even started, I still had *Family Ties.* We returned to work in November, Meredith having delivered her twins, then broke for the holidays and came back the first week in January of 1985. This was the home stretch, the back nine of our twenty-two-show order. A return to business as usual, or so I thought.

A day or two after our Christmas break, Gary summoned me to his office for a meeting—there was something very important he needed to discuss with me. He walked me up to his second-story office adjacent to the NBC soundstage where he was producing the pilot for a new series. A bank of picture windows overlooked the set—perfect for surveying his ever-expanding empire. Gary walked around to the business side of his desk, opened a drawer, and pulled out a manila envelope from which he extracted a script. It was thick, too thick to be a script for *Family Ties*, or any other sitcom for that matter.

"I have a confession to make," Gary began. "Just before the start of the season, Steven sent me a copy of this script." Steven Spielberg and Gary were good friends and whenever Gary said "Steven," I knew he meant Spielberg.

"He's producing it and Bob Zemeckis, the guy who did *Romancing the Stone*, is directing. Steven and Bob really wanted you for the lead role. They came to me asking if there was any way I could let you out of the show. I didn't mention it to you then, because it was just impossible and I didn't want to disappoint you. I hope you understand."

I did, actually. With *Family Ties* on the threshold of breakout success, Gary would have been insane to jeopardize the show by risking the loss of what had by now become its main character. This was all starting to sound vaguely familiar though, and suddenly I remembered why.

"This is that *Future* thing, right?" I asked. "Eric Stoltz is doing that. I thought they started shooting a couple of months ago."

"They did," Gary replied. "But they're not happy with what they've got so far. Eric's great, but they don't think he's the right fit for the role. The more they thought about it, the more they kept going back to their original choice, which was you. It's going to be expensive, but they want to reshoot all of his stuff."

My head was spinning.

"You'd have to start work this week. But I want you to understand what this would mean. I can't disrupt our *Family Ties* schedule in any way, especially after what we've already gone through with Meredith this season. We're not prepared to write around you, or write you out of a single episode. You'll have to work your regular day on the show, then be picked up and brought to the movie set where you'll probably work until two or three in the morning."

(It would turn out to be more like five or six.)

"It's gonna be like that for the rest of the season. I've given this a lot of thought, and I don't want to take this opportunity away from you for a second time. If you think you can handle it, then it's fine with me."

"Yes . . . yeah . . . I think . . . I'm sure I can," I stammered.

"Well, first things first," Gary concluded. "The movie's called *Back to the Future*. This is it."

And with that, he tossed the script across to my side of the desk, where I caught it with nervously fumbling hands.

"Read it. If you like it, we'll see where it goes from there."

I held the screenplay and then balanced it on the palm of my left hand, weighing it and considering its heft. Looking up at Gary once more, a shit-eating grin now plastered across my face, three words tumbled out of my mouth.

"I love it."

. . .

I had little doubt that this was the feature film project I had been hoping and waiting for since day one, but I did, of course, hurry back to my apartment to sit down and read the thing. The story was fantastic, if a little difficult to follow on the first reading, and the character of Marty McFly—a skateboarding, girl-chasing, high school rock and roll musician—seemed like the kind of guy I could play in my sleep. That very nearly turned out to be the case.

The deal was made. Wardrobe fittings were arranged, as were meetings with Steven, director Bob Zemeckis, and his co-writer and producing partner, Bob Gale. Gary was right; within the week, I'd be picked up from finishing a full day's rehearsal on *Family Ties* and driven out to Pomona, where, at approximately 2:00 A.M., I would record my first shot of the picture. Encased in Guess jeans and a life-jacket-looking down vest and gripping a camcorder, I'd straddle one of two flaming tire tracks in an otherwise wet shopping mall parking lot and sputter, "You built a time machine out of a *DeLorean?*"

I called Canada to share the news with my folks. Mom didn't know Steven Spielberg from Cecil B. DeMille.

"That's great, honey," she said, adding, "just don't let them wear you out."

For the next three-and-a-half months, the combination of *Back to the Future* and *Family Ties* swallowed me whole. A teamster driver would pick me up at 9:30 A.M. and take me to Paramount, where I would spend the day rehearsing that week's show, culminating in a run-through at approximately 5:00 P.M. each afternoon. Then at 6, another teamster driver would pick me up and shuttle me to Universal Studios or whatever far-flung location we were based at that evening, where I would work on the film until just before sunrise. At that point, I'd climb into the back of a production van with a pillow and a blanket, and yet another teamster driver would take me home again— sometimes literally carrying me into my apartment and dropping me onto my bed. I'd catch two or three hours of sleep before teamster driver #1 would reappear at my apartment, let himself in with a key I'd provided, brew a pot of coffee, turn on the shower, and then roust me to start the whole process all over again.

Friday nights, we'd tape *Family Ties* in front of a live studio audience, so I'd start on *Back to the Future* later those evenings. But because I didn't have to work on the show the next day, we could compensate for the delay by working well past sunrise into Saturday morning. Each production operated completely independent of the other. The onus of coordinating between the two fell squarely on my shoulders. Not that there was anything either could have done to relieve my burden; both had schedules that had already been dramatically compressed by unforeseen circumstances—*Family Ties* by Meredith's absence, and *Back to the Future* by recasting its lead character and reshooting all of his scenes. Universal Studios reluctantly agreed to foot the bill to re-dress their casting misstep, but only on the condition that it not affect their summer release date. Bob Zemeckis had editors working around the clock to piece my reshot coverage into previously filmed scenes, and to assemble all of the new material to meet the deadline. So, in all fairness, it wasn't just me who was under the gun, although I was probably the only one who felt the cold steel of double barrels against the back of my neck.

While both Zemeckis and Goldberg seemed to be satisfied with the quality of my work, I was beginning to have my doubts. A few weeks into the process, there were times when I would badger Bob Z.

about the outcome of the previous day's filming—scenes I sometimes couldn't even remember shooting. During one audience taping night at *Family Ties,* I panicked backstage. Just about to make an entrance into the kitchen, I searched the prop table frantically for Marty McFly's camcorder. I didn't even know where the hell I was anymore. How could any of this shit be any good?

And so, in London, perched on the edge of my hotel bed, my left hand gripping the telephone receiver, the heel of my right palm kneading my eye sockets in an attempt to short-circuit the shooting pain of my hangover, I could formulate only one response to Peter Benedek's announcement that he had just seen *Back to the Future.*

"I'm sorry, Pete, I know I sucked. I'll do better next time."

"You're crazy," Pete laughed. "You did a great job. I'm telling you that the movie is going to be a monster. Universal wants you to do some press to support the release. And since you'll still be in England when it opens, they need to send some reporters over and set up a couple of days of satellite interviews. Oh, and they're shipping a print of the movie over so you can see it before you talk to the press. Okay?"

I agreed to do the interviews, of course, never wanting to be accused of being anything but a team player. I passed on screening the print, though. I didn't want to see it. Not yet, anyway.

"You can only see something for the first time once," I explained to Pete. "And I want to see it for the first time with a real paying audience back in the States."

The truth had more to do with fear. The phone call had been like a lightning bolt. It suddenly all made sense. Now I could connect this free-floating sense of doom I'd been carrying around with me through the past few weeks with an actual, impending event. It was a sensation that would repeat itself over the course of many movie openings in the years to come. I was approaching a moment of truth: a crucible. There was absolutely no way I could affect the way it played out. It wasn't so much, as I had suggested to Pete, that I had a low opinion of what I had done, but more that I could barely remember having done it at all. This sense of disconnect cut both ways, however; it was at once the source of my anxiety (was I any good?) and my security blanket, since the performance about to be judged scarcely felt like mine.

My success to that point had been so unexpected—I was nowhere near being able to process it—that I regarded the whole thing as a matter of luck. Would the luck hold? That seemed too much even to ask for.

In Chilliwack, when I was four years old, my mother took a job for a time and would leave me in the care of a baby-sitter, one of the other mothers in the neighborhood. It was all well and good for me to wander off whenever I wanted, but I didn't appreciate it much when the adults in my life did the same thing. This is when my four-year-old mind discovered the power of reverse psychology. From about four o'clock on, I'd stand in the baby-sitter's front yard, tears streaming down my face, chanting the same mantra over and over again: "My mom's not coming back—my mom's not coming back." But of course she always did—a miracle that I credited to being pre-pared if she didn't.

Maybe that's what I was doing in the days before the release of *Back to the Future*. My luck was about to run out, I told myself, the other shoe was set to fall. And when it did, I wanted to be adequately prepared. I said good-bye to Pete and hung up the phone. I shuffled over to the minibar, cracked open a bottle of beer. If this was the be-ginning of the end, I had to admit, it'd been a hell of a ride.

The ride, it turned out, was only beginning.

CHAPTER FOUR

Lost in the Fun House

An American Newsstand—Circa 1986

GQ: "The Rise and Rise of Michael J. Fox"
US: "Michael J. Fox—Back to My Future"
People: "The Secret of His Success"
Rolling Stone: "The Hot Issue—Michael J. Fox"

Playgirl: "On the Prowl with Michael J. Fox"

Bop: "Who's Cuter? Kirk Cameron or Michael J.—You Decide!"

There's a newsstand in my old Studio City neighborhood, on the southwest corner of Van Nuys and Ventura boulevards. Every now and then during the post–*Back to the Future* eighties, I'd stop by and—baseball cap tugged down low on my brow, sunglasses snug to the bridge of my nose—discreetly scan the racks. No, I wasn't checking out *Hustler* or *Juggs* or any of the other girlie magazines, but surveying the versions of myself on display—*People, US, GQ, TV Guide, MAD, Cracked, AdWeek, Variety, McCall's, Family Circle, The National Enquirer, The Star, The Globe, Seventeen, 16, Tiger Beat, Bop,* and on and on.

Everywhere I looked, I saw my image reflected back at me. But that was the thing—none of them was a true representation of my real self, whoever *that* was; it was more like a hall of mirrors. These weren't reflections so much as they were different facets of my public persona, skewed by the various publishers and editors to best promote their point of view—not mine—and, most important, attract whatever demographic group they catered to. So on the cover of *People* I was the boy next door, *GQ* a well-groomed yuppie, *Playgirl* a sex symbol. . . . Some I recognized, others might have been aliens inhabiting my body—in fact, that might have been a headline on one of the tabloids.

That hall of mirrors on Van Nuys is a perfect metaphor for what my life had become as I found myself in the labyrinthine fun house of America mega-celebrity—a place where, I discovered, it is easy to get lost.

Here are the facts, a recap of my story thus far. In 1979, feeling constricted by the conformity in which I was raised and with dreams of becoming an actor, I left Canada for Los Angeles. Over the next three years, I enjoyed a modest, anonymous success, but by the spring of the third year was struggling. Winning the role of Alex on *Family Ties* in 1982 sparked a turnaround. Surrounded by talented producers, actors, and writers, I played a character who happened to strike a chord with viewers. I gained a certain notoriety—of the second-guest-on-Johnny-Carson, two-page-profile-in-*TV-Guide* (after the crossword puzzle) variety. Then, for the first time in my career, I started to receive film offers, adding that work to my TV commitments. In the summer of 1985, with *Family Ties* the second most-watched program in prime time, *Back to the Future* shot to number one at the box office, with *Teen Wolf* inexplicably holding number two. And so it was that in a brief six-year period I had become famous.

Here's the fiction: that was my plan all along.

Well, wait a minute, *wasn't it*? Didn't I set out for Hollywood at the age of eighteen to seek my fame and fortune, and three years later, after shooting the *Family Ties* pilot, report to Coady that I was "finally about to go large"? Wasn't my goal, all along—wasn't the whole idea—to one day become rich and famous?

It's not that simple. "Richandfamous" was as much a cliché fantasy to me as it would be to a truck driver from Peoria. So, sure, inasmuch as "richandfamous" implied freedom, it held an appeal. But if the cliché is broken down into synonyms like, for instance, *millions* and *adoration*, then, no, I don't believe that either of those words, together or apart, were prime motivators.

Rich, relative to my background, meant buying my own food and clothing and being able to pay the rent. Fame, to me then, meant something as basic as not having to constantly explain myself, earning a reputation and, along with that, room in which to pursue my interests. I didn't want anyone to kiss my ass, I just wanted to get to a place where they couldn't kick it.

Simply put, my highest ambition was to be an actor. I was focused on getting work, not gaining wealth. The law of averages suggests that a career as a performer is not a likely means to that end. And, as for fame—were that the only objective, there might have been an easier route, though none so direct as exist today. Now I'd just have to go camping with a group of equally machiavellian narcissists in Bora Bora or the Australian Outback, eat a few rats, a handful of blowfly larvae, and, *bam*, every talk show and magazine in the country would come calling.

What I really desired—and for a long time even this seemed too much to wish for—was for acting to be a means to a *means*. I wanted whatever part I was playing to lead to another, and so on. And, hey, if something happened, well, that would be too good to be true.

Something happened.

I'm about to take you on a brief tour—highlights and lowlights—of the *Being-Famous-in-America Fun House,* a shape-shifting world where only one thing is perfectly clear: there is no way to prepare for the journey.

No maps or guidebooks are available, and few who have experienced the maze leave behind helpful advice or even the most cryptic clues regarding pitfalls or shortcuts. I was pretty much on my own. I had to rely upon whatever moral and ethical compass my family provided me (here, I was lucky), or trust my impulses (in this department I was not so lucky).

Also, contrary to popular opinion, before you enter the fun house, you aren't handed a waiver to sign titled FAUSTIAN BARGAIN: *You want to be an actor? Fine, but by choosing such an undignified and, worse yet, selfish (admit it, bub, you just wanna be* richandfamous*) vocation, you hereby waive any right to complain about, contest, or place conditions upon whatever might happen to you. Just put your autograph right here on the dotted line* . . . I'm not complaining, but I sure as hell don't remember signing anything.

It should come as no surprise that fame—showbiz fame anyway—is so disorienting. After all, the theater, where it all begins, is founded on a conspiracy of mutual deception. The performer pretends to be someone he is not, and the audience willingly suspends its disbelief. It's a confidence game in which both parties risk the humiliation of being played for a sucker. The actor makes himself vulnerable to the embarrassment of failure by trusting that the audience will grant him the time and attention to craft his lie. In return, the audience depends upon the actor's gift to keep them from feeling like fools for believing. Artfully transacted, this is one con where the potential exists for everybody to win. The payoff is an hour or so of collective—and harmless—magical thinking.

The symbiotic relationship between the entertainer and the entertained goes something like this: The audience witnesses its darkest fears and deepest fantasies being played out in a safe environment—

experiential enrichment without emotional risk. The performance holds out a mirror in which we can observe the most secret parts of ourselves without the risk of anyone else recognizing our reflection. The actor is rewarded with applause and his cut of the price of admission—fame and fortune at its most basic.

Once you get beyond the physical and temporal boundaries of the playhouse, however, the deal gets more confusing. With TV and film, for example, the sense of scale is thrown so completely out of whack that the whole idea and value of the mirror is lost. Take the film actor—blown up to fill a twenty-foot-high film screen, he assumes the dimensions of a god. Some in the audience, viewing him from the darkened, churchlike environment of the cineplex, might even begin to regard him as such—hence, matinee *idol*. In contrast, the television actor is miniaturized, omnipresent as a new member of the viewer's family. But there's a godlike power in this illusion as well, turning on its ubiquity, and the sheer number of lives that the performer can touch in the intimate space of their living rooms.

These perceptions are amplified by all of the other forms of mass media—newspapers, magazines, radio, books, and the Internet. By now, almost all of the boundaries of the original theatrical conceit have vanished, and the theater of celebrity expands to become the whole world. In this new multimedia realm, there seems to be no beginning or end to the performance, no backstage or onstage, no proscenium. Everything is now part of the show—the performer's private life included.

So much of this magical thinking is unbidden and beyond the control of the celebrity. Fame is not something you *do*; it's a perception that originates and resides not in the mind of the celebrity, but in the collective imagination of the public. Over time, the rewards to the performer and the expectations of the audience grow unchecked, and everybody, each for their own reasons, is happy to forget that the whole exercise is based on illusion. A simple magic trick confined to a theater or television screen has mutated into a society-wide epidemic of magical thinking.

Odd as this might sound, becoming famous is something that

happened to me in the same way that Parkinson's disease is something that happened to me. I'm not saying celebrity is a disease, but it can trigger an abnormal psychological condition not unlike mania or amnesia. I became so intoxicated on the nectar of money and the ambrosia of unlimited possibility, that I fell completely under its influence, forgetting for a time that it wasn't real.

Fortunately, someone came into my life to remind me that the whole thing was hocus-pocus; that while it might be okay to get caught up in the wonder of it all, I should never forget how the trick works. Like many others in the same position, I eventually had to make a choice: either live in a world where I believed in the illusion, and accept privilege as entitlement; or reject magical thinking and do my best to keep my feet planted in the real world. I'm embarrassed to say it wasn't an easy choice, but I ultimately went with the second option. It's a good thing that I did—because if I were still living according to the fun house rules when I was diagnosed with Parkinson's disease, it would, I'm sure, have destroyed me.

IT'S GOOD TO BE THE KING

Don't get me wrong—I had a really, *really* good time.

When I was growing up, I was crazy about girls. I can remember the specific crush I had in each year of grade school; I could even give you names. But by the time I was a teenager, I felt shy around the opposite sex. Maybe it had to do with an insecurity about my height. I'd also resigned myself to the fact that, in school anyway, girls go for the jocks, not the theater geeks. Still, while I was hardly a lothario, I did date a little, and by the time I dropped out of high school, I was going out with Diane, my first long-term relationship.

By the mid-eighties, it was a whole new ball game. You know that old sentence that starts with "girls who never used to give me the time of day . . ."? Well, I'd end it with ". . . were now inviting me home to read it off of their bedside alarm clocks." And as for the question, "Does it bother you that maybe she just wants to sleep with you be-

cause you're a celebrity?" My answer to that one was, "Ah . . . nope."
Mel Brooks as Louis XVI in *The History of the World: Part I* said it best
when, arms wrapped around the waists of a pair of corseted ladies-in-
waiting, he gushed, "It's good to be the King."

·   ·   ·

I may have felt like a king, but I was out of my league in the company
of a real princess. I returned to England in the fall of 1985 for the royal
premiere of *Back to the Future*. Princess Diana was in attendance. Upon
arriving at the theater, Bob Zemeckis, Steven Spielberg, the cast, and
other invited guests were ushered into a reception area off the lobby.
The chief of royal protocol prepped us for our formal introduction to
Diana. Sweating bullets in my starched, rented tuxedo, I probably had
more reason to be nervous than the others in our party. I was Canadian after all, and therefore a royal subject. This was my future Queen
I was about to meet. It occurred to me that Nana might be watching.

While we waited at the bar to be escorted to the receiving line, I
made the critical mistake of downing a couple of beers to calm my
nerves. I didn't get drunk, but that's not the only consequence of
poorly timed beer intake.

The Princess was cordial, and she looked even more beautiful—
sexier—than I'd expected. She was wearing a backless blue silk gown,
a generous strand of pearls wrapped once around her long, elegant
neck and then draped down the length of her spine. I wanted to mention that, in my humble opinion, this was a really good look for her,
but the opportunity didn't present itself. The protocol guy had been
exacting in his litany of dos and don'ts, and I'd followed them to a tee.
To everybody's relief (maybe even Nana's), I made it through the introduction without a serious gaffe.

I'd soon get another shot.

The royal party was shown into the theater, and once they were
settled, the ushers came back for our group. I was led to my seat and
almost went into cardiac arrest. It was right next to Diana's. I was
going to spend a night at the movies with Princess Diana. *Jesus*, I
thought, *except for the fact that she's married and is the Princess of Wales, this*

is practically a date. Well at least I could pretend, couldn't I? As long as I didn't get carried away, fake a yawn, and leave my arm draped across her shoulder. *What if it got caught in all those pearls?* I was sweating all over again.

In the moments before the movie started there was a flurry of small talk, initiated by the Princess. That was part of Mr. Protocol's whole riff, along with all the honorifics you had to use when addressing her. You couldn't speak to her unless she spoke to you first; if seated, you weren't allowed to rise until she did; and never, ever, did you turn your back toward her. I didn't anticipate any problem adhering to these guidelines until the lights went out and *Back to the Future's* opening credits scrolled across the movie screen.

Then it hit me: a sharp and unmistakable discomfort—I had to take a leak. Urgently. Made sense—the anxiety, the *goddamn beer*—but what the hell was I going to do? I was a hostage to etiquette. She'd be too polite to speak during *my* movie, and if she did say anything, *whatever* it was, "Excuse me, Your Highness, I have to go wring it," was not going to be the appropriate response. I couldn't just get up and leave unless she did. And even if I could, I'd have to back away, tripping over the other people in our row and probably falling on my ass. There was, of course, one final option—but that was unthinkable.

And so my fantasy date with a princess turned into two of the most excruciating hours of my life, a timely reminder from nature not to get too carried away by my heady circumstances. No matter how many people were eager to let me believe otherwise, I was only human. There'd soon be more reminders. I'd need them.

Though not a king, or even a prince, I was quickly gaining the means with which to live uncommonly well. By late 1986, the driveway of my Laurel Canyon home resembled a luxury car lot. I owned a Ferrari, a Range Rover, a Mercedes 560SL convertible, a Jeep Cherokee, and a Nissan 300ZX. I can't remember the intricate decision tree I had to climb in order to determine which one I'd drive to work on any given day—it probably had something to do with the weather, or which car had more gas in the tank, or upholstery that best matched whatever shirt I happened to throw on that morning.

Then there was the house itself. I had some remodeling done during the summer of 1986 while I was away making two films back-to-back, *Light of Day* in Chicago and then *The Secret of My Success* in New York City. The bungalow already had three bedrooms, so additional sleeping quarters weren't called for. At a cost of almost a half a million dollars, I commissioned a massive addition to the main bedroom, creating a master suite with retractable skylights and a jacuzzi/steam room area complete with fireplace, two TVs, and a full wet bar. For a twenty-five-year-old lottery winner, money was no object—and neither was good taste.

I remember a *Saturday Night Live* bit from the early eighties in which Eddie Murphy puts on white-face and discovers a different America. His first stop, post-makeup chair, is an office building newsstand. He picks up the morning paper, waits for a black customer to finish making a purchase, and then puts his paper down on the counter, along with a quarter. The vendor is confused at first, and only after nervously checking to make sure that the black customer is gone, smiles and pushes the money back toward Murphy. "You're kidding me, right pal?" the newsy laughs. "*You* don't have to pay for this. Take the paper . . . it's okay. Just take it." Later, at a savings and loan, when an African-American loan officer asks the Caucasian Murphy for his credit history, a white banker has to come to the rescue. Once they're alone, the banker apologizes with a wink and pulls out stack after stack of fresh $100 bills. "And don't worry about paying this back . . . Need more?" Whenever African-Americans aren't present, Murphy learns, white people give each other things *for free*. But that's not all. On his way home, the subway car he's riding discharges the last of its nonwhite passengers and then erupts into a spontaneous cocktail party, complete with champagne, hors d'oeuvres, and a jazz quartet.

So what does this satire about the African-American experience have to do with my story? Well, on a political level, not much. But like Murphy's astonished black Everyman, I was experiencing the shock and vaguely illicit thrill of an unexpected crossover into a parallel universe, one that I had no idea even existed.

Like the white people in the *SNL* skit, celebrities are the recipi-

ents of a hell of a lot of free stuff. At a time when I could finally afford
to buy whatever shoes I wanted, I'd be invited down to the Nike
showroom in Santa Monica, handed a huge canvas duffel bag, and invited to help myself to all the swoosh-emblazoned swag I could stuff
inside. Nike's motives were obvious: even one published photograph
of a celebrity wearing those free shoes had the value of an advertise-
ment without the expense of an endorsement fee. Once, on the
Tonight show, Jay Leno asked me how I liked living in the States. "It's
great. Except for the beer. American beer's a little watery," I confided.
"So I drink Moosehead Ale, imported from Canada." A week later, sitting at my kitchen table, I heard the grinding of a large vehicle laboring up my driveway. Drawing aside the curtain, I peered out the
window to see a green beer delivery truck with the giant Moosehead
logo painted on the side. "There's lots more where this came from,"
the delivery guy said, handing me a business card. "Just give us a call
when you run out."

I had stumbled upon one of the lesser-known truisms of American society: *those who got, get*. No wonder I could afford a black granite steam room—I was paying for little else. There were free meals,
first-class travel, luxury hotel rooms. From my time in London's pubs
to the day when I finally quit drinking altogether, I don't recall many
bar tabs being slapped down on the mahogany in front of me, Moosehead or no Moosehead.

Even better than *those who got, get* is the real prize in this particular box of Cracker Jack: *the wink*. You can't buy the wink—the
unspoken acknowledgment from almost everyone you encounter
(shopkeepers, bouncers, maître d's, airline ticket clerks, and even the
uncivil civil servants in the Department of Motor Vehicles) that
you've been deemed worthy of a new set of privileges; that for you
the usual norms don't apply. You are no longer just plain folks.

What was astounding was how many just plain folks were willing
to play along in a game whose rules were tilted so absurdly in my
favor. And if I wanted to bend those rules further, or break them, or
ignore them altogether, the world seemed happy to oblige. Any direction I chose to move in became the path of least resistance. Maybe this
is the true root of the expression, "life in the fast lane."

The cool thing was, I could still be a nice guy. I didn't have to sacrifice my Canadian politeness by demanding anyone get out of my way. Though I do have to confess to feeling a secret indignation, after a while, when people didn't jump. A guy can get used to this treatment.

.   .   .

I loved my automobiles, but once I'd selected which one to drive to work in the morning, freeing it from the rest of the fleet was a chore. I felt like an overpaid valet parking attendant. The solution to the problem (some problem!) was this: I still went home to Canada regularly—almost every holiday, long weekend, or hiatus—so the next time I'd just drive up there in the 300ZX and leave it behind for use during future visits.

I'd be retracing the twelve-hundred-mile route that I'd taken seven years earlier with my father, only now my big brother Steve would co-pilot. Steve arrived on a Friday afternoon flight in late August of 1986 only to turn around and hit the road again after that night's *Family Ties* taping. Our plan was to drive nonstop, L.A. to Vancouver in less than twenty-four hours.

Driving the first shift, I set a fast pace heading out of the city. In a literal manifestation of my figurative life-in-the-fast-lane attitude, I quickly grew frustrated whenever slower cars wouldn't let me pass. One slowpoke was particularly stubborn. No matter how often I flashed my high beams or how close I edged my turbo-charged sports car to his rear bumper, Mr. Where's-the-Funeral? refused to get out of my way.

"What the hell is this guy doing in the fast lane anyway?"

Steve, whose wit and timing had been my model for Alex Keaton, leaned over, glanced at my speedometer, and then at the car in front of us.

"Oh," he answered, "about 90."

In preparation for the drive to Canada, I'd had a radar detector mounted beneath the dashboard of the 300ZX. I can't vouch for its effectiveness—it never beeped once on the entire trip. But the very fact that I used such a device meant I recognized the rules of the road, even if I was trying to circumvent them. Experience would later teach me that maybe I didn't need to bother.

Early one afternoon, I was barreling down Ventura Boulevard in my Ferrari; I was late for an appointment at one of the studios in the Valley, a casting session. I wasn't auditioning—I hadn't had to audition for anything in years. Now the roles had been reversed; actors were coming in to read with and for me in hopes of a part in my next film, since I had casting approval. Still, I had fresh memories of what it was like to be in their position, and what an ordeal it was to be kept waiting. So I wanted to get there as fast as possible, and by applying $100,000 worth of Italian automotive engineering to the task, that was damn fast.

It had been a weird morning. After flying in from a New York press junket, I was still a little jet-lagged when, in the limo on my way home from LAX, I got a frantic call from my assistant. Burnaby, my until-now perfectly friendly and harmless pit bull, had chosen that morning to munch on the neck of a neighbor dog and was, as we spoke, mid-munch. In a surreally one-sided phone conversation, I was shouting the word "Release!" over and over into the mobile phone while on the other end my assistant was holding the receiver up to my dog's ear. When I arrived home, Burnaby was back safely inside the house and the neighbor dog, while sporting a little unwanted ventilation in its larynx, appeared likely to survive. Its owners were rattled, but not especially angry. Their Siberian husky had, after all, wandered into my yard, a trespass which, I guess, had triggered Burnaby's territorial attack instinct.

As friendly as my neighbors were, I'd been a public figure long enough to recognize them as potential complainants in a dog-bites-dog lawsuit. So, as I climbed into the Ferrari and roared down the driveway for the meeting at the studio, I punched the number of my attorney into the car phone to give him a heads-up. Ironically, we were still talking when, going in excess of 80 mph down a stretch of Ventura Boulevard, I saw the flashing blue and red lights of an LAPD patrol car strobing in my rearview mirror.

"Shit. You're not going to believe this," I said to my lawyer. "Hang

on . . . I may need you in a second." I pulled over and in my side mirror, marked the cop's progress as he made his approach—left hand on
the butt of his revolver, and right hand tracing the smooth line of the
black Ferrari. Maybe he needed to convince himself that it had actually stopped; even parked, the car looked like it was doing fifty. His
opening remark made it clear that I was screwed.

"Do you even *have* a driver's license?"

I sit low in a car seat anyway, and in a Ferrari, built to ride close
to the road, I must have looked, from his perspective, like a high
school kid on a joyride. It wasn't until he'd studied the photo ID I'd
handed over with trembling fingers—panic, not Parkinson's—that we
actually made direct eye contact. His stone face now dissolved into a
smile.

"*Miiike*," he said, peeling off his sunglasses. "You gotta take it easy,
buddy. This is a big heavy car, and we sure don't want to see you getting hurt."

"I'm sorry," I stammered, even though his cheerful admonition
hardly demanded an apology.

"Okay now," he said, reaching in to return my license and shake
my hand. "You have a nice day, and take it easy. My wife and I wanna
be able to keep on watching *Family Ties*. We love that show."

I've been issued plenty of traffic citations—all deserved—but
there had been just as many instances like this one, though maybe
none quite so egregious. I felt a tremendous wash of relief followed by
the exhilarating rush of knowing that I'd gotten away with something
I shouldn't have. Then it started to freak me out a little. I mean, I was
happy to take the free pass and go. It's not like I called the cop back
and insisted that I had a ticket coming to me and, goddammit, he'd
better write me up. But, on a commercial boulevard, with stop lights
at regular intervals, in lunch hour traffic on a weekday, traveling at
over 80, I was brazenly flouting the rules that every other citizen of
Los Angeles was bound to comply with. Add to this my state of mind
at the moment—jet-lagged, harried, preoccupied by that morning's
chaotic events—and I deserved not only a ticket, but to be barred
from the public roadways altogether. But as soon as that cop recog-

nized the perp in the Ferrari as that funny kid from the box in his living room, the menace became "*Miiike*." I couldn't help but wonder, as
I slowly pulled out into the flow of traffic, "How fucked up was *that*?"

YES-MAN

I don't know about your kids, but the first word each of mine mastered
was "no." The same was true for me as a kid, and probably for you as
well. From the corrective ("No, you can't have cake for dinner") to the
protective ("No! Johnny, never pee in the wall socket"), "no" is how
we establish and begin to comprehend boundaries. But this doesn't
mean "no" is only about limits. By giving a child the means with which
to define his or her own unique identity and sense of self, pronounc-
ing the word *no* marks the first step on the road to autonomy.

Still very much a kid in my mid-twenties, I was no longer hearing the word *no* very often, if at all, and frankly, I was too blissed out
to care—at first. All yeses, all the time, worked just fine for me. "Well,
Mr. Fox, we are totally booked for the evening, but, *yes*, we can seat
your party of ten. Right this way." "Why *yes*, a twelve-hundred-
square-foot lavatory tacked onto your bedroom would be a *wooonder-
fulll* idea." "*Yes*, here's my phone number. Call me anytime."

As a young child, I dreamed and spoke incessantly of a world of
limitless possibility. And now, it turned out that such a world did exist,
and this was it—I'd arrived in the magical realm of "yes" that they'd
told me existed only in fairy tales. Yet there are times when any sane
person, no matter how spectacular their box office or Nielsen ratings,
expects to hear "no"—as in "No, you can't drive twice the legal speed
limit on a city street."

These were the moments when I first started to sense the implications of a life with no clear boundaries. Wall-lessness didn't just
mean freedom, I slowly began to realize; it also meant vulnerability. It
took me a while, but eventually I started to ask and then answer two
terrifying questions: Do I deserve all this? And if I don't (and who
did?), what happens when everybody finds out? So I developed a

threefold strategy for protecting myself against whatever nasty, humiliating, ride-stopping no was lying in wait at the end of this long string of yeses.

First, in order to assuage any creeping guilt I felt about never hearing anyone say no to me, I all but banished the word from my own vocabulary. Whatever anybody asked of me or wanted from me, I figured the safest thing to do was to say yes. Be a nice guy, go along, get along. Of course, if you hear only yes and say only yes, you're apt to find yourself stranded in the middle of nowhere, with no fixed boundary between yourself and the outside world, unarmed.

The people I said yes to most often, and most happily, were fans. After all, their response to my work (a sort of huge collective yes) had made my success possible. Some had known me for years from *Family Ties*; others only recently through *Back to the Future*. It was always easy to tell one from the other. *Ties* fans would be animated but friendly and relaxed; in fact, my first instinct would often be to infer from their backslapping familiarity that I must know them from school (however brief my time there). By contrast, movie fans would react as if they had just spotted Sasquatch during a picnic in the woods. Given my visibility on both the big and small screen, there were those, of course, who had feet in both camps—the ones who weren't sure whether to tap me on the shoulder or tear my shirt off.

I didn't mind. Look, how often do plumbers have strangers approach them on the street to compliment them on their latest pipe refitting? With a "thank you," a smile, a willingness to take a photograph or sign an autograph—a simple "yes"—I've been able to literally make someone's day, and I've always regarded that as a privilege. Sure, sometimes the encounter is inconvenient or awkward. The cameras, for example, never seem to work right the first time. Hastily pulled from pocketbooks and fumbled nervously from one giggling friend to another as each in the group takes their turn beside me, inevitably the camera's flash won't go off or the film runs out. Just a quick tip: those little cardboard throwaways need to be rewound after every exposure.

Signing autographs can sometimes be just as comic—long moments spent laughing with people as they scramble to find a pen, pencil, crayon, or eyeliner—whatever works. And then what exactly is it that they want to have signed? A business card, a matchbook, a child's wallet portrait from Sears, the bill of a baseball cap, an exposed body part, or, in the case of the well-prepared, an autograph book. Some actors, even the most gracious of them, like my friend Alan Alda, refuse to sign autographs at all—in the belief that the ritual creates a barrier that separates them from the experience of meeting people. I remember ending up in hysterics one night in a Chinese restaurant in New York as Alan tried to explain to an uncomprehending Cantonese kitchen crew, using pantomime and pidgin English, why it would be better to just shake hands. I was mercilessly teasing him as I scribbled away, obliging each and every one of them.

"I respect your principles, Alan, but your dumplings are getting cold. Just sign already!"

I can see his point, though; after all, what is an autograph, really? A signed contract wherein some guy from TV verifies the existence of Phil from Ohio? Just another example of magical thinking, I guess. But, for me anyway, signing autographs is a painless way simply to say yes, and thank you.

There were other requests, some more sobering. Foundations like Starlight and Make-A-Wish, established with the purpose of fulfilling the desires of catastrophically ill children, called regularly, to arrange for me to spend time with these kids and their families. When I was on the road, I'd routinely schedule visits to that particular city's pediatric hospital. I've met children with leukemia and other cancers, kids with cystic fibrosis who fight for every breath, juvenile diabetics on dialysis battling the odds that a donor kidney will be found and transplanted before time runs out. Without exception, they faced their circumstances with a grace and dignity that any adult in the same situation would be hard-pressed to match. Many times their biggest concern wasn't for themselves, but for their parents and siblings. These are kids who know all about no, and who understand the unfairness of limitation. At the time, their lessons in courage and acceptance were humbling. But only more recently, as I've struggled with the no of P.D., have their lessons really sunk in. I am grateful to each of my young teachers. If every time I said yes to one of these young people was a gift, then the true recipient was me.

Those are the times when I would have said yes, regardless. But there's a longer list of things I agreed to do, purely to keep the success machine well-oiled and running smoothly. Yes to interviews and personal appearances, yes to studio requests, yes to network requests, and when there were conflicts, "Yes, don't worry, I'll make it happen." The royal premiere in London, for example, took place on a Sunday night before the start of a rehearsal week. That meant that I had to leave Heathrow on the Concorde the following morning at 8:00 A.M., GMT, arrive in New York at 10:00 A.M., EST, get on another plane and be on the *Family Ties* set immediately following the lunch break at 2:00 P.M., PST. Sometimes political, always exhausting, my policy of routinely responding in the affirmative was crucial to my three-part strategy of self-preservation.

Which brings me to the second part of my survival strategy: work. I felt a special obligation in the case of *Family Ties* to be amenable and diplomatic. Gary had drawn a lot of flack from his industry peers for letting me do *Back to the Future*; and once the film was a hit, they chided him for his foolishness. "That's it," they'd say, "you're never getting the kid back. He's going to be so *gone* he won't even show up in reruns." But whenever people would ask me if I was going to stay with the show, my answer was yes—absolutely. This was my home, these were my friends, Gary gave me my big break, and besides, I loved playing Alex Keaton.

Without compromising my commitment to *Family Ties*, I filled much of my time away with extra projects. Sometimes moonlighting, as in the case of *Back to the Future*, sometimes making two films during a single hiatus, hedging my bets by doing one drama and one comedy, such as *Light of Day* and *The Secret of My Success*. It's not just that I remembered the grief of unemployment, but keeping my nose to the grindstone, I figured, was one way to lessen the risk of having my head exposed.

Those times when I wasn't pressing the flesh, promoting one project or another, politicking or otherwise busy, I was applying the third component of my three-part strategy for survival in Hollywood: partying my ass off. This was, after all, a time to celebrate—so much was going right, why shouldn't I be happy? My cup had runneth over, and I was trying to drink up as much of the overflow as humanly possible. I remember this period of my life—to the extent I *can* remember this part of my life—as one blowout after another; the booze was free and I was usually the guest of honor. For some people, excessive alcohol consumption is a means of escape, but at this point in my life, anyway, that was the last thing I wanted. Already inhabiting what was essentially a fantasy world, there was nowhere else I wanted to escape to. Alcohol being a preservative, I figured, what better way to preserve the happy illusion? And so, a lot of the time I was pickled.

I didn't drink when I was working or had other commitments. But conscientiousness wasn't the only motive for my discipline. When I was on the set, or performing some other function related to my career, the environment itself sustained the fantasy and the work was stimulant enough.

The key was staying busy—constructively or not. My credo during this period—work hard, drink hard, say (and hear) only yes—was really a way of making sure that no matter what the situation, I was always occupied and had as little time for reflection as possible. Perhaps because my success was so sudden and outsized, I had the feeling that I was getting away with something. Sometimes I felt like I did as a teenager, when I wanted to get the car keys without waking my father from his nap on the living room couch. I'd try to grab the keys from the coffee table, inches away from his sleeping form, without disturbing him and incurring his wrath. My strategy was basic: keep moving, *get in and out as quickly as possible.*

The expression that comes to mind is "as if," as in "act *as if* this were all normal." But, of course, it wasn't. At least not for me. I couldn't help feeling there was something *inauthentic* about the whole thing—if not the situation itself, then at least my position in it. Perhaps there was something you could do to be worthy of all of this—

the money, the attention, the indulgence—but had I met the criteria? And so in time I began to feel like an imposter. It's almost as if I expected someone, at any moment, to kick in my door and tell me the charade had gone as far as it was going to go. The jig was up; it was time to go back to Canada, and don't even think about bringing any of this stuff with you. I don't know who, exactly, I thought was going to come storming in with this ultimatum, but I figured I might as well be drunk when they got here.

I can remember visiting that newsstand on Van Nuys Boulevard one day, and there among all the teen magazines, gossip tabloids, and other periodicals splashing my face on their covers, was one in particular that paralyzed me with fear. I was convinced the dreaded moment had arrived—that this was it, that they'd finally nailed me. For what other reason would I be on the cover of *Psychology Today*? I grabbed the magazine and frantically flipped through its pages until I found the cover story.

Turned out it had nothing to do with me specifically—it was just a general essay on the pervasiveness of celebrity in American culture. I don't even think my name was mentioned once. They were just using my face to sell a few copies (if you can't beat 'em, exploit 'em). For a second there, though, I had no doubt that I'd been totally and righteously busted.

I'M FAMOUS, YOU'RE FAMOUS

My wife Tracy, a lifelong New Yorker, cracks me up with her pithy observations about L.A.—especially regarding the lengths to which that city will go in catering to its more celebrated citizenry. "I'm surprised they don't have celebrity parking," she once mused. "You know, like handicapped parking, only more convenient." She went on to say that these choice spots could be marked with signage bearing not the customary star, but an even more appropriate image: a silhouette of a baseball cap floating over a pair of sunglasses.

What intrigued me, as I increasingly found myself in settings rife with famous people, was how many of them seemed to be friends with one another. I was struck, too (and, okay, flattered), by how many of them knew who I was. Some movie star, whose work I'd been watching for years, would just sidle up to me and start chatting as if we'd been in Little League together. It gradually dawned on me that while a certain percentage of these relationships were genuine, a lot of what I perceived as friendship among the famous was, like so much else in this industry, an illusion. By this, I'm not implying a society of duplicitous backstabbers; only that, in many cases, these people "knew" each other in the same way that you might know any one of them—for the simple reason that they are well-known. The twist is, they each know that they themselves are well-known, so in that way, two celebrities not only know each other, but have some-thing in common: they know that the other knows what it is like to be known by everyone else. This results in a certain bond, and a strangely easy sort of camaraderie. This is the phenomenon that Tracy (who else?) refers to as the "I'm famous, you're famous" club.

While I've never been particularly star-struck, there were times when I couldn't help but be impressed by the company I was keep-ing. In March of 1986, I traveled to Las Vegas with Sugar Ray Leonard. Though we'd never met before, we were co-investors on a real estate deal along with a rich entrepreneur, on whose private jet we were traveling to see that weekend's Marvin Hagler/John Mugabi fight. Thrilled to have a ringside seat, I was even more thrilled to be in the company of one of my favorite boxers.

Following the fight, we were escorted into the casino. In an area sectioned off by velvet ropes, crowded around the high-roller tables, was a particularly glittering crowd—the "I'm famous, you're fa-mous" club on a weekend road trip. Here were old friends, many meeting for the first time, and I was amazed at how easily I could slide into their ranks; how matter-of-factly they accepted me, a newcomer. The party continued until 5:00 or 6:00 in the morning, and as it broke up, earnest promises were made to "get together" and "do lunch" back in L.A.

Of course, not everyone in this elite club is eager to see the membership rolls expanded—believing there should definitely be velvet ropes inside the velvet ropes—and these people are quick to send that signal. At that year's Oscars, I presented an award and backstage afterwards I passed Cher, in full diva regalia, waiting by an elevator. "Hi," I said, extending my hand. "I'm Mike Fox."

Maybe it had something to do with my being roughly the same height as Sonny, or the fact that she had starred in *Mask* with Eric Stoltz, the actor whom I'd replaced in *Back to the Future*, but Cher seemed less than thrilled to meet me.

"I know who you are," she said flatly across an imaginary velvet rope, and without stopping to shake my hand, turned and stepped into the elevator. *I'm famous, you . . . not so much.*

The reason Tracy's appellation for this separate and insular fraternity is so canny is that like "I'm okay, you're okay," "I'm famous, you're famous" suggests a kind of support group. Interacting with others who, in many cases, do the same thing for a living, and for whatever reason have been afforded the same privileges, reinforces the idea that this ethereal existence is a normal state of being.

Maybe I just wasn't that good at it—at lowering my voice so that others would have to strain to hear my pearls of wisdom. Because as time went on, I found I wasn't getting any more comfortable in the role of "star," and I knew I was approaching a moment when I would have to make a choice: to stay in the real world, or set up permanent housekeeping here on the other side of the looking glass.

Not that life on the other side didn't have its temptations. Magical thinking is infectious, and there were many moments I succumbed, though one in particular stands out. Growing up in Canada during the sixties and seventies, I idolized Bobby Orr, the legendary Boston Bruins' defenseman. As any Boston hockey fan could tell you, the day he was traded to the Chicago Blackhawks set off a long period of civic mourning. So when, in the mid-eighties, years after Orr had retired because of bad knees, it was announced that he would be leading a team of Bruin old-timers against a team of celebrities in a charity hockey game at the Boston Garden, the event sold out immediately. I was ecstatic at being asked to play, and literally dumb-

struck when, minutes before the game, Bobby Orr came over to
speak to me.

George Wendt of *Cheers*, our team's honorary coach and a fellow
Orr worshipper, was the one who tapped me as I was lacing up my
skates, excitedly indicating the approach of the hockey god himself.
Orr was genial and down-to-earth. But as he started talking to me, I
realized I was too excited to comprehend what the hell he was saying.
I just nodded my head.

After he left, George sat down beside me again. "What were you
guys talking about?" he asked.

"I have no idea," I admitted. "But that was *so* cool."

Toward the end of the first period of play, the Bruin old-timers
were forcing the play in my team's end when I stole the puck, and,
skating toward Orr, who was guarding the blue line, executed a quick
fake, tucked the puck between his feet, glided around him and picked
it up on the other side, breaking away toward the opposing goal. My
blade caught an edge and I fell briefly, but recovered before anyone
caught me and sailed a wrist shot past their net minder.

This was easily one of the most thrilling moments of my life. I was
almost hyperventilating when I returned to the bench. As I took a big
gulp of water, I was thinking, *Holy shit, I just faked out Bobby Orr and
scored on a breakaway!* Then it hit me—what Bobby Orr had said to me
before the game:

"Near the end of the first period," he'd said, "I'm gonna let you
put the puck between my legs, break away, and score."

I know, it was only a charity hockey game, and gimme goals are a
staple of those kind of events. But the fact that I was able to fool myself about what had just happened, however briefly, stands as an em-
blem for me of the seductiveness of magical thinking, and just how
easy, and perilous, it is to accept the fantasy of this life as reality.

"FOUR FEET TALL"

Steve and I managed to arrive safely in Vancouver that Saturday in August of 1986—this despite my penchant for driving too fast. As it

turned out, my unquenchable need for speed allowed us to shatter our twenty-four-hour drive time estimate: we crossed the border in just under eighteen hours.

I not only loved these trips home to Canada, I had come to depend on them. Ironically, the sheer ordinariness of life in British Columbia, the same normalcy that I had found so restricting as a kid, was something I now craved, at least in small doses. My time away, and the extreme nature of my experience, had given me a fresh perspective. Happy for, if surprised by, my success, my family never tried to co-opt it, take advantage of it, or pass it off as their own.

My parents did allow me to do some things for them: help them pay off the mortgage on their old home and move into a new one, fix Dad up with a fancier car and talk him into an early retirement—in effect providing that pension he'd kidded about before the 1979 trip to Los Angeles. I was insistent; they'd worked so hard their whole lives. While these gestures were accepted, my parents made it clear they were never expected. In fact, my earlier attempts at largesse were politely, but firmly, discouraged. In the heady first years of *Family Ties*, for example, I'd come home at Christmas and shower the whole family with inappropriately lavish gifts—household appliances like big-screen TVs and side-by-side washer/dryer units. We'd all sit around the tree after Christmas dinner, awkwardly avoiding the subject of my unseemly swag crowding out all the other gifts, and drink B-52 shooters chased with beers—a kind of bizarro reenactment of my father's ancient Christmas Eve tree vigil, though now with me as the prime-time paterfamilias. Eventually I'd pass out—or, worse, puke on the rug—and they'd put me to bed. My family always made me feel that home was a place where it was still safe to be myself.

But by the time Steve and I rolled into town, at the tail end of our sprint up the West Coast, the whole fame thing had gotten too big to leave at the border; there was no refuge from the ubiquitous reminders of my celebrity. In retrospect, I obviously had some ambivalence about leaving it behind—why else would I have gone to the trouble of driving my flashy sports car all the way up here?

Vancouver was the home of the World's Fair that year, Expo 1986, and an attempt to walk the grounds with my family proved impossible.

I was attracting so much attention that security eventually had to intervene and quickly arrange a private tour for us, using back doors and other behind-the-scenes approaches to bypass public entrances to the exhibits.

Just before things started to get out of hand, however, I noticed a souvenir photo booth—one of those setups where folks can stand next to a cardboard cutout of a celebrity or famous politician and have their picture taken. There, between Rambo and Reagan, was a likeness of me—actually, Marty McFly in the looking-at-his-watch pose from the movie poster. My family thought this was hilarious, and goaded me into posing with myself. Keeping my head down so that the photographer wouldn't get what was happening until the last second, if at all, I gave him the five bucks and stepped in front of the camera. I remember a burst of laughter from my dad, who had been the first to notice: the cardboard me was a good six inches taller than I was. *Maybe so,* I thought to myself, looking over the one-sided cutout, *but at least I have an ass.*

A few weeks later, I was back in Los Angeles—Pasadena actually—at the Civic Auditorium. I was up for the Lead Actor in a Comedy Emmy. I'd had a shot at an award the previous year, in the Supporting Actor category. I hadn't expected to win, and didn't. This year, in a more competitive category, I was even less confident, but I had been on such a freakish lucky streak that anything seemed possible. I had no speech prepared—an obvious jinx—but there was a line, a short joke, I'd been kicking around in my head since the day the nominations came down. At first it seemed like a simple bit of self-deprecating humor, a play on the fact that so much attention seemed focused on my height, or lack thereof. Jokes like the one I was considering have two purposes: they show that you're willing to laugh at yourself, and they make a preemptive strike—say it about yourself before somebody else gets a chance to.

And so, when fellow Canadian Howie Mandel opened the envelope and announced, "The Emmy for lead actor in a comedy series goes to . . . Michael J. Fox," I bounded to the stage, accepted the statuette, ran my fingers through my hair, made some brief, inarticulate crowing noises, and sputtered "I don't *believe* this." Then, steadying myself, my gaze panned the expanse of the auditorium, and I said it: ". . . I feel four feet tall."

In the years since, it's become clearer, to me at least, that the joke was about much more than my height. I was expressing just how over-whelmed by my success I was feeling, tacitly acknowledging that I didn't feel worthy of everything that was happening to me. I didn't measure up.

During my next hiatus, I brought the trophy back to Vancouver—in part, to share the honor with my parents, but also, frankly, to show it off. Mom gave Emmy a place of honor on a table in the entry hall to their home, directly across from the front door. That night, my brother and sisters gathered at Mom and Dad's. There was lots of laughing and celebrating. Experience had taught me, though, that somewhere in all this backslapping, Steve, or somebody, would come up with a way to tweak me—bring my balloon back down to earth. When the shot hadn't come by the time my beer intake went critical, I made my way downstairs to the guest bedroom in the basement and fell asleep.

The following morning when I stepped into the entry hall where the Emmy had spent the night, I burst out laughing. Surrounding the gold-plated statuette, as if to subdue its gaudiness by the force of sheer numbers, were my brother's fifteen-year-old boxing trophy, Mom's bridge trophy, Dad's curling trophy, my sisters' bowling and swimming trophies, plus a few other tokens of their individual triumphs. Perfect.

It was this sort of simple but pointed comic gesture that provided me with reassurance. If the entire dizzying ride came to an abrupt end, if the other shoe dropped and I was exposed as an imposter, I still had a place to go back to. I still had a home in the real world.

Although just a couple of weeks later, I wouldn't be so sure. My folks came down to visit me in L.A., and they brought the Emmy with them. As soon as my parents arrived at my door, I could see that my father was distraught. Something terrible had happened. We hugged in the driveway, and Dad excused himself, carrying his lug-gage, as well as a carry-on bag, into the house ahead of us. Mom touched my arm, wordlessly requesting that I stay back with her a moment; that there was something she needed to tell me.

"There was an accident on the trip down here," she told me. "It's your Emmy. It's pretty badly broken. I don't think it can be fixed." The overnight bag with the statue in it had been tucked into the overhead compartment, she explained, and another passenger's luggage shifted during the flight, crushing it.

"Is *that* what Dad's so upset about? That's crazy!"

When I got into the house my dad was sitting at the dining room table. I hadn't often seen him quite this shaken. The whole scene had a strange sort of upside-down feeling to it. I looked at him and thought of myself as a kid, all the times I had bashed in the fender, bumper, or door panel of his car and waited, miserably, for him to come into the room and confront me. It rattled me to see him so near tears.

"Dad." I smiled, reaching down to him for a hug. "Forget about it. It's a trophy. It's just a piece of metal. And, besides, I've heard of this happening before—they just give you another one. Don't worry about it, okay?" His relief was instantaneous and palpable.

The incident stayed with me because it drove home how the fantasy of celebrity could hold even the most levelheaded in its grip. Here was my dad, erstwhile ambassador for the reality principle, treating this hunk of laminated tin as if it were a sacred relic. As if it somehow embodied success, or power, or *me*. If he, of all people, had bought into this sort of magical thinking, then everybody in my world had succumbed. Who would have thought that in my entire family, I would be the sole surviving skeptic?

But this time I had found another ally, blessed with a healthy dose of skepticism and a clear understanding of the unique pressures I was facing. This lifeline to the real world had been in place for a year already at the moment my parents and I huddled around the mortally wounded Emmy—I just didn't know it yet.

TRACY

At the end of the summer of 1985, as the 1985–1986 *Family Ties* season was getting under way, something big happened: Alex Keaton got a girlfriend. A budding romance with Ellen, an art student he'd met at college, immediately captured the imagination of the show's audience—the ratings picked up where they'd left off at the end of the previous season, and climbed even higher.

For me, the effects would be more far-reaching. I suddenly had a partner. As an actress, the young woman cast in the role had an earthiness, integrity, and talent that demanded I push my own work to a higher level simply to hold my place onstage with her. She, as much as anyone, would be responsible for my bounding up those stairs in Pasadena a year later to accept an Emmy. Later, as a friend, she'd help me to ask and answer many of the questions I was now grappling with. There was no way to foresee it then, but in a couple of years I'd have a question for her, she'd say "yes," and, as my wife, she'd love and stay with me through challenges that neither of us had easy answers for. Tracy Pollan had come into my world.

I'd read with Tracy before she'd got the part of Ellen. Almost as soon we began to go through the lines, we found a rhythm, a give-and-take that worked—not because we were approaching the material from the same perspective, but because our styles were in many ways so different. Having trained in the New York theater, Tracy brought a grounded, disciplined quality to the work that was in stark contrast to my instinctive, unschooled, just-go-for-the-laugh approach. She was not, to put it mildly, the typical sitcom actress. Her beauty—shoulder-length blond hair, cut into bangs and framing a delicate face with high cheekbones and riveting wide-set eyes—was unusual for network television. This was not the sort of Chiclet-toothed cutie you'd see chirping "Welcome to McDonald's" in a burger commercial.

Plus, she was nice and funny and smart.

Tracy was involved in a relationship during her time on *Family Ties*, and I was seeing someone myself on a fairly regular basis, but I can easily pinpoint the exact moment I fell for her, the onset of my crush. While it would go unrequited for a long time, it never faded (and still hasn't).

For lack of a better name, let's call this lightning bolt The Scampi Incident. First, some context: At the beginning of the 1985–1986 *Ties* season, *Back to the Future* was still the undisputed number one movie at the box office. On the set of the show that summer/fall, I was welcomed back like the proverbial prodigal son. I'd always had a great relationship with the cast and crew—we shared a raucous and good-naturedly sarcastic camaraderie. Everyone cut me plenty of slack, now more than ever. I was "the star," after all; this set was my domain, and while I would have never dreamed of lording it over anyone, the fact is, I could get away with the most outrageous behavior. Despite the best efforts of our stage manager, I pretty much determined the pace of rehearsal—when we buckled down and pushed forward, and when we would stop for extended telephone breaks or dissolve completely into near-apocalyptic food fights. On one occasion, I had Woody Harrelson wander over from the *Cheers* set and, for an entire scene, replace Tina Yothers, acting out the Jennifer part up to and including sitting on Michael Gross's lap.

One day about four weeks into the season, Tracy and I were rehearsing a scene when we broke for lunch. By now, we'd struck up a friendship and spent a lot of time on set talking, getting to know each other, but we tended to go our own ways during the lunch break. That day, Tracy had spent hers in an Italian restaurant. After lunch, we picked up where we had left off, Alex answering a knock at the Keatons' living room door, opening it to reveal Tracy. The moment she said her first line, I detected a hint of garlic, and sensed an opportunity to have a little fun at her expense.

"Whoah. A little scampi for lunch, babe?"

At first she said nothing. Her expression didn't even change. But before long it became clear that my remark had surprised and hurt her. Here I was, a fellow actor whom she was just learning to trust, and maybe beginning to like, and I had ambushed her with my insensitivity. Looking me dead in the eye, she said slowly and evenly in a voice too quiet for anyone else to hear, "That was mean and rude, and you are a complete and total fucking asshole."

I was floored. *Nobody* talked to me that way; not lately anyway. This woman was completely unintimidated, unimpressed by whomever I thought I was, and even less by whom everyone else thought I was. A pig is a pig, no matter how many hit movies he's just had. I felt a rush of blood redden my face. I was overwhelmed by an emotion I was surprised to discover was something other than anger. I wasn't pissed off, I realized—I was *smitten.*

I apologized. She accepted. We got back to work, and The Scampi Incident was never mentioned again.

At the beginning of the Alex/Ellen relationship, Alex falls for Ellen hard, only to learn that she is engaged and leaving school to get married. Devastated, he pursues her to the railway station, where she is preparing to board her train and leave his life forever. While funny, the scene, as written by Michael Weithorn, was also tender and emotional. In the hands of an actress less capable than Tracy, it might have been overplayed to the point of sappiness. During the taping, I can remember momentarily losing the sense that I was actually in the scene myself and instead just watching her, as captivated as the rest of the audience. My reverie couldn't last, though, because working with Tracy demanded an attention and a degree of honesty from Alex that I hadn't felt pressed to reach for in the first three seasons. That scene, like every scene I've ever played with Tracy, pushed me to be better than I'd ever been before.

Tracy was offered a contract to come back for a second season, but she missed New York, her family, and the theater, and was wary of being pinned down to a long-term television commitment. It's hard to believe, looking back on it now, that she appeared in only seven *Family Ties* episodes. Her impact was tremendous—not only on the show and my character, but on the way I would think about my craft from that point on. Which is why I give Tracy so much credit for the Emmy I received that season.

But she left me with much more to think about than my acting. When we weren't rehearsing, taping, collaborating to get the most out of every script and bring as much color and nuance as possible to the Alex/Ellen romance, we'd hang out on set together a lot. Talking backstage, or lounging in the audience bleachers during breaks in the action, a friendship developed. I valued her sense of humor and intelligence as well as her sophistication, which was free of any taint of cynicism.

Tracy's seven episodes were spread out over the course of that entire season, giving her a front-row seat from which to view the whirlwind my life had become since the release of *Back to the Future*. While most of the people around me saw only the upside of this spectacular success and presumed that I could only be ecstatically happy—as I was, much of the time—Tracy alone appreciated the toll it was taking. Having grown up on Manhattan's Upper East Side (Park Avenue, to be precise), and attended private school with the sons and daughters of more than a few household names, Tracy was not particularly dazzled by the trappings of success. She was astute at seeing the person behind the personality, and although she was not the least bit pushy or intrusive about it, she did drop the occasional hint that I might want to pay a little more attention to some of my life choices.

She was particularly disturbed by the amount of drinking I was doing, and was one of the first people I can remember ever suggesting to me, however tentatively, that alcohol was something to be careful with, and that I might want to ask myself if drinking was becoming a problem. We also talked about the pressure I felt not to let anyone down, to prove myself deserving of the opportunities that were coming my way, and to choose projects that would guarantee success after success, even if that meant cheating myself of opportunities to grow as an actor.

Before she headed back east, as an expression of friendship and hope that I'd make my way safely through the Hollywood minefield, Tracy left me with a gift. She was returning to her life in New York, and had already told me that while she had had a good time, she didn't think she'd stay with the show. We promised to keep in touch, but, assuming as we both did that this was the end of our time together, she told me there was a song she wanted me to listen to.

As it happened, I was about to pull out of the Paramount parking lot in my ridiculously accessorized 300ZX when Tracy walked by on the way to her rented Volkswagen convertible. It was at the end of one our last days of working together, and she leaned into my car, handing me the cassette she had been talking about. I invited her to get in and we'd listen to it right there in the parking lot. She slipped in the tape, music immediately booming out of the speakers, including the gigantic bass woofers factory-installed in the car seats. Embarrassed, I hurriedly dialed down the volume on the speakers, switching off altogether the ones that were vibrating the seats so violently that our spines were quaking. The voice of James Taylor, now at a decibel level more appropriate to his particular stylings, filled the car.

My own musical tastes ran more to The Clash—maybe Elvis Costello in my more moody, reflective periods—so I couldn't imagine what exactly Sweet Baby James could say to me that would have any significant personal relevance. But when I heard the following lines, which I understood to be about John Belushi, I immediately grasped the message she'd wanted me to hear. Like other comedic actors of my generation I had a fascination with the late comedian; a framed Ron Wood lithograph of Belushi hung in my dressing room. Tracy had mentioned that as a teenage waitress on Martha's Vineyard in the early eighties, she had met Belushi several times, by way of urging that I not let alcohol do to me what drugs had done to him. The fatal mistake, she was suggesting by playing the song, would be to lose myself in the middle of the party that was now my life. By being all things to all people all of the time, I could end up being nothing to myself.

> *John's gone, found dead*
> *Died high, he's brown bread*
> *Later said to have drowned in his bed*
> *After the laughter, the wave of dread*
> *It hits us like a ton of lead.*
>
> *It seems, learn not to burn*
> *Means to turn on a dime.*
> *Walk on, if you're walking*
> *Even if it's an uphill climb.*
> *Try to remember that working's no crime.*
> *Just don't let them take and waste your time.*
>
> *That's why I'm here . . .*

I thought about this song, and Tracy, a lot during the crazy year that followed. In the spring of 1987, Tracy, by now unattached, came in to read for a role in *Bright Lights, Big City*, a film I was about to shoot in Manhattan. She got the part, and by the end of filming, we were falling in love and into the relationship that we'd been pretending to have in the seven episodes that played out on America's TV screens. House hunting in Vermont in October, engaged at Christmas, we were married the following summer.

And that's a story in itself. . . .

A MATTER OF CHOICE

Arlington, Vermont — July 1988

Tracy and I were married on July 16, 1988, and the reviews were terrible. *The Globe* announced on its front page that the wedding had been "a fiasco." *The National Enquirer* quoted an "insider" who reported that "people were nearly fainting as they staggered out after the ceremony. They were fanning themselves and gasping." People objected to our wedding attire, surprising considering that no one from the magazine had seen it. "Hush-hush nuptials turned into a circus," said the front page of the *Star*, whose article began, "Teensy-weensy actor Michael J. Fox . . ." Whenever a newspaper or magazine is annoyed with me, I immediately begin to shrink. In the coverage of our wedding, I was microscopic.

That our nuptials were "reviewed" at all is pretty strange; Tracy and I had never conceived of our wedding as part of our *oeuvre*. Moreover, none of the supposed "reviewers" had witnessed any of the events they presumed to describe and deride. By anyone's standards, it was a small, intimate gathering, peopled only by immediate family and our closest friends—we hadn't even invited any aunts, uncles, or first cousins. This was a measure of Tracy's positive influence on my life; it was important from the outset of our life together that we carve out an intimate space for ourselves, apart from the tumult of our careers.

But by attempting to have a small, private wedding in Vermont, about as far from Hollywood as we could get, it seems we had unwittingly thrown down the gauntlet to the press. The tabloids launched a massive, multiple-front offensive to find out when and where the wedding would take place, and then to obtain a photograph of the event, no matter what the cost. Tracy and I were determined to keep to our original plans for a modest, untelevised family affair, and the result of this mutual resolve was an absurdly elaborate cat-and-mouse game that drove home to us just how difficult it was going to be to draw a line between our public and private lives.

At the time, the tabloids' intrusive—sometimes comic, sometimes dangerous—attempts to interfere with what we considered a private occasion, as well as their derisive comments in the aftermath of having failed to do so, pissed me off no end. A lot has changed since then. For one thing, I'm much less angry, if at all. For another, many of the practices the press engaged in on our wedding day are a thing of the past—at least in the entertainment press. The public furor that followed the tragic death of Princess Diana while being chased by paparazzi caused the press to tone down, if not totally renounce, many of the guerilla tactics they employed during the 1980s and early 1990s.

Last, and most important, I am grateful, because the wedding provided the occasion to make emphatic my decision to get the hell out of the fun house. This wasn't about my future, but Tracy's, as well. It wasn't just a simple matter of choice—I was going to have to fight to establish and protect our boundaries, the border separating public and private life. That meant being sober and determined enough to say no to some people who were accustomed to hearing from me only yes. We would make it clear to ourselves, to our families, and to anyone else who gave a damn, that regardless of what we did for a living, our new life together would have its address in the real world.

A month before the wedding, the *Enquirer* reported that Tracy and I would be getting married in Vermont on July 16 or July 17. We don't know where they got that information, but it was correct. To make sure we understood that they planned to be there, invited or not, they published an aerial photo of our new home in Vermont.

Soon after, my publicist got a call from the *Enquirer*; they knew all the details and had an offer. If we would grant them exclusive rights to photograph the wedding, they would pay us $50,000, and provide security so that no competing reporters or photographers would disturb the event. The aerial shot was, of course, intended as a veiled threat: either invite us to your party, or we'll crash it.

Then the other tabloids and magazines started to call. One of the glossy weeklies took what they must have considered to be the high road. Instead of money, they offered us "what we gave Burt and Loni." That meant security (as with the *Enquirer*, their first priority was protecting their exclusive), a favorable article, and our wedding picture on their cover.

In making their offers, the *National Enquirer* and the others cited my "obligation to the fans." They argued that the people most responsible for my success and happiness should be able to share in this happiest of days. This sounds nobleminded until you realize that these publications could care less about my relationship with my fans, except as they stood to profit by it. Suggesting I "share" my wedding with the public is really just a polite way of inviting me to collaborate in the packaging and selling of the event, and in turn, as much newsprint as possible.

Maybe we're odd, but we had trouble thinking of our wedding as some sort of NCAA event to which we could sell the rights. If we were going to do that, why not also make a deal for corporate sponsorship (call it the Nike Nuptials), and hold the ceremony at Madison Square Garden, with Regis Philbin performing the ceremony and Bob Costas conducting the postcoital interview? Needless to say, we turned them down.

The battle lines had been drawn; if we would not sell them what they wanted, they were simply going to steal it. True, we could have changed our plans; we briefly considered an elopement to Vegas. But taking such a reactive stance in planning the wedding seemed wrongheaded. We decided to go forward as scheduled—there's always a chance, we thought, that the press knew less than they were letting on. In the event that they did show up, though, we'd be prepared. We

hired Gavin De Becker's firm to provide security (and were happy to
pay for it out of our own pockets).

The ceremony itself was to take place on Saturday, July 16, under
a tent adjacent to the West Mountain Inn in Arlington, Vermont. The
inn itself was a cozy bed-and-breakfast-type place, nestled in twenty
acres or so of bucolic Vermont countryside. The only access to the Inn
was a driveway that bridged the Battenkill River and wound through
pastures where llamas grazed.

During the week leading up to the big day, things got progressively weirder. A reporter virtually set up camp outside of Tracy's
apartment in New York, asking everybody who went by if they knew
her and, if so, had she spoken to them recently about any of the up-
coming events in her life. In Vermont, the *Enquirer* established a command center at the Equinox, in Manchester (the same hotel, as it
happens, where Tracy and I were staying). They staked out all of the
other hotels, motels, and inns in the area too, promising cash to employees in exchange for details about the comings and goings of our
friends and family members. A man claiming to be Bill Fox, my father, regaled strangers with wedding plans (when tabloid reporters
aren't asking questions, they are laying out imaginative scenarios for
you to confirm). Dozens of reporters were roaming around both
towns offering bribes to anyone else who could provide further information. At one point, an enterprising tabloid reporter went so far
as to attempt an abduction of Tracy's eighty-two-year-old grandmother, trying to lure her into his car, ostensibly to give her a tour of
the local environs, but in reality, to pump her for information. They
deployed photographers in camouflage gear into the hillside surrounding the West Mountain Inn. We heard later that they'd even tried
to rent a llama costume to gain even closer access to the proceedings.

I woke on the day of my wedding to the sound of choppers overhead. In all, the various tabloids, magazines, and TV entertainment
news programs had chartered a total of six helicopters from local air-
fields. Some had obviously pooled their resources so that photographers and cameramen from competing entities were sharing a ride, but
still, the cost must have been enormous. The *Enquirer* booked two for

themselves alone, one of which was to remain overhead at all times on Saturday. These helicopters had absolutely nothing to do with getting pictures of our wedding—the reporters knew we were going to be under a tent, and who gets married at 9:00 A.M. anyway? No, the helicopters were strictly a form of psychological warfare. The idea was to keep up the pressure until I backed down and allowed them a photo opportunity. They would be just as pleased, I assumed, if I stomped out of the tent à la Sean Penn and shook my fist at the sky. But the helicopters were never that bothersome to me, although there were disconcerting moments when the realization sunk in that these giant steel-bladed contraptions were competing for a tight quadrant of airspace directly above the people we loved and cherished most.

So why didn't Tracy and I at some point just give in? Step out of the tent and wave? Or stroll down to the end of the driveway where scores of press (and few, if any, actual fans) were gathered? Why couldn't we have simply allowed them to have one wedding picture and made everybody happy? First, after all the tabloids had done, we were in no mood to reward them. And second, there was no way a single, nonexclusive photograph would have left them satisfied. Next they'd go after the cake-cutting shot, the "exclusive" wedding-night shot, and then the honeymoon swimsuit shots.

Tracy and I understood that to surrender at this point would have been to give up much more than a simple photo opportunity. It would have been a vote for magical thinking; a place where you live and die by your press clippings, ratings, and box office—a place where the performance is twenty-four/seven. A decision to stroll down that driveway would have been a choice to stay in the fun house forever and kiss the real world good-bye.

During the ceremony, the helicopters came out in force. Under the tent it was warm, but certainly nobody fainted or gasped for air. We had the flaps down on the side of the tent open to the sky, but on the opposite side (where the helicopters couldn't approach because of the terrain), the tent was open to let in the breeze. If anything, the external craziness only sweetened the event by drawing everyone even closer together.

Unimaginable though it may have been to the uninvited gathered outside, it was a great wedding, a tremendous success. In spite of their bribes, their helicopters and subterfuge, all of their combined resources hadn't bought them as much as a single photograph. So, we paid for our privacy in the coin of bad press, the tabloids projecting the embarrassment of their failure directly onto us. It was a price well worth paying because it enabled us in a single moment not only to join together in the ritual of marriage, but to draw a line and create a space apart for ourselves. A place of our very own that, unbeknownst to us then, would help us to weather a much more serious storm ahead.

The Michael J. Fox Collection

CHAPTER FIVE

Reality Bites

Studio City, California — January 6, 1990
As the limousine traveled the quarter mile from our home in the hills
down to the intersection of Laurel Canyon and Ventura boulevards,
the sky darkened into night, the streetlights came on, and a gentle rain
slicked the roadways. The traffic signal went to yellow as we ap-
proached Ventura, the driver wisely choosing to slow to a stop rather

than trying to beat the red. There were young kids in the car, and though he knew we were in a hurry to get to the airport, he also knew the purpose of our trip. Why risk adding tragedy to tragedy?

The five of us needed to catch the next flight to Vancouver, where my father had been rushed to the hospital. Dad hadn't been feeling well for the last month or so; not that he had ever felt physically great throughout most of his adult life. He chain-smoked, and over time packed in excess of 300 pounds onto a frame so naturally slight it once earned him mounts as a jockey. His body, on this, the first Saturday of the new decade, had finally surrendered after a sixty-one-year assault. His heart gave out first, then his kidneys began to fail. At last report, he was still alive, but barely.

Tracy and I sat on either side of my sister Jackie, who was weeping softly. Tracy held Jackie's hand. Across from us on the rear facing bench behind the driver, our seven-month-old son, Sam, strapped into his car seat, had already nodded off to sleep. Next to him, Jackie's nine-year-old boy, Matthew, squirmed and fidgeted, using a shirt sleeve to wipe away tears of both fear and disappointment. Just old enough to recognize that his grandfather was very sick, Matt was still young enough so that to him, understandably, the more immediate crisis was the sudden cancellation of the rest of his California vacation, including the next day's trip to Disneyland.

As we waited in the idling limo for the light to turn green, a white sedan rolled to a stop beside us—a white, 1987 Chrysler Fifth Avenue, to be exact. I knew the year and make instantly because, from the ivory Naugahyde of its landau roof down to the whitewall radials and maroon pinstriping, it was the same car I'd bought for my father on his fifty-ninth birthday. This was Dad's car. Except of course, it wasn't.

I looked to my left and directly into my sister's face; she was staring past me out the window and at the car. Though tears rolled from her eyes, her mouth formed a smile.

"It's a good sign," she whispered.

"Yeah," I said, though as I embraced her, my eyes met Tracy's. She was crying too, but not smiling. She didn't think the ghost car was a good sign; not a good sign at all.

At LAX, my family boarded the plane while I stayed behind in the lounge to return a phone call. There'd been a message waiting for me from a close friend of the family. As soon as I reached him his first words were "I'm sorry," and I knew that Dad was gone. I couldn't help but think of the white car when he said that Dad had passed while we were making our way to the airport.

I joined my family on the plane. The attendant offered cocktails; I ordered a Jack Daniel's and a Bacardi. The drinks came, and I drained the bourbon and carried the rum across the aisle. Placing it on the tray table in front of Jackie, I sat down next to my sister and told her the news that our father had died.

.   .   .

The four years following my father's death could not have been more different from the four years preceding. Yet at the same time they present a kind of a mirror image. For me, Dad's death is a bit like the folded crease down the center of a Rorschach test, or perhaps more appropriately, a fulcrum uneasily balancing two opposing but closely linked worlds. Although I didn't appreciate it until much later, the four years I'd just spent struggling to make my way safely through the fun house of success, celebrity, and magical thinking would be child's play compared to the four years that lay ahead: a much more challenging struggle with the reality of mortality, maturity, and Parkinson's disease—real life's harsh answer to magical thinking. I couldn't know it that day in January 1990, but I was stepping across a threshold.

Burnaby, British Columbia—January 10, 1990
On the morning after the memorial service, Steve and I went to the funeral home to collect the impossibly small carton containing Dad's ashes. On the way back to the house (Mom's house now), me driving and Steve in the passenger seat of Dad's (Mom's) Chrysler, we were at once appalled to find ourselves laughing at the realization that this was the only way Steve and I could ever share the car's front bench seat with Dad. Similarly, we were surprised to find ourselves stifling laughter a few hours later when, after Mom had asked

us to gather up some of Dad's things, Steve and I came across a cache of our father's heart pills.

"What do we do with these, do you think?" I asked.

"Throw 'em out, I guess," Steve replied. Then, after a beat, "I mean, it's not like they *worked*."

Anyone who's been through the grieving process will recognize moments like these. It's not that we didn't love and respect our dad, but that, shaken by his sudden departure, at times it seemed our most natural reactions were just what Dad's would have been: whenever possible, we had to find *something* to laugh about.

It's just as common, however, when families join together in mourning for the result to be as divisive as it is cathartic. A scene played out at my mother's home later that evening that unexpectedly erupted into anger.

It was late, almost midnight; Mom had gone to bed, and Tracy and Sam were asleep in the downstairs guest room. It was just my brother, sisters, and I grouped around the kitchen table, some sitting and some, like me, wandering to and from the refrigerator or just pacing the line where the linoleum met the kitchen carpet. The discussion was about, among other things, how best to carry out my father's final wishes.

Dad didn't want us to feel tied to the ritual of visiting a gravesite or monument. He had loved ones in nearby cemeteries and felt remiss that he'd rarely found time to pay his respects, so he'd asked that in death he be cremated, and that we spread his ashes over those graves. This ceremony would take place the following morning, with only my mom and the five kids taking part.

While we worked out the logistics for the next morning, Kelli and my older sister Karen were clipping copies of Dad's obituary from a stack of newspapers. Karen asked if I wanted her to save one for me. In truth, I had already slipped a copy into my suitcase that morning, but, exhausted and a little punchy, I said something meant as a throw-away bit of levity that came out sounding all wrong. "Don't worry about it," I said, "I'm sure my clipping service will pick it up."

Jackie's rebuke was particularly angry and took the form of a command. "Michael," she barked, "sit down and shut up."

By now, I was even less accustomed to such scoldings than I was four years earlier on the set of *Family Ties* when Tracy lit into me during The Scampi Incident. This *did* piss me off, and I decided that it was time for me to go to bed, but not without a parting shot.

"Hey, Jack," I said as I turned to walk toward the basement door and make my way down to join Tracy and Sam in the guest room, "screw you."

The remark was neither diplomatic nor witty, I admit, but I never expected it to spark the sudden explosion I heard from behind me. When I wheeled back around, Steve had bolted to his feet, almost overturning the kitchen table in the process, and was coming at me—fast.

I only had a second to set myself, and as he reached for me I gave him a defensive shove, intended to buy myself enough time to get to the basement door. I love my brother, I certainly didn't want to fight him, then or ever—it would be the last thing my father would want to see happen. Besides, let's face it, the guy had three inches and sixty pounds on me. But as I made my second break for the door, he grabbed hold of my T-shirt—actually, one I'd borrowed from Tracy. As I pulled away, it tore all the way down the front. He stayed with me, my sisters following closely behind, until we reached the entry hall at the top of the stairs.

And there we stood in an uneasy standoff, the four of them encircling me in a tableau eerily reminiscent of an earlier one, a few short steps away and a few short years back. I'm thinking of that tabletop in my parents' hall, where my siblings' hastily assembled collection of trophies had outnumbered and surrounded my brand-new Emmy award. In retrospect that very image points to the drama *within* the drama—how awkwardly my fun-house self now confronted real-world disaster. When I think back to the events of those days and begin to see them from my brother's point of view, I wince—and can easily understand how things got to this pass.

·   ·   ·

Steve had been at the house when Dad rapidly began to deteriorate. He'd called the ambulance. He'd held and comforted our frightened father as EMS attendants punched needles into his arms and loaded him onto the gurney before speeding off to the emergency room. Steve was the point man at the hospital, conferring with the doctors, and relaying the grim prognosis to Mom, while trying to keep her as calm as possible. Then he had to make the phone calls to the rest of us, relaying the news that not only was Dad very sick, but he was fighting for his life.

By the time Steve's call had reached me, I'm sure he was down to his last reserves of physical and emotional strength. My reaction, given his understanding of the direness of the situation, must have seemed ludicrous. But I was drawing on what I thought were *my* greatest and most available strengths: money and influence.

"He should have the best doctors, Steve," I said. "If he needs to be transported, get a chopper, send him to Seattle if you have to. Jackie and I will be right there. I'll make some calls, see if we can get a private jet."

Steve must have been shaking his head. It's a measure of his grace under pressure that he didn't take that opportunity to rip into me, let his big-shot little brother know that even *he* couldn't buy, bribe, or bullshit his way out of this mess.

"You and Jackie just need to come home," he said simply. "As soon as you can."

While I made a series of futile attempts to contact friends and studio executives with access to private jets, Tracy called American Airlines and made the reservations we eventually used to fly back to Vancouver that evening.

My mother's quiet devastation; the expressions on my sisters' faces, as if they'd been suddenly and violently slapped in the middle of an otherwise pleasant conversation; and Steve's anguish as he recounted the ordeal of our father's final moments—this is what greeted me at the door in Burnaby, and immediately it grounded me in a landscape of loss, a landscape dominated by the absence of my father. It was the harshest reinforcement yet of the truths I had been grappling with. Money, property, and prestige were no protection from reality.

As awful as the situation was, the bottom feeders of the tabloid press did what they could to make it even worse. As far as they were concerned, this wasn't a private tragedy, but a public story. Their intrusive phone calls upset my mother, and a few even showed up at her doorstep in the guise of condolence callers. Gavin De Becker's office sent security personnel from California; a sound move as it turned out, for in subsequent days, tabloid photographers were caught smuggling cameras into my father's viewing and attempting to crash his wake. More theater of the absurd from the folks who brought you llama suits, dueling helicopters, and kidnapped grandmothers. What was astounding was that they could make no distinction between *my* wedding and my *father's* funeral. According to their twisted logic, anything that *involved* me was *about* me. But how could my family understand this, and why should they have to?

At the wake, close friends of the family approached and spoke to me as if I alone was heir to the mantle of familial responsibility; that it was all in my hands now. Not only was I was in no way fit to take on that role, but these well-wishers, however well-intentioned, were being grossly unfair to Steve, who had already so ably shouldered so much of this burden and was, after all, eight years my senior. It must have stung.

All of this brought Steve and me to the precipice that night in my parents' house. I'd come home, I thought, wanting simply to be present, a grieving son and brother. But evidently I carried a lot of extra baggage with me—at least in the eyes of others, including my family. The effect was to open a gulf between my siblings and me, which was the last thing any of us needed.

It was Tracy who wordlessly defused the confrontation. She had been awakened by the fracas, as had Sam, whom she carried on her hip as she rose up the stairs behind my brother. When I saw her, I released my grip on Steve's shirt. He noticed the shift in my gaze and let go of the shreds of mine, then turned to make way for my wife and son. Tracy knew better than to involve herself in a family feud. Taking my hand, she simply led me down the steps into the guest room. I began to blurt out my side of the story. Tracy closed the door, put Sam in his crib, and crawled back into bed.

"Tell me about it in the morning. You need to sleep." She switched off the bedside lamp and I lay down beside her in the darkness. She draped an arm across my chest.

"You know," she said, "that *was* my favorite shirt."

I knew, even the next morning, as my siblings and I made our somber rounds of the local cemeteries—speaking to each other only through our mother—that the wounds of the previous night's encounter would eventually heal. (About this, I was right.) The focus of my attention returned to my father. The way I understood things then, there was no more *eventually* for him and me: our relationship would forever be what it was on January 6, 1990. Future events could have no bearing. (About this, I was wrong.) I was grateful that my dad had lived long enough to know Tracy and to hold our son Sam. Their presence in my life represented a personal accomplishment that was more powerful and, quite possibly in his view, just as unlikely as my worldly fame and fortune. I doubt he expected I'd ever choose a mate as grounded as Tracy, or so eagerly embrace the responsibilities of fatherhood.

My career did impress him, though, and I felt glad he'd lived long enough to enjoy it. Given his cautious nature, the risks I took (albeit with his solid if reluctant support) were outrageous, but they had paid off. Obvious in his pride and generous in his praise, the entire tone of his relationship with me changed—though, truth be told, not until after I had become successful. The bottom line: I was untouchable now, and he knew it. Getting Dad to relax and just go with the ride will always stand as one of my most unlikely and gratifying achievements. My dad, as would be most evident with the fractured Emmy incident, had bought into the magic.

So what would he have made of events to come? And how would his reaction have colored my own? I worry that my dad would have taken my diagnosis as a confirmation of his darkest views of the world; proof that happiness and success were not to be trusted. He believed life operated according to an inflexible system of compensation, in which each of life's gains had to be paid for by an equal amount of loss. Though obviously I can't know this for sure, I suspect he may have interpreted my P.D. as the cosmic price I had to pay for all my success. That would not have been helpful to me. For one thing, there have been times when I have felt as much myself, and the belief—which after all is nothing but superstition—has only gotten in the way of getting better.

So much good has happened since the dark days of this period in my life that I wish my father could have lived to see. He died just as the shit was about the hit the fan, and there's much I'm relieved he didn't have to live through, much I'm not proud of. I remember thinking soon after he died that at least he lived long enough to see the magic, to enjoy and take part in his son's success. And yet, as I can see now, there was an even greater magic to come, and I so wish I could have shared that with him too.

DIAGNOSIS: DENIAL

New York—October 1991
One morning, less than two years later, I found myself wandering the halls of New York City's Mount Sinai Hospital. The name of the doctor and his office number—listed on the directory in the building's giant atrium lobby—matched those on the scrap of paper I'd brought with me to the hospital and slipped into my left pocket. Now, after ten minutes of exploring the medical center's maze, I'd forgotten the room number altogether. No big deal, *right?* Just refer to the paper again.

Well, that was one of the things I was having a hard time getting used to: there were still times, particularly midmorning, when I was relatively free of symptoms, and could use my left hand much as I had for the first thirty years of my life to do things like, for example, casually tuck a slip of paper in my jeans pocket. But then, with no obvious cue, the symptoms would fire up again, my left hand would begin shaking uncontrollably, as it was now, and the process of retrieving that slip of paper from my left pocket was anything but casual. It required a right-handed cross-body grope that was awkward, at best, and, at worst, vaguely obscene.

White-jacketed nurses and doctors scurried back and forth

through doorways and along the length of the corridor. Any one of them would have recognized the name of the physician I was looking for and been able to point me toward him, but that was the problem: as likely as they were to recognize his name, they were also just as likely to recognize *me*. I didn't want any water-cooler gossip about why Michael J. Fox was seeing one of the preeminent neurologists in North America, a renowned figure in the treatment of Parkinson's disease.

A week or two had passed since my initial diagnosis, and I'd still told very few people beyond my family. I didn't want anyone not directly involved in my care to associate me with the illness. I just needed Dr. Big Muckety-Muck to offer what would now be a *third*, and hopefully final, opinion so I could retreat once more to the privacy of my apartment.

After a few more minutes of slapping shoe leather against institutional floor tile, I arrived at the Department of Neurology, and finally the door of the doctor himself. His waiting room was empty—a relief. I was seconds away from the inner sanctum of his office and the protection of doctor-patient confidentiality.

The nurse/assistant at the front desk showed me into an examining room. She informed me that the doctor would be in shortly, and as I was shedding my coat and baseball cap, she noticed the shaking in my left hand.

"It's okay," she said. "You don't have to be nervous."

Confused for a second, I suddenly realized she was talking about the tremor.

"Oh," I responded. "That . . . That's why I'm here. In a neurologist's office, I mean."

After a second of mutual embarrassment, she left, closing the door behind her. Minutes later, it opened again, and in walked the legendary neurologist himself, just as wizened, curmudgeonly, and all-business as he'd been described to me.

"Says here you've been diagnosed with Parkinson's disease," he grumbled with some incredulity. "How old are you?"

Thirty, I told him, and he shook his head as if he was pissed off at me for wasting his time.

"Well . . . I doubt you have P.D.," he said. "Essential Tremor, maybe. Possibly something else. It's very unlikely that a fellow your age has Parkinson's. But you're here, so let's have a look."

I would have hugged him if he hadn't immediately ordered me to drop my trousers and hop up on the examining table. He was about to lead me through the battery of tests that I knew so well by now that I could have conducted them myself. But I was hopeful. *Finally*, I thought, *we're going to get to the bottom of this. This guy knows what he's talking about. This whole Parkinson's thing has been a colossal mistake.*

In a practical sense, the initial diagnosis had been a nonevent. Telling Tracy, and then my mother and family, had been gut-wrenching— a lot of crying and hugging. But after that, how was I supposed to act on this information?—if, in fact, it was true and I chose to believe it. (Those were two very big ifs.) I played at being the patient, took to bed—as though putting a name to the physical sensations I'd been experiencing for over a year now suddenly made them ten times worse and demanded an entirely new protocol. But this didn't feel right. In fact, it felt downright silly.

In a classic case of shooting the messenger, I resisted following up with the diagnosing neurologist—never consulted with him again, in fact. Illogically and irrationally, I was just plain pissed off at the guy for having the balls to suggest such a fate was mine. In the short term, I would get a second opinion, and if that didn't put an end to this farce, I'd get a third.

During this time, it made sense to do a little personal research. But not with the purpose of finding facts about Parkinson's disease that I could relate to; more to find reasons to disqualify myself as a probable victim. The handiest resource was, of course, Tracy's *Columbia School of Medicine Encyclopedia of Health*. What the book had to say about P.D. was sandwiched between Stroke and Epilepsy. This is the entry's first paragraph:

Parkinson's disease, sometimes called shaking palsy, usually begins between 50 and 65 years of age. The disabling symptoms include muscular rigidity, slowness and poverty of movements, and tremor. Other signs of the disease may have been present, in retrospect, before the diagnosis is actually made. These include diminished blinking and reduced spontaneity of facial expression, stiff postures, loss of ease in changing positions (such as attempting to sit or stand), and a tendency to remain in a single position for unusually long periods of time. It is usually a shaking tremor of the hands, however, that finally brings the patient to a physician.

Contained in this first sentence was the one shining fact that I was pinning my hopes on: ". . . usually begins between 50 and 65 years of age." My symptoms, if that's what they were, showed up in my late *twenties*. How could I possibly have this old person's disease?

In the days and weeks following my diagnosis, I observed what seemed like dozens of people with the symptoms of Parkinson's, all of them elderly. It's amazing I hadn't noticed so many before, although I'm sure my obliviousness could be attributed to what I call the Baby Effect. When I was single, babies were all but invisible to me. Then Tracy became pregnant with Sam, and all of a sudden everywhere I looked there were expectant mothers, mothers nursing newborns, pushing strollers, loading toddlers onto buses. Here was the same phenomenon, only infinitely more depressing. Those cardigan-wearing seniors I'd seen shuffling along Central Park West with their nurse-companions were often, I now understood, shuffling from the effects of Parkinson's disease. Courtesy had always taught me to allow old people to board elevators first, but I'd never realized that the reason it took so long for some to step inside, to find and push the proper button, was the debilitating hesitation of P.D. When I'd switch seats in a diner booth so I didn't have to watch the old woman across from me mismanaging her plate of eggs and bacon, not once did it ever occur to me that I might be turning away from the ravages of Parkinson's.

Chalk it up to the arrogance of youth, I guess. You might pay attention to this stuff if it's your grandparents—but otherwise, *don't bother me. I'm young, I'm healthy, I've got other things to worry about.*

Young Onset Parkinson's (the appearance of symptoms in people under forty), the diagnosing physician had explained, is rare. These patients make up less than ten percent of the overall Parkinson's population. This, I'd learn later, made me one of only a hundred thousand or so North Americans in my predicament. Just this once, though, I got no satisfaction from defying the odds.

I tried to remember if I'd ever met anyone under the age of seventy who might have been afflicted, and only one came to mind. A journalist—mid-forties maybe—who'd interviewed me for a magazine piece at a Greenwich Village coffee shop. The conversation was pleasant enough, but I remember feeling a guilty impatience with the distraction of her movements, the rattle of her sugar packet as she labored to open it and pour the contents into her coffee, and the irregular rhythm of her spoon clinking in the cup—she wasn't actually stirring, just holding the utensil and allowing the shaking of her hand to blend in the cream and sugar. Like the neurologist's assistant, I assumed what I was witnessing was nervousness, and remember feeling mildly flattered that I might have that effect. But after a while I realized this wasn't a case of nerves. Nothing the writer said indicated that she was flustered in the least; to the contrary, she was all confidence and utterly professional. This was probably my first brush with Young Onset Parkinson's disease.

So, okay, obviously it was theoretically within the realm of possibility, but still . . . "usually . . . 50 and 65." There could still be another explanation. Yet with each subsequent sentence, the *Columbia Encyclopedia* described a condition unmistakably like my own. "Symptoms include muscular rigidity, slowness and poverty of movements, and tremor." All of these features were definitely present, predominantly in the left hemisphere of my body. The "poverty of movement" (I thought I'd left poverty behind back in the slums of Brentwood) was what had so shocked Tracy when she interrupted my Martha's Vineyard jog—the left arm barely swinging and out of sync with the rest of my body. There was also a rigidity in my hip, creating a barely noticeable hitch in my gait, plus I'd wake up in the morning with a stiffness in my neck and left shoulder, as well as my knee, wrist, and ankle joints.

"Other signs of the disease may have been present, in retrospect, before the diagnosis . . ." I reviewed my recent history for evidence that this might have been true and, regrettably, came up with quite a few hits. I considered the first example: *diminished blinking and reduced spontaneity of facial expression*. This could easily be confirmed through a review of my work by screening, in chronological order, a series of videotapes. I wasn't about to do that—only my mother could stomach that much of me—but the description of symptoms did resonate. I'd always thought, however, that my "diminished blinking" and "reduced spontaneity of facial expression" marked a growing comfort in front of the camera, less mugging, hamming it up—in general, an improvement as an actor. "No," this book was telling me, in so many words, "you weren't getting *better*—just *sicker*."

As for "stiff postures, loss of ease in changing positions (such as attempting to sit or stand)," my past work experience provided another clue. My favorite part of the original *Back to the Future*, filmed in 1985, was the Johnny B. Goode sequence during the "Enchantment Under the Sea" dance. As a frustrated musician, I was in my glory, learning the guitar chords and lead solo arrangements, as well as working with a choreographer to mimic and incorporate into the production number the signature styles and stage moves of my rock and roll heroes. Shooting this scene over the course of two days was sweaty, exhausting work, but I was young, in great shape (I thought), and it didn't feel especially grueling.

Four years later, for 1989's *Back to the Future II*, I had to reprise the Johnny B. Goode number, duplicate it right down to the tiniest detail. Not only did I find the moves much more difficult to pull off, but the physical toll was shocking. For weeks afterward, I was achy. At the time, I wrote this off to merely being four years older, but four years couldn't account for just how difficult it was for me to repeat the scene.

The last few words of the penultimate sentence in the encyclopedia's paragraph—"a tendency to remain in a single position for unusually long periods of time"—were also on the mark. They made me think of Tracy, or at least something she always kidded me about. Trying to reconcile the hyperactive blur I could sometimes be with the lumpen sloth I was at other times, she'd say, "You're the textbook definition of inertia. Once you start moving, you can't stop; but once you do stop, it's almost impossible for you to start up again." It was an apt portrait and, unfortunately, a fairly good description of everyday life with Parkinson's disease.

What I now understand only too well is this: the reason that the symptoms were presenting in such a gradual (my own characterization would be *insidious*) fashion had to do with the effect of the disorder on the mechanics of the central nervous system. A part of the brain known as the *substantia nigra* contains a group of cells that produce a chemical called dopamine, which acts as a messenger, transmitting signals within the brain. When, for whatever reason, these cells begin to die, the result is a gradual reduction in the amount of dopamine manufactured. The messages aren't being delivered properly, if at all, to certain nerve cells in the brain, or neurons, critical to motor function, and they start to fire out of control. As a result, the brain's owner (in this case, me) is no longer the final authority over the movement of his body. Like a car without motor oil, a brain without dopamine is going to slowly but inevitably break down. The physical changes I had failed to recognize as symptoms were like the red light on the dashboard, but who knew to look? Come to think of it, I'd always ignored all those little red lights on the dashboard—much to my father's chagrin.

It's possible that I'd actually had Parkinson's for five or even ten years before I noticed the twitching in my pinkie that morning in Florida. Scientists believe that by the time a patient notices even the tiniest tremor—the blinking red light, if you will—as much as eighty percent of the dopamine-producing cells in the substantia nigra are already dead, totally lost without any possibility of recovery.

Which brings me to the final sentence of the paragraph: "It is usually a shaking tremor of the hands . . . that finally brings the patient to a physician." It was bad enough that I might have a chronic progressively degenerative brain disease, but did I have to be so *god-*

damn predictable on top of everything else? This predictability was no small part of the entire horror show. One of the things I'd be losing here was *freedom*, and I don't just mean loss of physical freedom as a result of the demise of thousands of tiny brain cells. If this diagnosis was correct, if I had this disease, then I would forever be locked into a prognosis, and with that, an identity I'd had no part in creating. I'd be tracked and studied, compared against others *just like me*, and the findings would be scrutinized to see if or how I varied from the *norm*, in what way my progress differed from *projections*. And all the while, I could be counted upon to go through a by-the-book coping process: Elisabeth Kübler-Ross's five stages of grief (denial/isolation, anger, bargaining, depression, and acceptance); my most trying personal experience reduced to a common laundry list by some Swiss woman I'd never even met.

I can't overemphasize what a blow this prospect of being so unfailingly predictable was to my sense of myself as an individual. And further, if my diagnosis got out, it wouldn't be simply a matter of my employer knowing and perhaps judging me differently. Or Mrs. Jones, the neighbor across the backyard fence, gossiping with the other parents in the carpool. No, the *whole world* would know. After my wedding and my father's funeral, I knew full well how the tabloid press would run with a story like this—possess it and thereby possess a greater part of me than I was willing to let go of. I wasn't just losing my brain, I was losing my *franchise*.

Back to that very first sentence: "Parkinson's disease, sometimes called shaking palsy, usually begins between 50 and 65 years of age." Here was the escape clause I clung to like a life raft; my only hope for salvation. Like the doctor said, it was very unlikely that a fellow my age could have Parkinson's.

At Mount Sinai Hospital, even as I was finishing the last of my finger taps and nose touches for the great doctor, the ultimate authority on Parkinson's disease, I knew I had failed miserably. So it came as no surprise when, after dressing and stepping into his private office, he asked me to sit down in the chair across from his desk.

"I'm very sorry," he said, his earlier impatience giving way to sympathy. "But it's clear to me that you do, in fact, have Young Onset Parkinson's disease."

Now what?

THE ESCAPE ARTIST—REDUX

Once Dr. Muckety Muck had rendered his verdict, I had little choice but to go with the consensus that I was in the early stages of Young Onset Parkinson's disease. *Go with,* mind you, is a long way from *accept*—as Ms. Kübler-Ross could tell you, I'd have a great distance to travel before I finally reached *acceptance.* Sure, I understood that the medical facts all pointed toward a confirmed diagnosis; that I would have to at least behave as if I really had this disease, research the proper medications, take whichever one was indicated, and so on. But I hadn't really fully surrendered my denial.

Stubbornly, I clung to fantasies of escape, hoping against hope that somehow my diagnosis would turn out to be a mistake. Or, better yet, having defied the odds by being one of a tiny population of young adults with Parkinson's, I would further defy the odds by being the only reported case of the condition magically disappearing. I'd have a couple of symptom-free days, let's say, then Tracy would casually drop that she'd switched toothpastes—did I notice the difference?—and I'd slap my forehead and say, "*Jesus, honey,* the toothpaste! That was it! You've cured me!" I know it sounds nuts, but hey, you've read the first half of the book.

Exasperation, frustration, and fear were my constant companions in those early days, but I never once found myself resorting to blame. Who was there to blame? God? My notion of spirituality was different then than it is now, but even if I'd been the most fundamentalist of believers, I would have assumed that God had better things to do than arbitrarily smite me with the shaking palsy. I was no Job.

Blame assumes causation and, in that respect, Parkinson's remains a murky matter. Researchers have not yet found the exact cause of Parkinson's disease. Most believe a combination of genetic and environmental factors are involved, but no definitive data exist. There was no history of Parkinson's in my family, for example, but that doesn't mean there wasn't a genetic predisposition toward developing Parkinson's if exposed to certain environmental pollutants such as pesticides.

It's come to my attention, all these many years later, that at least three other people who worked with me at CBC's Vancouver Studios, where we taped *Leo & Me* in the mid-seventies, have all been diagnosed with Parkinson's at an age that would put them in the Young Onset category. Was this mini-cluster a coincidence, or evidence of a common environmental cause—a "sick building" or chemical exposure? The last I heard, an investigation by research scientists was under way, and I have an obvious investment in their results. I'm curious about what they conclude, though not because I'm looking for someone to blame, a bad guy on whom to vent my anger by means of a well-lawyered class action suit. The real reason I'm curious is that their findings may provide one more clue in solving the mystery of causation, and discovering the cause is the surest road to a cure.

The doctors had asked me if I'd ever worked with or been exposed to a litany of metallic-based chemicals or abused any opiate-based drugs such as heroin, laudanum, or morphine compounds; some young heroin addicts have developed advanced Parkinsonism after using a synthetic version of the drug containing the chemical compound MPTP. The answer to all of these questions was no. There was also the possibility a head injury had been responsible; I'd suffered several concussions playing hockey, and I couldn't help thinking of Muhammad Ali, whose Parkinson's I assumed, perhaps falsely, may be related to the countless punishing blows he received in the ring. But the doctors all seemed quick to dismiss head trauma as a factor in the development of my symptoms.

Even if I hadn't knowingly done something stupid to put me at risk, there were times when I did fault myself. My culpability, as I saw it, had to do with my failure to anticipate this calamity. For all the fretting I'd done about the ultimate No—the looming disaster that would offset all my halcyon fun house years—I'd never prepared myself for anything quite this bleak, this *perfectly* shitty. Why me? Why *not* me? It's human nature to search for meaning, and I was sorely tempted to see my illness as a metaphor (a tendency Susan Sontag brilliantly dissected in her book *Illness as Metaphor*). My Parkinson's represented the dropping of the other shoe. It was payback. It was the bill being brought to a sloppy table after an ill-deserved and underappreciated banquet. Such a turnabout I had no choice but to consider fair play. I should have seen it coming. In a way, this was my father talking, but there were times when the sentiment was mine.

Angry or not, my only immediate recourse was to just get on with it until I could figure out some way to get out of it. I wouldn't begin regularly seeing a neurologist for several more years, but the original diagnosing physician had given me prescriptions for two different P.D. medications: Sinemet, the brand name version of levodopa or L-dopa, and another called Eldepryl (generically known as selegiline hydrochloride). Each acts differently within the brain to help mitigate symptoms, and they are just two among an ever-increasing number of commonly administered pharmaceutical therapies that include: Comtan (entacapone), Parlodel (bromocriptine), Requip (ropinirole), Permax (pergolide), and Mirapex (pramipexole dihydrochloride), Artane (trihexyphenidyl), Cogentin (benztropine), and Symmetrel (amantadine). Some of these work better than others, some not at all, depending on the patient and the severity or idiosyncrasies of what is, for all practical purposes, his or her own personal disease. Over the years, at one time or another and in various combinations, I'd take a turn on the dance floor with almost all of these drugs. None is, of course, a *cure*. There is, at this writing, no such thing.

The doctor wanted me to start on Eldepryl, which can ease symptoms by delaying the breakdown of what dopamine the brain still produces. I took Eldepryl for a while, maybe a week, and found it had only a minor effect on the escalating tremor in my left hand. Again, it's important to emphasize that every patient experiences a unique manifestation of the constellation of symptoms that fit under the general umbrella of *Parkinsonism*. By the same token, every patient reacts differently to treatment, so it's crucial that he or she work closely with a neurologist to find the most effective way to manage the disease, not to mention strike a tolerable balance between the benefits and side effects of the various drugs. If I had followed this sensible advice, my experience with Eldepryl might have been more successful, but I was looking for more immediate results. Basically, I just wanted the symptoms to go away so I could forget about the whole mess for as long as possible, and, even more important, keep anyone else from noticing. So it was on to the next drug for me.

The first drug approved specifically for Parkinson's (in 1970)— and still the most often prescribed P.D. medication—is Sinemet (levodopa). Sinemet is taken up by the brain and changed into dopamine, the neurotransmitter that a Parkinson's patient can no longer produce in sufficient quantities. In most patients, Sinemet significantly improves mobility and allows them to function almost normally. As Parkinson's disease progresses, however, the drug often proves less effective, making it necessary to take larger doses, thus heightening the risk of debilitating side effects like dyskinesias—involuntary movements and tics. For this reason some doctors try to postpone their patients' use of Sinemet for as long as possible. It's also an accepted truth that if Sinemet succeeds in relieving your symptoms, that removes any doubt you have full-fledged Parkinson's disease. So I had decidedly mixed feelings the day I first took a half a Sinemet pill and, after approximately thirty minutes, found that the tremor had vanished, and didn't return for almost five hours. The bad news was obvious: here was yet another confirmation I had Parkinson's disease. The good news was, now I could *hide* it.

Given what I do for a living, the very notion of hiding seems, on the face of it, ludicrous—the expression "hide in plain sight" pushed to the extreme. But, I never gave a second's thought to sharing my diagnosis with anyone outside of my inner circle of family, close friends, and trusted associates. I saw absolutely no compelling reason to do so. I didn't, and still don't, feel as though I was *deceiving* anyone by not immediately going public—this was my problem, I'd deal with it. With Sinemet, I now had the means to completely mask symptoms. If my employers didn't notice any difference in the way I performed my job—and, for the time being anyway, there really was none—then I had no compunctions that I was somehow peddling damaged goods.

Since I didn't yet have a neurologist (I didn't even have a regular internist in New York, where I was living most of the time), I had my general practitioner from California prescribe Sinemet whenever I needed refills. I carried them around, loose and broken in the pockets of my shirts, coats, and trousers, popping them in an admittedly haphazard fashion until I achieved the desired result. I was a young man with a brand-new family, I had work to do, and I intended to pretend as if none of this was actually happening to me. Although, knowing what I knew, my life now could hardly go on business as usual.

Following his surprise pronouncement that I had P.D., that very first diagnosing neuro offered what I assume he considered an upbeat prognosis. "With proper treatment," he promised, "I see no reason why you can't have another ten good years of work ahead of you."

Ten years? I had just turned thirty.

There was a rueful irony in the prospect of having to retire at forty. Jokingly, I had been announcing for years to disbelieving friends that forty was the age at which I intended to pack it all in, retreat with my family to our farm in Vermont, and pursue other interests. We'd all share a laugh. It was, of course, an idle threat, a fantasy of seizing control over the vagaries of show business: *I can quit and live life on my own terms.* But now, confronted with terms far harsher than those dictated by a fickle public or the box office bottom line, what had been a hypothetical and voluntary fallback position was suddenly my fate. Forget *abdication*, this was a *coup*, and in my panic I decided to break out the pillowcases, loot the palace, and escape with whatever I could carry.

There is never a good time to find out that you're incurably ill, but from a career perspective, I felt especially vulnerable. After *Family Ties*, my future in the business would be built upon film work, and that foundation was already showing signs of cracking. While *Doc Hollywood* had been a modest hit for Warner Brothers, the Universal action comedy that preceded it, *The Hard Way*, had been a dismal failure. In ideal circumstances, I could address this stutter in my career in one of two ways: The first scenario would be to draw a measure of confidence from past successes, without trying to duplicate them, and proceed to reinvent myself—take interesting chances, choose lower-profile projects with greater artistic, if not commercial, ambitions. Or I could simply try to repeat myself, and pray lightning would strike twice. This meant chasing my tail, playing it safe by doing formulaic romantic comedies that had a shot at doing blockbuster business.

Creatively, the first option was obviously preferable, but could I afford the time it would take? *Ten years*, the man had said—*ten years to do whatever work I was ever going to do*—ten years to build on whatever financial security I had provided for my wife, son, and future children. How arsty-fartsy could I afford to be? So when Universal came to me post–*Doc Hollywood* (and, unbeknownst to them, post-diagnosis) with an offer of an eight-figure deal for three pictures over five years, my instinct was to leap. Tracy, however, was adamantly opposed.

"You'll be trapped," she warned.

I argued that that wasn't true, since the contract allowed me to work on outside projects. She countered, rightly, that most of the writers, producers, and directors I'd want to collaborate with had exclusive deals at other studios. They couldn't come to Universal, and they wouldn't wait for me to be available for their films. And we both knew what Universal had in mind—keep remaking *The Secret of My Success* over and over until it paid off again.

"You don't understand." The words sounded strange to me, even before they left my lips. Had I ever said *that* to Tracy before? "I only have a limited window of opportunity here. This deal is giving me a chance to crawl through it and come out with something on the other side. I'm taking it."

THROUGH A GLASS DARKLY

Los Angeles/New York City—Spring/Summer 1992
In the days leading up to preproduction on *For Love or Money*, the first film of my Universal contract (more or less a remake of *Secret of My*

Success), I busied myself with other projects, some personal, some professional. Tracy, Sam, and I flew to California (we still, at that point, kept a home there) so I could direct an episode of *Brooklyn Bridge* for my old friend and *Family Ties* mentor, Gary Goldberg. It had been a year since I'd directed the episode of *Tales from the Crypt*, and I jumped at Gary's offer; directing had gone from an interesting sideline to a future career option. In addition to this work, and in an attempt to distract myself from my health problems and lose some weight, I threw myself into a maniacal fitness regimen.

It wasn't enough that my drill-sergeant trainer pounded on our door every morning at four A.M. to lead me on a run around the UCLA campus and up and down the bleacher stairs of Drake Stadium, before dragging my ass back to my garage for a grueling half hour of weight repetitions—it was his diet that was killing me. Restricting myself to portions small enough to emaciate a hamster was one thing, but limiting my alcohol intake to one day of drinking a week—well, *that* was torture.

Without really understanding what the hell I was doing, I realize now I'd entered, all too predictably, into the third stage of Elisabeth Kübler-Ross's paradigm for coping with loss—after denial and anger comes bargaining. Though I couldn't yet comprehend the ultimate outcome of Parkinson's takeover of my body and, with it, my life, my instincts told me to start negotiating now, fiercely, for preemptive control in whatever areas that was still possible. If P.D. was going to rob me of the ability to work in front of the camera as an actor, I'd establish a role for myself behind it as a director. To offset the eventual financial losses, I'd accept the assured payday from Universal at the price of my creative freedom.

As for the fitness training, I theorized that this self-imposed ordeal would strengthen my position on two fronts. I convinced myself that my conditioning, endurance, and increased physical toughness would somehow serve as a bulwark against neurological erosion. It would also, I calculated, fool other people. Even as I was growing sicker, those who didn't know my true condition might interpret my improved outward appearance as evidence that I was healthier than ever.

For some, drinking alcohol only one day a week would be no hardship at all—they probably wouldn't think about it one way or another. I had trouble maintaining this discipline. Once, downing a few cold ones with Pete Benedek, my agent, while watching the Redskins humiliate the Bills in the Super Bowl, I expounded on my experience with the rigors of temperance and heard myself utter this priceless bit of drunkard's logic:

"I'm glad I don't have a drinking problem," I confided, "because I don't think I'd ever be able to quit."

Succeeding at my drinking career had taken some doing, even perseverance. I was never really cut out for drinking—I just wasn't that good at it. I was too small, got hammered too quickly. There was always a good reason to hoist a few, though. In the late seventies it was youthful rebellion—booze was an antidote to the self-consciousness that consumed me as an eccentric teenager in search of an identity. Then, in the eighties, as the range of my experience and the scale of my accomplishments exceeded my wildest imaginings, alcohol (all that free Moosehead) became an essential ingredient in what was ostensibly a decade-long victory party.

I say "ostensibly" because the deeper purpose of all that celebrating may well have been to obliterate feelings of unworthiness and fear. But make no mistake, on the surface—and what were the eighties about if not surface?—the presiding mood was hedonistic abandon. This was a two-fisted, *yee haw!* scramble on top of a big oak bar with a magnum of Cristal champagne, leading a hundred or so of my closest pals in a chorus of "We Are the Champions"-type social drinking. And other than occasionally waking up with an army of fire ants colonizing the inside of my skull, there never seemed to be any major repercussions. Everybody knew who I was, how hard I worked—that's Mike, just blowing off steam. "I was drunk at the time" became my ever-ready, all-purpose excuse for any indiscretion.

As the eighties gave way to the nineties, my marriage to Tracy—a glass-of-chardonnay-with-dinner type whom I don't think I've ever seen inebriated—led to a voluntary change in my drinking habits. I was ready to embrace a quieter life. My days as a backstage regular at rock concerts, a New York nightclub VIP lounge habitué, were over. I was happy to trade beer blasts with the boys for time alone with my bride, and soon after, our baby. Though my new lifestyle was decidedly less social, drinking still had its place. Rarely, if ever, intoxicated around Tracy, I'd just have a glass of wine or two at dinner—as if I actually subscribed to her belief that there was a purpose to drinking other than getting blotto. I'd still tie one on occasionally, usually when I was traveling, and might even go on prolonged benders if I was out of town working on a movie. Overall, though, the party was over, and I was okay with that, as long as they didn't shut down the bar completely.

With my diagnosis in 1991 came another shift in my relationship with alcohol. The quantity of my drinking was still down from eighties levels, but the quality of that drinking had changed ominously. I always knew, somewhere in the back of my mind, that my drinking was about filling a void, masking a need to be something more than I was. Now, without the pretense of celebration and camaraderie to veil the abuse, I craved alcohol as a direct response to the need I felt to escape my situation. Joyless and secretive, I drank to disassociate; drinking now was about isolation and self-medication.

.   .   .

We returned to New York from Los Angeles early in the spring of 1992. Tracy was in rehearsal for a new Neil Simon play, *Jake's Women*. There'd be an out-of-town run in North Carolina for a few weeks before it opened on Broadway, roughly around the same time I was to begin shooting *For Love or Money* in the beginning of May.

As soon as we began shooting, I was miserable. In the midst of all this inner turmoil and psychological negotiation, it probably was no coincidence that I agreed to play this particular character—a wily and hyperactive concierge at one of New York's luxury hotels. A concierge, or at least the one represented in our movie, is a wheeler-dealer, a calculating operator who will do whatever is necessary to please his hotel guest clients and thereby extract as big a tip as possible. He aspires to own his own hotel someday, but becomes so frantic and so fearful of failure, that he can think of nothing better to do with his life except to keep moving—just keep on dancing as fast as he can and hope folks keep throwing nickels. For me, this was like method acting in reverse.

As an actor, I did feel that I was repeating myself, but I didn't dare complain to Tracy. I was afraid that she would come back at me with some variation on "I told you so." And whether or not that was fair of me, it deepened my sense of isolation. At the end of the workday I'd drink a couple of beers in my trailer, having a couple more as my teamster driver shuttled me home. At dinner, I'd ask Tracy if she wanted wine. If she said yes, I'd select a bottle, pour us each a glass, then take the bottle back into the kitchen under the pretense of returning it to the refrigerator. In my other hand, I'd be carrying my own wine glass. Once in the kitchen, I'd quickly polish off the bottle, throw it in the recycle bin by the service elevator and extract an identical bottle from the wine rack. I'd open it and swill enough to lower the level of liquid in the second bottle so it matched that of the first when I'd left the living room. Returning from the kitchen, as if I'd spent the last five minutes checking on the pot roast, I'd ask Tracy if she wanted me to freshen up her glass, do so, and then refill my own once more.

For all my sneakiness, I knew I couldn't be hiding my drinking all that well. By the end of dinner, my voice would be inappropriately loud and my words slurred. There were nights that I'd get out of bed after Tracy had fallen asleep and continue drinking. On those occasions when Tracy confronted me, I'd become angry and defensive. The distance that my behavior was opening up between me and my young family frightened me—but this was dwarfed by the greater fear of the other shoe dropping; the bill that had finally come due but which I had no way to settle.

What could I say to Tracy; how could I explain? There was no explanation for anything. Nothing made sense. "You don't understand" had evolved from a phrase I rarely, if ever, uttered to my wife into a virtual mantra. She didn't understand; nobody understood. Even *I* didn't understand what Parkinson's would do to me, how it would change my life. But when I was drunk, it was all a little easier to ignore.

If this downward spiral had continued much longer, I'm sure that there would have been an intervention of some sort. But in June of 1992, just before I finished work on *For Love or Money*, there would be one more bender, one last morning of awakening to feelings of confusion, fear, and remorse, not to mention a crippling hangover. And then, in a moment of clarity, something I can now attribute only to grace, I'd decide to put a stop to it.

That summer, Tracy spent most nights on the Broadway stage, and I'd be on the film set all day long, so we saw less of one another than usual. But as *For Love or Money* prepared to wrap before the second week of July, we'd made the typical end-of-production shift into night shoots. On Friday the 26th of June, it happened that Tracy and I were leaving for work at the same time, she to the theater and me to the set. I'd been told to expect to work until 5:00 A.M. and advised Tracy that she probably wouldn't see me until the following morning. Our plan that day was for me to take Sam up to Connecticut, and for Tracy to join us on Sunday—Sunday and Monday being dark, or off, days for most New York theaters. But as soon as I got to work, I learned that there'd been a scheduling mistake. I wouldn't have to work through the night after all; in fact, I'd be finished by 9:30 or 10:00 P.M., and home before Tracy.

Under normal circumstances, in less troubled times, this prospect would have cheered me and I'd have hurried home, glad for found time together. But at home was my new reality, my P.D. And so, my first impulse was this: *I said I wouldn't be home until morning, and so now I have five or six hours that I don't have to account for—prime drinking time.*

There was an urgency, an edge to that night's partying, as if somehow I knew it would be my last. Even as I stood in front of the camera—all I had to do was a two-page twilight scene on a Tribeca street corner—a few of my crew buddies were picking up a quart bottle of Tequila, a bag of limes, and commandeering a blender. We were on our third pitcher of margaritas by the time the assistant director called "wrap."

By 10:00 P.M. we had taken over a small restaurant/bar in the village, the name of which, along with many other details of that evening, is now a blur. It must have been a Russian place because I remember throwing back shots of chilled vodka. The transition from tequila to vodka had been cushioned by a brief interlude of beer guzzling. I don't know whether it was the custom of the joint, or something we had simply improvised and the management tolerated, but as we tossed back each shot of vodka, we hurled the tiny glasses into a fireplace where they'd explode into crystalline splinters. This bacchanal went on until well after closing time, when we circled back to my trailer in Tribeca to polish off the beer in the mini-fridge.

I don't remember being driven home, only stealing in sometime before sunrise. Nothing is quite so noisy as a stealthy drunk. Tracy's head soon peered from behind the bedroom door.

"Mike, is that you?"

"Yeah . . . just got back from work," I lied.

"Okay. Come to bed," she said, and closed the door. I knew she'd be asleep seconds after she slipped back under the covers.

I made a beeline to the fridge and grabbed a beer. The trip from the kitchen to the living room sofa must have been a bumpy one because when I popped the tab, the sixteen-ounce Coors sputtered and foamed. I took a long sudsy draw, and then collapsed onto the sofa, propping my feet up on its upholstered arm—I still had my shoes on. I put the beer can on the floor within arm's length, but I never reached for it again. I passed out with the taste of that final swig still in my mouth. A watery Coors tallboy: what a pathetic end to a drinking career.

SOBER AS A JUDGE

"Wake up . . . Daddy, wake up . . . let's go to Coneck-ti-kut."

I was fully clothed and slick with sweat. The sofa faced the big picture window of our West Side apartment, which looked across Central Park. While I'd been sleeping it off, my body had been cooking in the glare of the summer sun as it rose over the East Side.

I came to slowly, incrementally piecing together fragments of my present situation.

Sam, my three-year-old son, my baby boy, whom I loved so much, was at that moment nothing more than a giant gnat, climbing all over me, buzzing in my ear, irritating me into consciousness. I wanted to swat at him, push him off me and onto the floor. Instead, I sat up painfully and positioned him beside me on the couch. I resisted fully opening my eyes; the room was too bright, its millions of lumens like tiny needles piercing my brain. My fuzzy gaze went to the carpet where the tallboy lay, no doubt toppled over hours ago by a flopping arm. I used it as a point of focus, to orient myself. A damp stain in the rug fanned out from the hole in the top of the can.

Then I saw feet. Tracy's feet. The feet had on shoes. *Shit. What time was it?* She was probably on her way back to the theater for Saturday's matinee. I'd slept all morning—been passed out all morning, more like it. I kept my eyes open as I hoisted my gaze from her Nikes, past her knees, her handbag, and steadily upward. I braced for what I'd find when my eyes finally met hers. She was going to be pissed off, disgusted. I was about to be ripped into big-time, and I knew I had it coming to me.

But when I finally summoned the courage to look her in the face I found no expression of rage. Here was something far more disturbing. She was meeting my sorry state with a calmness approaching boredom. No, it was worse than boredom; it was *indifference.*

"I have to go to the theater," she said flatly. "Are you still going to be able to take Sam to the country?"

"Yeah," I stammered. "I just . . . just give me a second to get . . . listen, last night . . ."

"I don't want to hear it," Tracy said, still eerily calm. She turned for the door and then looked back, fixing me with another look. "Is this what you want?" she said. "*This* is what you want to be?"

It wasn't a question. And then she was out the door. My hands started to tremble, but not just from some fucking brain disease. I'd never been so frightened in my life.

"Hitting bottom" is a term recovering alcoholics often use. It describes a place of physical, emotional, and spiritual despair that they had brought themselves to in pursuit of their next drink, a moment of realization that to slip any lower would be unbearable. At least as far as my drinking career was concerned, that morning on the sofa I hit bottom.

I was lucky. Compared to the experiences of others who've battled alcohol, mine was a pretty soft landing. I'm sure many people reading this now are thinking, "Shit . . . I *spilled* more than you *drank*." I have no doubt that's true. You hear stories of utter financial ruin, horrendous car wrecks, injury and death, prison sentences, wrecked marriages, degradation, and humiliation far beyond anything I'd ever experienced. But as long as I continued to drink, any one of those fates could have been mine.

At first I thought of alcohol as an ally in my struggle with Parkinson's. But as I lay there on the couch that morning with Sam crawling over me, I knew this couldn't be true. Alcohol had become yet another adversary—one that threatened to take away everything I cared about.

I couldn't do anything about P.D., but alcohol was different: here at least I had a choice, and that day I made it. Helping me to make that choice was the first thing I'd actually be grateful to Parkinson's for. Part of the disease's "gift" is a certain stark clarity about the rest of your life. P.D.'s brutal assumption of authority over more and more aspects of life makes you appreciate all those areas where you still have sovereignty. P.D. teaches you, perforce, to distinguish between the two and defend whatever you still can. Which meant the alcohol had to go.

Winding along the Saw Mill Parkway toward northwestern Connecticut that afternoon, Sam snoozing in his car seat, I wasn't thinking in those terms. To the extent that my mind was working at all, it was scripting snatches of contrite dialogue, excuses, apologies. Calling Tracy was my first priority once I reached my destination and I wanted to be ready with *something*. Flipping through my internal catalogue of *mea culpas* from hangovers past, I recognized that my motivation had always been to pacify her disappointed anger. But I had nothing with which to answer that look on her face. Tracy seemed all out of fight, resigned to view me as a lost cause. *Was that what I wanted? That was what I wanted to be?*

Tracy was between the Saturday matinee and evening show when I reached her on the phone. I offered a sheepish "hi" and she responded with a noncommittal "hello." I realized that the deadly pause that followed was all mine to fill. And this is what came out of my mouth:

"I'm sorry—I just wanted to say that I have a drinking problem, and I'm ready to quit . . . if you know somebody I could talk to . . ."

"Stay by the phone," she said quickly, and before she hung up, "I love you."

Within minutes the phone rang again.

"Hi Mike," said a female voice I recognized immediately, a good friend to both Tracy and me. It suddenly dawned on me that, while we'd had dinner with this woman many times, I'd never once seen her take a drink, not even a glass of wine. I never bothered to wonder why—just more for me, I guess.

"Tracy tells me you think you've finally had enough?"

"Yeah," I said.

A brief conversation followed, a feeling-out session in which she asked a few questions and seemed convinced by my answers that I did, indeed, need help and was ready to accept it. We made plans to meet in the city on Monday. She had one more question for me.

"Think you can not drink before then?"

I held my reply for a beat. What was I doing? Was I really ready for life without anesthesia? Or was this just more bargaining? Something on the order of "Please, God, get me through this and I won't touch another drop"? What the hell difference did it make? My drinking days were over.

"Yeah, I think I can do that."

That unfinished Coors was the last drink I've had. Ten years have passed and I haven't had to reach for the next one, though this isn't an accomplishment I can honestly attribute to my own willpower. I met my friend on that Monday, and over the following days, months, and years, she, along with an ever-widening circle of new friends, all of whom prefer to remain anonymous, showed me that it was possible to live a life without alcohol.

You would think the decision to get sober would mark the beginning of an inspiring upward arc, but the truth is more complicated. There would eventually come such a well-defined turning point, when I would begin progressing toward a whole new way of understanding my disease and my life, but there were still a couple more difficult years ahead. As low as alcohol had brought me, abstinence would bring me terrifyingly, but necessarily, lower. Although living without the filter of alcohol provided an opportunity to examine every part of my life, it did not immediately equip me with the ability to understand what I was seeing, or to make reasoned decisions about how to react.

For the first year of sobriety, I focused primarily on just that—staying sober. At the beginning, simply going through the motions, one day at a time, constitutes a series of heroic acts. To survive any number of social occasions for the first time without the comfort of a drink marks a behavioral milestone. My sister Kelli's wedding at which I was, ironically, the toastmaster was a notable one. Then there was my First Sober Christmas, followed by a multitude of similar events and occasions, challenges and celebrations, where, previously, I would have felt the need to reach for a beer at the very least. In the twelve months since that final hangover, I finished one film, started and finished another, and began a third, all without touching a drop. Each of these small victories gave me some measure of satisfaction.

In the short term, though, paying such close attention to abstinence became nearly as much of an escapist distraction as inebriation had been. While I was doing something indisputably positive by quitting drinking, in the rest of my life, I was still pursuing the same fear-based agenda that had gotten locked into place in the days following my diagnosis. In my career, I stuck with my plan to do as many lucrative, broad-appeal comedies as possible. After *For Love or Money*, I exercised my option to work outside of my Universal contract, but instead of seeking out a challenge—a creative risk to counter Universal's safe commercial game plan—I accepted an offer from Disney to star in *Life with Mikey*, a sweet and squishy family comedy about a ne'er-do-well former child star whose pocket is picked one day by a young street urchin with star potential. She becomes his protégé and he becomes her agent. Yet another swing at the same old piñata.

Tracy's disappointment was obvious, but I refused to discuss the matter any further. "I know what I'm doing—trust me." But how could she when it was achingly clear that I didn't even trust myself? Booze or no booze, I was still isolating myself from my family and caught up in an inner turmoil that I could not comprehend, except to the extent that I was sure no one else could either. For her part, Tracy continued to work, traveling with Sam to Los Angeles for a tele-film while I spent the winter of 1992–1993 in Toronto on the Disney film. So, our deepening emotional distance was often compounded by geographical separation.

The year 1993 was turning out to be a dry version of 1992. I had a lot of time alone to think, but I spent very little of that time considering a future with Parkinson's disease. Mostly I plotted ways to busy myself with anything but. I made no effort to find a neurologist or to learn more about the disease. I signed on for another Universal comedy, *Greedy*, slated to start production in L.A. that May. With a different trainer, I started working out again—putting on pounds of muscle mass, and looking healthier than last time, even though my symptoms were getting worse. While filming *Greedy* in L.A. that summer, *Mikey* opened and bombed. When *For Love or Money* finally hit theaters that fall, it too failed to generate any business. In the same way I'd fired my old agent to jump-start my movie career with Peter Benedek, I now let Pete go and signed on with one of the big-three mega-agencies. Hell-bent on doing the same thing over and over and somehow expecting different results. By year's end, I'd begin to understand why this approach is often described by people in recovery as a sort of functioning insanity.

Charting the course of my emotions during this period is a grim and tricky task because it's not a time I went through with eyes wide open. In effect, I kept my head down and plowed forward, tensing in the anticipation of running into walls but lacking the clarity or wisdom to see them coming. It was not so much a journey as an experience of being lost in a no-man's land—far more disorienting than any hall of mirrors, a place where I'd at least recognize *some* reflection of myself, however distorted.

Though I didn't know it at the time, what I was in desperate need of was objectivity, an honest and thorough accounting of where I was in my life and how or why I'd arrived there. Only then could I move ahead safely. I needed to stop running and initiate a process akin to the one that lawyers call *discovery*—assemble disparate bits of raw information like time lines, paper trails, and anecdotal evidence in order to develop a persuasive theory of motive and method, action and consequence. "Discovery" completed, I then needed to sit still for however long it took, as if in a courtroom, and sift through the findings, connecting the dots until I grasped the truth. And that's exactly what happened. Although *I* didn't have to put myself on trial—somebody else was only too happy to do me that favor.

SO HELP ME GOD...

Los Angeles County Courthouse—November 1993
Remember that bachelor pad in Laurel Canyon—with the swimming pool in the backyard and the jacuzzi in the bedroom? Shortly after Sam was born, Tracy and I decided to sell the house and move back east. After the sale, the purchaser had some complaints and sued me. I don't need to go into the specifics of the lawsuit; civil litigation is exasperating, anguishing, and often boring. Though, as you will see, I learned a great deal from the experience, I'm in no hurry to repeat it.

The crux of the case was this: the buyer claimed that there were preexisting defects with the house and landscaping that I had willfully conspired to conceal, thereby committing fraud. Further, the suit claimed that as a result, I had caused emotional and physical distress. They were asking for several million dollars in damages, many times the value of the house itself.

Set against the backdrop of everything that was troubling me during the early nineties—the death of my father, the P.D. diagnosis, the downturn in my film career, and the rest—I was only peripherally aware of this gathering storm. As time went on, however, a court date was set, and I was called in for a deposition, as were some former employees. This wasn't going to go away, my insurance company's lawyers reported to me. They were as shocked as I was that not only was the complainant insisting on a multimillion-dollar settlement, but that the judge hadn't dismissed the whole thing outright.

Now I was angry. I hadn't defrauded or conspired to defraud anybody. The whole thing was ridiculous, and had evolved from a nuisance into a nightmare. They were counting on me to write a check and settle, but I told my lawyers not a chance, even if that meant going to trial.

The person suing me exercised their option to request a jury. That meant that the case could conceivably stretch on in court for at least a couple of weeks. No matter. I resolved to be there every day, for every minute of the trial no matter how long it took. The proceedings were set for November 1993, in the Los Angeles County Courthouse. As it happened, Tracy had to be in Los Angeles for another television movie during that time, so I cleared my calendar and the whole family set up housekeeping at a West Hollywood hotel.

The lawsuit would drag on until the second week of January 1994. Jury selection alone consumed the better part of a week. The plaintiff's attorney would grill each prospective juror, asking questions like, "Do you think Alex Keaton would ever lie?"—a negative answer to which would obviously allow him to force the court to excuse that juror from service. If they made it past the other side's lawyer, then my attorney would ask his own series of questions, ferreting out strategic disqualifications. Sometimes he'd let a potential ally get away. After my lawyer thanked and excused one elderly woman from the jury pool, she made her way past our table on her way out of the courtroom, leaned over, and pinched my cheek to say, "Ooooh, I just love you."

I turned to my attorney and whispered, "That's it. Let's just get on with this. Any twelve will do."

The whole thing felt ridiculous and overblown. This was no murder trial, just a ho-hum property dispute, yet there was no question that the presence of a celebrity in the courtroom had created a legal circus.

But if justice wasn't completely blind, she wasn't winking, either. In fact, this was the flip side of fame that I hadn't seen before. Being well-known wasn't going to earn me any special consideration, only more intense scrutiny. Cute wouldn't cut it; charm would be more of a liability than an asset, since in this setting it could be misread as guile. The obvious strategy of opposing counsel was to widen the rift between these honest working folks in the jury box and me, the arrogant boy prince of Hollywood. The strategy wouldn't succeed with the jury: they ruled against the plaintiffs on all the key issues—fraud, conspiracy—although I would end up paying for some repairs. But the plaintiff's strategy did succeed in creating a rare and unsettling opportunity for me to witness myself on trial. Day after day, I sat in the harsh light of the courtroom, watching the details of my life paraded before me.

The theme of my defense, the central truth that ultimately persuaded the jury I hadn't conspired to defraud, was just as powerful in making plain to me at last how pathetic my personal situation had become. That theme was ignorance—that is, lack of knowledge about my own life. How I could have conspired to misrepresent a transaction that I had barely any involvement in? I had delegated the selling of the house to others, signed the sales agreement that had been Fed-Exed to me, and moved on. I had never met or spoken to the buyer—hell, before the court case, I had never even met the realtor. Were there problems with the house? I didn't think so, and I would have had them fixed if I did, but those are the kind of details that, in my charmed existence, I would never have noticed.

To prove my innocence, I would have to demonstrate an entirely accurate pattern of detachment from the minutiae of day-to-day life, an absence of personal accountability that must have come as a shock to the men and women of the jury. I appeared before them on the witness stand, sitting on my quaking hands lest they mistake my Parkinsonian tremor for the nervousness of a liar, and laid out the intricate workings of the machinery I relied on to function in the world. I had agents, money managers, personal assistants to handle most of the practical matters of life—I was far too busy (playing make-believe for a living) to do much of anything for myself. At one particularly telling point in my testimony, I was forced to admit, "I don't even buy my own socks." Rather than testify at all, I could have just placed a portable stereo in front of the jury box and blasted out Joe Walsh's "Life's Been Good to Me." This was my "defense": my life had gotten away from me. No wonder I hadn't owned up to my diagnosis, taken a cold hard look at its reality. Why should Parkinson's be any different from anything else in my life? *Don't I pay someone to take care of this?*

I soon understood that the trial would drag on past the Christmas break, when Tracy and Sam and I planned to return to New York. After the holiday, she had to begin a new project. This meant I would have to return to L.A. alone in January for the concluding weeks of the case, a prospect I dreaded. *At least*, I thought to myself with a horrible sinking feeling, *I know I won't be missed.*

This was perhaps the most humbling aspect of the whole ordeal. If I thought that by dropping everything to make some grandstand defense of my personal integrity, the world would stop spinning, I was sorely mistaken. My absence—from my family, from my career—created no discernible void; as far as I could tell, it was barely noticed. There was no project that had to be put on hold—I was developing a feature film to direct, but that was almost a year away and, anyway, I had begun to doubt my ability to see it through. Another actor might refer to my current state as "being between jobs," but the average person would simply call it unemployment. I prefer the British term for it, "redundancy." That's exactly how I was beginning to feel—redundant, unnecessary.

Tracy was working through it all and apparently thriving. In the past, I'd always been pleased and proud of her when she'd be given a chance to show off her talent, but these were mean times. Every morning, by the time I'd slink out the door of the hotel on my way downtown to that dingy glue-trap of a courtroom to plead my "I'm not a fraud, just a *flake*" defense, Tracy had already left for the set. I have to admit, too, that for the first time in our marriage, I was feeling jealous. Her co-star, Peter Horton from the popular TV series *thirtysomething,* was ruggedly handsome, and not, as far as I knew, being sued by anyone. It was all making me nuts.

Tracy was well aware that I was mired in something awful. One evening, a few days before we traveled back to Connecticut for Christmas, she tried to get me to talk about what it was I was feeling. I didn't know what to say, and was as surprised as she was at the words I finally mumbled.

"I've never been so miserable in my life." I was close to tears.

"Honey, you've got to stop doing this to yourself. I think you should see somebody." Somewhere I had a piece of paper on which she'd copied down the phone number of a New York therapist who was supposed to be very good.

I shook my head. Tracy had proposed this once or twice before, and I'd never done anything about it. For that matter, she'd spent the last two years begging me to get a neurologist, and I'd shrugged that off too. In the days before I got sober, I'd occasionally consider making an appointment with a psychologist, but that plan was always stopped in its tracks by a clever little catch-22 I'd devised for precisely that purpose. In those days, any therapist that was worth a damn would probably tell me that the first thing I had to do was face up to my drinking problem, and I certainly didn't want to do that. Conversely, any mental health professional that spent more than an hour with me and *didn't* recommend I quit drinking wouldn't be worth seeing. Ergo, no shrink for me.

"No, I'll get through this on my own," I'd say to Tracy. I could see that she was far from convinced.

"Just don't give up on me," I mumbled, not really comprehending that this time I was talking to myself.

HAPPY X-MAS (WAR IS OVER)

Los Angeles—December 1993

Each day spent in court dismantling my elaborate network of de-
fenses, ostensibly to convince the judge and jury that at the core existed no intent to defraud, laid bare a man hard even for me to
recognize. This was my life we were talking about, but I felt as though
I didn't truly *own* it. And that realization made it excruciatingly difficult to leave the courtroom each evening and pretend as if I did.

By December 1993, I had reached bottom, the winter of my disconnect. Returning to the hotel, I'd hug Sam, but felt far too dispirited
to engage in any sort of play. With Tracy, I'd try to be polite but brief.
The anger I was feeling—at the trial, at myself (and no doubt at
Parkinson's, but I wasn't quite there yet)—was so inchoate that it could
uncoil and spark arguments as nonsensical as they could be bitter. My
self-esteem by now was so negligible that even when I'd try to be
sweet or romantic, I felt as though I was cursing her with my affection.
My appetite was nonexistent, and I used that excuse to avoid joining
my family for dinner, which seemed to me a false and pitiful attempt
at normalcy.

What I would do instead is retreat to the bathroom, and run a
bath. As I sloughed off whatever outwardly respectable shirt-suit-and-
tie combo I'd worn to trial that day, I was careful to avoid catching a
glimpse of myself in the mirror. When the tub was full and the mirror
fogged from the stream, I'd turn off the lights and slip into the hot
water; as naked now as I'd felt in the courtroom, but safer. The bathtub became my refuge, my hiding place.

My body ached. For weeks in court I'd been manipulating it, con-
torting it into intensely uncomfortable positions in order to mask the
tics and tremors. I was well-practiced at this deception, but on a film
set I'd have breaks, minutes and hours when I could retreat to my
trailer and let my symptoms run riot. I'd get a heads up on when
they'd need me next, and then time my P.D. meds accordingly. But
trapped in the wooden chair at my lawyers' table, there could be no
such respite. Squirming and fidgeting in this room where it seemed as

though I had exposed so much already, I was not about to let anyone—jury, plaintiff, judge, or lawyer—see what I was still not willing
to look at myself. Against the surface of the warm water, I could hear
the muted splash of my trembling hand, feel my left side twist below;
but with the lights out, I was spared the sight of it.

This is what my lifelong search for room to maneuver had come
to: a box of water in a lightless, windowless nine-by-sixteen-foot
room—afraid to leave my artificial womb, to go outside where I could
only cause trouble, disappoint my family and myself. Best, I thought,
to stay right here where I couldn't fuck anything up. And stay I
would, day after day, sometimes three or four times on weekends, for
hours at a time, just trying to keep my head *below* water.

Connecticut—Christmas Eve 1993
It was the night before Christmas and I was making a list.

Everyone else was sleeping in the weekend home Tracy and I kept
near her parents' Connecticut farm: Tracy, Sam, and my mom, who'd
traveled east from Vancouver to be with us for the holidays. I couldn't
sleep. I was restless, but not in the excited way that I had been during
the Christmas Eves of my childhood, tossing and turning in anticipation of the biggest holiday on the kid calendar. Unable to quell the
dyskinesias in my body, I had gotten out of bed, and careful not to dis-
turb my wife, slipped out of the bedroom. My first impulse was to
head for the bathtub, but the house was so small and the plumbing so
ancient that to run the water risked waking everyone up, and I sure as
hell didn't want company.

I soon found myself in the sitting room, pen in hand, hunched
over a loose collection of scrap paper I'd gathered up and laid out on
the coffee table. The only light in the room was a dim floor lamp that
I'd moved closer so that a soft glow was cast over my improvised
work space.

What I was furiously scribbling wasn't quite as orderly as a list; it
was really more like what my anonymous nondrinking buddies would
call a long-overdue fourth step, an inventory of my life to that point.
But even that sounds too linear. It was more like the minutes of the

raucous committee of voices chattering like spiteful monkeys inside my head. Maybe if I could get all of this down, I thought, then read it over and pick it apart, I could find some peace or, at the very least, some notion about where to turn next.

The next several hours produced a remarkable, disturbing document: a rambling, occasionally incoherent autodissection, a ledger of faults and failures, resentments and recriminations. The words that spilled out on the page chronicled not only my present situation, but also alluded to the past: growing up small, having to constantly prove myself, overcome circumstances I couldn't control; how having done that, I'd blown it all, pissed it away. I wrote about my dad, his swing from unfairly doubting me to believing that I'd become something more than I had. And I wrote about missing him, acknowledged my love for him. I noted that having my mom there with me at that time was incredibly difficult. Her faith in me was so absolute that I wondered if she was able to see the incredible pain that I was in. I wanted to protect her from it, which was a ridiculous idea, given that I myself was overwhelmed by it. As for Tracy, I kept writing the words "does she still love me" and if she did, "how is that possible?" Over and over, I professed my love for her, and the hope that I could earn back her trust. We had always talked about having more kids after Sam, and I noted, bitterly, that she didn't talk about that so much anymore. What kind of father could I be in the future? For that matter, what kind of father was I now? I apologized to Sam. I realized I put a lot of pressure on a four-year-old to deal with me and what I was going through in a way that even the adults I knew were incapable of.

Bleak as these pages were, there are some things in them that manage to make me laugh. Throughout I keep referring to an intense desire to be "more low-maintenance"—someone who was more dependable and self-reliant. Three or four times this phrase appears, and finally, after the last reference, I'd scribbled in parentheses "is that how you spell 'low-maintenance'?"

Eventually I tired of writing, or my hand cramped, or I just didn't have the strength to go on. I looked over what I'd written, and wept. Whatever else this was, I realized, it was an instrument of surrender.

The next day I'd find that phone number Tracy had written down for me weeks earlier—the one that belonged to the shrink in Manhattan. I'd call her—Christmas Day or no Christmas Day. I just couldn't handle this by myself anymore.

Reading it today, what's perhaps most astonishing about my manifesto is the one thing it failed to mention:

That I had Parkinson's disease, and it wasn't ever going to go away.

© Mark Seliger

CHAPTER SIX

Year of Wonders
(Or: The [Real] Secret of My [Real] Success)

Connecticut—December 26, 1993

I had spoken with an analyst once before—but that was in a sitcom.
During the fourth season of *Family Ties*, Gary Goldberg and producer

Alan Uger co-authored a one-hour script called "A—My Name Is Alex." Alex's best friend dies in a traffic accident while moving some furniture—an errand Alex was supposed to be helping him with, but had weaseled out of at the last minute. Wrestling with profound survivor's guilt—compounded by the realization that he was spared only through an act of selfishness—Alex seeks the counsel of a psychotherapist. For Alex P. Keaton to admit a need for this sort of help was completely out of character. Self-reliance, after all, is the cornerstone of the swaggering boy-wonder persona he presents to the world; unstoppable, Alex ascends on a straight line toward the future of his choosing.

The death of his friend stops him in his tracks, though, and poses questions that, for once, he can't glibly answer. As the episode's schoolyard-rhyme title suggests, Alex now has to retrace his steps through life, beginning with early childhood, in order to reconcile the fear and self-doubt he feels on the inside with the admiration and praise he's always received from the outside world. The episode was shot in a theatrical *Our Town* style in which the therapist is never seen on camera; Alex looks directly into the lens as he answers the probing questions put to him by a disembodied male voice.

That episode won me an Emmy, but now, immersed in this dauntingly real version of my alter ego's anguish and reaching out just as he had for professional help, the only reward I sought was relief. In many ways I could relate to Alex's confusion. Like him, I never thought I'd have anything to do with psychologists or psychotherapy. I was always a figure-it-out-myself kind of person, but it was painfully clear to me that this time I didn't have a clue about where to start. Like Alex, I had a great deal invested in being regarded as a winner, by myself as well as others; to find myself this beaten down and vulnerable made me feel as though I'd somehow, at last, come up a loser. But losing is one thing, and quitting is another: thankfully, something deep inside would not allow me to quit.

Unlike the disembodied voice in the "A—My Name Is Alex" episode, the one on the other end of the telephone line was female and belonged to a nonfictional human being—that therapist in New

York whose number I had saved and finally dialed on the day after Christmas 1993.

Joyce is a Jungian analyst who practices on the West Side of Manhattan. When I asked her recently about that first phone call, she told me that I sounded like "a little boy who'd rather die than admit how scared he was." My voice shaking (Joyce said I was "barely audible"), I recall telling this stranger on the phone that I felt "like my life is in flames." Interestingly, neither of us remembers any mention of Parkinson's disease during that first of what would turn out to be hundreds of conversations.

I had an immediate, visceral sense that I had done the right thing in reaching out for help. All I wanted to know now was how soon could I get in to see her. Joyce reminded me that I had called during the holidays and she had no appointments scheduled until the following week. Still, she had been listening carefully to both what had and hadn't been said, and quickly determined that I was in crisis and needed to see somebody right away. Never one to believe in coincidence, Joyce also gave no small weight to the fact that although she was supposed to be out of the city that day, she happened to be in her office when my call came.

"I can see you this afternoon at three," she offered, and gave me the address. There was a pause. *That afternoon?* We hadn't planned on returning to the city so early—my mother was visiting, it was the day after Christmas, and anyway, I was counting on an hour or two in the bathtub.

"I don't know if that time works for me," I replied.

On her end, Joyce must have been incredulous. Here I was with my life in flames, and I was *haggling* with her about appointment times.

"Do you have anything later in the day or maybe tonight?" I couldn't help it. Negotiating had become reflex for me.

Joyce held firm. "Three P.M.," she said. "Today."

M—MY NAME IS MICHAEL

December 26, 1993–Spring 1994

My anxiety was liquid; the phone call to Joyce had primed the pump—and it was ready to flow. I showed up at her office at 2:55 P.M., and seconds later we were seated across from each other, she with a notepad on her lap and me with my head in my hands. Recalling that first session, Joyce says I arrived "defenseless," as if "all of my skin had been peeled away." I started to tell my story, haltingly at first, and then in a torrent. I didn't leave until 6:00 P.M.

Before that first meeting with Joyce, what little I knew about psychology, psychiatry, therapy, and/or analysis I had read in books and magazines or seen (or acted out) on television; and then there were all those Woody Allen movies. I'd laughed at the *New Yorker* cartoons—a man lies on an analyst's couch, fingers knitted across his middle above a caption that reads: *I had a dream I was getting results.* Freud, I'd heard, called analysis "the talking cure." Joyce's approach followed Carl Jung; but whatever school it was that I had stumbled into, I'd soon be doing a lot of talking, having a lot of dreams, *and* getting results.

How did it work? The author E. B. White said about humor that examining it too closely "is like dissecting a frog. Few people are interested, and the frog dies of it." I think the same is true for analysis. A lot has to do, after all, with the therapist, or more specifically, the fit between analyst and analysand. With Joyce and me, the connection was almost immediate. After having lain bare so many details of my misery in our first encounter, I was relieved in subsequent sessions to spot no red flags warning me that my trust had been misplaced. I sensed no judgment or criticism, and no dogma. Joyce, I'd learn later, has a background in the theater, so when I'd talk about career issues, no translation was necessary. Still, this wasn't friendship—she made it clear I couldn't charm, smart-ass, or bullshit my way out of confronting my demons, or what Jung would call "my shadow."

I have to give myself some credit, though. Once I embarked upon this process, I made a commitment to it, seeing Joyce three times a week. This wasn't quite as time-consuming as it sounds, however. Those three hours freed me up to live the rest of my life, react to whatever I might encounter without feeling its weight exaggerated by the emotional burden I was carrying. Joyce's office became a place to, as she puts it, "hold the energy," a sanctuary where, once having unlocked the doors to my unconscious, and exposed the fear and uncertainty within, I could safely leave all of it there until I could return to explore more thoroughly. I didn't have to hide in the bathtub anymore, worried that I was going to say the wrong thing. I could say the "wrong" thing all I wanted to, fifty minutes a session, three days a week. Rediscovering the shower—a cleansing rinse instead of a long wallowing soak—was not only a time-saver, but an indication of a new outlook.

The smoke was beginning to clear. I could see that my life wasn't completely in flames, but was beset by a series of small fires that, with Joyce's help, I set about extinguishing. Old patterns crumbled, sometimes forcibly. A couple of weeks in, my assistant called to reschedule an appointment. Joyce asked that I call her myself. When I did, she told me, in so many words, to erase her number from my assistant's Rolodex. If I had something to say to her, I'd have to speak for myself. Similarly, when she handed me her first bill and I gave her my accountant's address, she refused it, saying, "No, this is between us. I bill *you, you* pay me." Joyce subtly but firmly established the rules of the partnership in ways that confronted the trouble spots in my dealings with the world outside of her office. Basic Adult Responsibility 101, I was beginning to understand. *This is the way most people live. No bubbles.*

Parkinson's was not a fire that Joyce and I could put out, but we could work on my denial. The first step was for me, at long last, to claim my Parkinson's diagnosis—to own it instead of continuing to let it own me. Acceptance didn't come without flashes of anger and sieges of pain, psychic as well as physical. Joyce reminds me that when my left arm would tremor violently during sessions, I would punch it with my clenched fist—sometimes pummeling it until I raised bruises. Within weeks of beginning my work with Joyce, I went, at her prompting, to see a new internist, Dr. Bernard Kruger in Manhattan. He referred me to Dr. Allan Ropper, a top neurologist in Boston. I scheduled an appointment (myself!), and the first week of February 1994 took a shuttle flight up to meet him in his office.

The sort of doctor whose bearing automatically conveys both authority and reassurance, Allan Ropper is one of the co-authors of *Principles of Neurology*, a doorstop of a book that is the neurologist's bible. During one of our visits many years later, Allan was trying to explain to me why I was responding to a certain medication in a particular way. He opened that giant textbook, flipped through its pages, and muttered without a trace of self-consciousness, "I can't remember what I wrote about that."

Dr. Ropper conducted his examination, then we sat down in his office to talk. He wrote out some new prescriptions. He had some ideas about different medications and how to titrate them in order to maximize their benefits and smooth out the transitions.

He explained the reasons for many of the symptoms I'd long contended with, gave terms to tics and behaviors that I hadn't even realized were part of the disease. For example, my tendency to bring the thumb and all four fingers of my left hand together in a point, like I was creating a shadow puppet of an ostrich's head, was a phenomenon called "tenting." The fact that I was experiencing symptoms only on my left side was also typical, he said. The initial stage of Parkinson's disease is almost always asymmetric, or unilateral; it's not at all unusual for a patient's symptoms to remain limited to one side of the body for many years (though inevitably, the symptoms will spread to the other side). Dr. James Parkinson himself had noted this phenomenon when he first described the disease in 1817.

All of this information helped chip away at my uncertainty and sense of isolation. What I was experiencing was real, that much I knew; but the doctor served as a conduit to a broader body of knowledge about P.D. This helped me to see the disease itself as a fact apart from my own experience with it. I was not an anomaly. All this was happening to others, too. And while I gained no particular satisfaction from that, it did help me understand that it wasn't *personal*.

To my surprise, Dr. Ropper was also complimentary. He looked past all I didn't know about Parkinson's, the gaps in knowledge that, given how long I'd been diagnosed with the disease, were inexcusable, and instead offered praise for my ability to notice and describe my symptoms. "Being an actor makes you inherently very observant about your behavior. The manner in which you felt and expressed the experience is very different from most patients. It puts you at an advantage in managing it."

Oddly, I found comfort in my conversation with Dr. Ropper. It had been so long since I had talked to a neurologist, or for that matter anyone with more than a layman's understanding of Parkinson's disease. For one thing, he forthrightly addressed that prognosis I'd received when first diagnosed—that I had "ten good years" left to work, a deadline that, I was acutely aware, meant that by now, I was down to seven. *How about a little extra time added on? Let's be honest, the last three haven't been all that "good."* Dr. Ropper dismissed the whole notion of a timetable, except to say that all indications suggested mine was likely to be a slow progression given that other cardinal features, like rigidity, were still minor relative to the tremors on my left side. "I don't think anyone knows how much time they have. The rate in younger individuals is known to be slower and more unpredictable. The only thing you can predict is that, like aging, it's going to go on."

Pre-Joyce, pre-Ropper, my unarticulated belief was that by thinking about Parkinson's, I was hastening its arrival. It was as if I could choose between staying in the past where P.D. didn't exist, or a future where I would be overwhelmed by it. Life had become a set of unbroachable predicaments, events, and outcomes that I was racing from or toward, or, worse, that I feared were *racing toward me.* This defensive, compartmentalized attitude toward life with Parkinson's also infected my career, and my most important personal relationships. I'm thinking especially of Tracy and Sam.

If I can't fix it, I don't even want to talk about it. As a personal doctrine, this one is seriously flawed, but carried into a marriage, it is pure poison. Sadly, I thought I was doing Tracy a favor—after all, there was no way she could do anything about my illness, so why burden her by talking about it? But with a problem so huge, *not* discussing it meant not discussing much of anything. Even small talk was risky, because who knew what bigger issues that could lead to? Bad enough I had allowed P.D. to own me, but by my silence—cutting my wife and family off from the experience—I had made them slaves to it as well. And however dire my circumstance, that obviously didn't preclude Tracy from having travails of her own. God forbid Tracy came to me with unrelated questions about challenges she was facing in her own life. Unless the answer was immediately obvious to me, I felt as though she was bringing up the problem for no other purpose but to confront me with my ineffectiveness.

If I can't fix it, I don't even want to think *about it.* I knew, of course, that that wouldn't stop Tracy from thinking about my illness. Without ever directly enquiring about them, Tracy's thoughts on this subject, whatever they were, became my obsession. Session after session spent working through these issues in Joyce's office helped me to see that I was setting a trap for Tracy by never addressing the subject head-on, and my self-isolating behavior did nothing to invite disclosure. Questions like, "Does my being sick make you afraid? Are you disappointed that I'm different now from when you married me? Are you worried about the future? Would you love me if you knew that *I'm* afraid, *I'm* disappointed, *I'm* worried about the future?" all went unasked. But that didn't stop me from filling in the blanks myself. Tracy's answers, as I imagined them, devastated me. It was unfair for me to assume the worst—*she hadn't left me; how could I look past that?*—but in my war with P.D., the first casualty had been trust. No one was to blame for my disease, not even myself, yet it still left me with a sense of betrayal—and in time, I came to project that onto everyone else, even the person closest to me. I was beginning to understand how unfair this was. But, if it was wrong to simply invent a point of view for Tracy without giving her the opportunity to accept or disavow it (or maybe even offer a point of view of her own) in one area, her silence itself did speak volumes: she never talked anymore about having another child together. Enough *not* said.

. . .

I think it was when that huge, sad silence was finally breached late that spring that I realized the work I'd been doing with Joyce, and the progress I'd made in beginning to accept my diagnosis, had brought a sea change to my life. It's impossible to attribute this reawakening to a specific breakthrough or insight—I didn't suddenly burst out of a cocoon of fear. Neither was it a linear progression, an easily followed map of self-rediscovery. As Joyce might say, it all came down to showing up for my life—and doing the work.

This is how Tracy remembers those first few months of 1994, the gradual change in my outlook: "Your hopefulness came back, your sense of humor. Everything wasn't so thick with tension. You weren't so angry all the time. It was like this wall just started to crumble, and you weren't trying to build it back up again."

Late one spring afternoon, as we sat on the grass watching Sam lead a younger cousin on a chase through the butterfly bushes in their grandmother's Connecticut garden, Tracy smiled at me and said, "Sam's going to love being a big brother."

"CHOOSE A JOB YOU LOVE . . ."

Manhattan—March–April 1994
Before Parkinson's, when so much of my identity was tied up in my acting career, the question that burned inside me was, *How long can I keep living like this?* Then came P.D., with its slightly more pressing question: *How long will I be able to keep on living any life at all?* My sense of what really mattered had been turned upside down, and I came out of this period of self-reflection with a completely new perspective on my life and work.

In March of 1994, *Greedy*, the Kirk Douglas–led ensemble comedy I'd made the previous summer, opened and sank without a trace, just as the advance polling had suggested it would. I'd had box office failures before, but there was something different about this one. It wasn't just that Pete Benedek didn't call early Saturday morning, somberly intoning, "I'm sorry, man." Even if Pete had still been my agent, I doubt I would have been standing by for his consoling phone call. After everything I'd been through, the ups and downs of show-biz just didn't seem that important anymore.

Bryan Lourd and Kevin Huvane, my new agents at CAA, faced a couple of stiff challenges. The first, and most obvious, was finding a way to restore my status in the movie business—especially now, in the wake of another box office bomb. But these guys knew that *Greedy* was going to tank before they signed me, and resuscitating a once-promising career was exactly the kind of high-wire act they'd made their reputations on. The greater challenge was this: How do you find a job for someone who doesn't want to work?

Well, it wasn't quite as clear-cut as that. As the Confucian epigram advises, "Choose a job you love, and you will never have to work a day in your life." I wanted to find a job, it would just have to be a job that I *loved*. The urgency I'd felt about my career in recent years had less to do with the work itself than with the desire to distract myself from the more difficult trials of my day-to-day life. I was back in my life now, living in real time, and savoring the days with Tracy and Sam in a way I never had before. I was wary of letting all that slip away again. The lyric in the old James Taylor song Tracy had played for me in the Para-mount parking lot never rang truer: "Try to remember that working's no crime, just don't let them take and waste your time."

"Forget about chasing hits, forget about making more money," Tracy had told me so many times. "Unless you really think we need to live like Donald Trump for the rest of our lives. Do only what you have a passion for—you've earned that right." She didn't say what we both knew: that I'd already tried it my way, and it didn't work. What Tracy was saying had always made sense; now I was finally hearing it. But *did* I still have a passion for work? Did I still love acting?

Believe it or not, even after *Greedy* I was still getting offers, albeit not necessarily top-shelf material: a high-concept action comedy based on a popular children's toy; a couple of scripts inspired, if that's the word, by classic TV comedies of the 1950s and 1960s; and other similar factory-to-you Hollywood products. These were the kind of scripts I had no problem picking through and quickly passing on. To their credit, the boys at CAA weren't crazy about this stuff either.

"You'll see," they promised. "Better things will come along."

"Yeah, well, I want to take it easy for a while anyway—be with my family," I told them. "Just let me know if Woody Allen calls."

Invoking Woody Allen's name was a shorthand way of conveying a message to my agents. I no longer felt driven by the need for commercial success. What I craved now was a new kind of creative experience with a director, actor, or writer who didn't give a damn about anything other than telling an interesting story in a compelling way. Allen, being all three rolled into one, was the first name that popped into my head. (Or maybe, after spending so much time in analysis, I just wanted to work with someone who could relate.) Still, whatever Woody Allen's next project was, I didn't imagine that "Michael J. Fox" would be the first, second, third, or even forty-seventh name that would pop into *his* head. So maybe I was just buying more time to consider my future.

And then Woody Allen called. Okay, Woody himself didn't call, and it would probably be more accurate to say that Bryan and Kevin called him; or at least, his producers. My agents had heard ABC had a deal with Allen to produce, direct, and star in *Don't Drink the Water*. There was a part in the script for me, and they went after it.

Allen was adapting his classic stage comedy for television, with himself as the obnoxious patriarch of the Hollander family, American tourists mistaken for spies while visiting a fictional Iron Curtain country during the 1960s. They take refuge, and wreak havoc, in the American embassy, which is temporarily being run by the Ambassador's incompetent son, Axel McGee. This was the part Allen offered me. Shooting would begin in New York the first week in April.

The job meant going back to TV for the first time since *Family Ties*. The money was lousy—SAG scale—and they couldn't even promise me a dressing room. Here was a job I could love.

And love it I did. Filming so close to home (at Seventy-ninth and Fifth Avenue, right across the park from our apartment) allowed me to zip back to our place for lunch with Tracy and Sam almost every day. Breezing into our lobby one afternoon while still in my vintage 1960s wardrobe (Bobby Kennedy–style suit—narrow lapels, straight-leg trousers, white tab-collared shirt, and skinny tie), the doorman stopped me. "Looking sharp, Mike."

I touched the lapel. "Oh, the suit?" I said. "Yeah, not bad, huh? I don't think it's even been worn since 1963."

"No kidding?" he replied. "Still fits you good."

Don't Drink the Water, like most of the feature films Woody Allen directed around that time, was shot in a loose cinema verité style. Long uninterrupted takes with no cutaways forced cinematographer Carlo DiPalma to swim through and around the actors, swish-panning his handheld camera in rhythm with the scene. While some audiences find this herky-jerky "you are there and this is all happening now" style a little unsettling, to participate in it as an actor was a dizzying thrill. No scene ever played out the same way twice. The pace, intensity, and even the dialogue varied wildly from take to take. That was fine with Woody Allen-the-writer, who was anything but protective of his screenplay. "Just throw the script away," he'd tell us. "Say whatever comes to you in the moment." Far less accomplished writers often insist that actors treat their work as gospel, and here was Woody Allen telling me to "throw the script away." *I appreciate the trust, Woody, but your words are just fine with me.*

Woody Allen-the-actor, however, gave you no choice but to wander from the text. Underestimated as an actor, I think, because of the ease with which he can meld the idiosyncratic elements of his persona into a fluid performance, Allen is a gifted and hilarious improviser. Since it was impossible to know what he was going to do next, it was futile to try to plan my own performance in advance. There were no close-ups, no pickups. Each actor had to go all out every time or feel the cold breeze of Carlo's camera swish-panning elsewhere. Even when it seemed obvious that things were falling apart, we'd keep going, because in this kind of improvisational free-for-all, the comedy often comes out of the chaos.

There was something else apart from the performing that I'll never forget. Remember that at this time, spring of 1994, Woody Allen's private life was in turmoil and on very public display. To watch him act and direct, you'd never think that just that morning you'd seen his face and his tribulations splashed across the front pages of New York's tabloids. I was amazed at how completely he was able to throw himself into his work. At a time when my own struggles were never far from my mind (and thankfully, still out of public view), I drew inspiration from his focus.

I took one other thing away from the experience, unexpectedly and quite by chance. On the set one afternoon, a few of us in the cast were distracting ourselves between setups by playing a game of hypotheticals. We'd come to the question, "If you could live in any era other than the present, what would it be?" Everyone tossed in their ideas and then Woody, who had been hovering distractedly at the fringe of the conversation, decided to weigh in.

"I wouldn't want to live in any time prior to the invention of penicillin," he said.

Everybody fell out laughing—it was such a perfect, in-character response. With everything that Woody Allen was going through that spring, there was still nothing more terrifying to him than the prospect of incurable disease. And then suddenly it hit me. *Hey, I have an incurable disease—and I'm laughing anyway. I must be doing okay.*

Los Angeles—October 1994

Dog-eared from repeated readings during the flight from New York and stained with brown circles from my soda can, my copy of *The American President* screenplay was firmly tucked under my arm as I entered Rob Reiner's office. Maybe, finding it hard to believe that such a terrific script had actually come my way, I wanted to protect it, guard against the possibility that it might still be taken away.

"It's not an offer yet," Kevin had told me before I left. "Rob just wants you to look at it and fly out to L.A. for a meeting." *Yeah, well, I looked at it and I liked what I saw. So make me an offer Rob, but I should warn you, I won't do it for a penny less than "Free."*

I didn't say that, of course, but neither did I make any secret of the fact that I thought the screenplay by Aaron Sorkin, known then for *A Few Good Men* and today for television's *West Wing*, was among the best I'd ever read. It mattered little to me that the role he was considering me for wasn't a lead; Michael Douglas, as the President, and Annette Bening, as his lobbyist girlfriend, were well worth supporting.

Rob Reiner and I talked about movies and our kids, but the conversation grew most animated when the topic turned to politics. Newt Gingrich and his "Contract with America" were dominating the national headlines, and the Democrats were only weeks away from losing control of the House. The director's face, so familiar from *All in the Family* that I felt as though I knew him far better than I did, ran the gamut of emotions as he passionately voiced political opinions very near to my own. His reasons for wanting to direct this film were obvious. A clever romantic comedy, it was also a timely commentary on how cynicism can sometimes be passed off as patriotism in Washington politics. So I was thrilled when he asked me right there in his office to play the part of Lewis, a fictionalized version of a well-known aide to Bill Clinton.

But I wasn't home free yet. Weeks later, just after a cast read-through in a boardroom at Rob Reiner's Castle Rock Productions, something happened that terrified me. For the first time I was convinced that Parkinson's disease was about to cost me a job.

There was a lot of happy hubbub as the actors and production staff rose from the conference table after the read-through. The morning had gone well and the mood was relaxed, though I felt a mild urgency to say my good-byes, leave the building, and get into my car. Caught up in the reading, I had forgotten to take my Sinemet; tremors were about to kick in and I wanted to be safely alone and out of sight when they did. Before I could make my escape, however, the production manager asked for the cast's attention.

"We want to get your insurance company physicals out of the way today," we were informed. "Please wait in the lobby and the doctor will see you one at a time."

I was stunned. *Nobody warned me.* But why would they have?

Preproduction physical exams are routine nonevents, perfunctory once-overs by doctors working for studio insurance carriers. Usually consisting of nothing more than saying *aaaah* and checking blood pressure, exams are just a way for film companies to avoid hiring someone who might croak midpicture and bog down production.

My left hand began to slap uncontrollably against my thigh. I hid it in my pants pocket, dry swallowed half a Sinemet, and quickly revised my exit strategy. Now I stalled, slowing to a crawl; maybe if I was last in line the synthetic dopamine would reach my brain before I reached the doc.

I had made great strides in dealing with my illness, but I still wasn't sure how anyone else would. Better to keep it to myself. Sinemet consistently worked for me and I knew how to control my symptoms well enough that they were still years away from interfering with any production schedule. Would P.D. scare them out of hiring me? Knowing what I know now about the better side of most people, probably not, but at the time, I wasn't prepared to find out. One day I'd share my diagnosis with future employers, but it wasn't going to be today.

"Michael Fox."

My turn. I pulled my hand out of my blue jeans. Steady as a rock. I'd dodged the bullet.

Filming *The American President* spanned from December 1994 through March of 1995. I enjoyed every scene, every one of the superb actors I worked with, and every day spent on the set. What I didn't enjoy so much were the days off the set. Stuck in Los Angeles and separated from my family, who had remained in New York (for reasons I'll explain later), I'd spend hours watching television, eating the same old room service meals, and trying to catch up with Tracy and Sam on the telephone. Sam was never much for talking on the phone, especially as a preschooler. In order to get any information out of him at all, I'd sometimes pitch my voice a couple octaves higher and pretend I was Mickey Mouse.

Working so far from home was hard, but what else was I going to do? Having narrowed my employment possibilities down to only those jobs that I *loved*, was I now going to narrow it down further to only those jobs that I loved that filmed in New York City? How about only jobs that I loved that filmed in New York City with schedules that meshed perfectly with the rhythms of my family? There were only so many projects made in New York, and none of them would have production schedules that were that predictable, nine-to-five, day in and day out. That just didn't happen in the movie business.

But in television . . . it just might be possible.

I floated the idea to my agents—who were horror-struck. Having finally positioned me in an "A" picture with a big-name director, and picking up a lot of good buzz from the studio about my performance, they felt returning to television now would be exactly the wrong thing to do. To their chagrin, I kept bringing up the subject. Sure, the conventional wisdom about returning to television was that, having already made the jump to feature films, it would represent a backward career move. But, if I had learned anything over the last four years, it was this: *whatever anyone else thinks about me is none of my business.*

To satisfy my own curiosity, I had them put out feelers in the television community. What I heard from the creative side was that a number of first-rate writer-producers would be interested in working with me on a new sitcom. The word from the networks was that I could essentially write my own ticket. I wasn't thinking about the money necessarily, but I was intrigued to learn that no one would have any objection to my doing a show shot entirely in and around New York City. And, incidentally, should the show succeed, the money would be pretty damn good.

I spoke to Tracy about the idea. She was hesitant: she didn't want to see me get trapped again, committed long term to something that was going to make me unhappy. But she loved the idea of us living in one place, having as regular a family life as possible.

In the short term, however, that would remain a fantasy: before production had even started on *The American President*, I'd agreed to make another film in April of 1995. The third and final commitment in my Universal contract, *The Frighteners*, would be filming in New Zealand, of all places. Why, you might ask, in light of my desire to be at home, would I have ever agreed to do a film so far away, in another country, another hemisphere, another antipode? It's a long story, but suffice it to say that life doesn't always follow a straight line. In my case, the line took me *way* off course for five months. But at least by the end of the experience, I knew exactly where I wanted to go.

Cut to New Zealand. I'm living in a rental house outside Wellington, spending hour after hour watching videotapes sent to me from home. On each tape are different versions of the same thing: sitcoms—*Seinfeld, Friends, NewsRadio, Frasier.* In the six years since *Family Ties*, I'd watched very little television and I was amazed, sitting here all alone at the bottom of the world, to see how much better American TV comedy had become. Now I knew why I could never find any funny film scripts—all the truly gifted comedy writers were busy doing television.

Somewhere about halfway through my time down-under, I made up my mind. When I got back to the States, home to New York, I was also going home to television.

A couple of other factors weighed in favor of this decision. This time around, I wouldn't be working *for* anyone but would go into the venture as a full partner. Whoever my partners turned out to be, I would tell them up front about my diagnosis. Dr. Ropper had said there was no reliable timetable for the progression of my symptoms, but even at my most optimistic, I figured I only had another six or seven years of steady work left in me. Six or seven years, though, was the exact definition of a successful run on network television. Offering me a regular schedule, dependable hours, partners who understood my situation, proximity to my doctors, and the support of my family, a TV series represented the very best possible option for enjoying the time I had left to work at my craft.

There was this too: as I watched those tapes alone in my rented house down-under, laughing at the sophistication of this new brand of TV comedy, and taking in the laughter of the studio audience, I felt envy for the actors. They were doing what I used to do, what I loved to do, and couldn't wait to do again. So, ultimately, I heeded Confucius: I chose a job that I loved.

SUMMER OF SAM

New York — 1994

SAM: Why do you keep wiggling your hand like that?

ME: I'm not really wiggling it, it just wiggles all by itself.

SAM: Is something wrong with it?

ME: Yeah . . . well no, not my hand. You know how every time you want to run or jump or throw a rock you have to tell your brain first, and then your brain tells your body what to do?

SAM: Your brain won't tell your hand to quit wiggling around?

ME: Exactly . . . the part of my brain that talks to my hand doesn't work too great.

SAM: You don't *always* wiggle.

ME: No, if I take a pill, it can fix the broken part of my brain for a while. But sometimes all I have to do is play a trick on it to make it stop.

SAM: You can trick your own brain?

ME: My own brain and my own hand—both at the same time. It's kind of a secret, but if I show you how, will you help me do it sometimes?

SAM: Yeah!

Parkinsonian Tremor is often referred to as a "resting tremor." That is, it occurs when the affected limb is at rest, or in an attitude of repose. (Interestingly, this doesn't apply to sleep, when, in all but the lightest phases, decreased brain activity virtually eliminates any muscle contraction and the tremor disappears.) Any willed movement can diminish or even suppress the tremor, at least momentarily, though it will reassert itself as soon as the limb settles into a new position. This is why, especially in the earliest stages, I was able to mask trembling through the most basic of manipulations: by picking up and putting down a coffee cup, twiddling a pencil or threading a coin through the fingers of my left hand. To keep this up at work or in public—another tiny repositioning every four or five seconds for hours at end—was an effective bit of sleight of hand, but it also exhausted me. And it was lonely work; whatever anybody *thought* I was doing at any given moment, I was at the same time also busy doing something else. I was, literally, driven to distraction.

In the spring of 1994, as I became more willing to recognize and accept P.D. as a fact of (my) life, I realized that I had been playing these tricks on my family as well. My unwillingness to let Tracy and Sam see a version of me any less than ideal put a certain distance between us that, I decided, would no longer do. So I lowered my guard at home, allowed myself to be open with my symptoms around my family. What a relief it was to relax for a change. Their reactions were a welcome surprise. Tracy, of course, didn't see anything she wasn't already acutely aware of. She was simply relieved and encouraged by my renewed trust. For Sam, now, the revelation of my symptoms was not the source of concern that I'd feared it would be; it was more a point of interest and curiosity of the kind that sparked the conversation at the top of this section. The utterly straightforward thrust of his questions taught me much about my son, and the way I found to share my reality with him taught me a lot about myself.

This is how it happened that when Sam was not quite five years old I taught him that if he saw my hand wiggling he could squeeze my thumb, or twist it slightly to make it stop.

"Then," I instructed, "count to five and give it another squeeze or twist, and you can trick it into staying still."

He experimented for a few minutes, at first counting aloud, and then in his head, making eye-contact and nodding to let me know it was time to give a squeeze. I could see his delight in getting the timing down, short-circuiting the wiggle every time. But once he understood that it *always* came back, I detected a slight look of *uh-oh, what have I gotten myself into?*

"You know, Sam," I assured him, "this doesn't mean you have to do it every time. Not like it's your *job* or anything, only when you feel like it." His face brightened again.

"You can do it yourself still, right?"

"Right," I said.

Sam thought this over and then, "But I do it better."

"Definitely," I laughed. "And besides, I just like it when you hold my hand."

Sam's childlike willingness to accept my condition without dwelling on all its implications had a powerful influence on me. I'd conditioned myself to relate to the symptoms of the disease strictly as evidence of loss, of facility and freedom being taken away, but Sam's reaction suggested other possibilities. His curiosity awakened my own. If my condition could provide an opportunity to communicate so honestly and intimately with my son, what else might it bring? Clearly, to Sam, I was still "Dad," just "Dad with a wiggly hand." Was it possible that I could look at things the same way, that I was still *me*— just me plus Parkinson's?

Often that spring, I felt like a younger version of myself—like the Chilliwack me, pedaling my bike across the back lawn while dangling a garter snake, consumed once more with the possibilities of today. Yesterday's losses and tomorrow's trials were no longer the only poles of my existence—there was another place I could settle, and Sam had a lot to do with showing me where that was. The threat of time passing, hurrying me toward an uncertain fate, began to fade.

"Never play the result" is one of the golden rules of acting, itself perhaps the most childlike of all professions: exploratory play, *let's pretend*, are at its heart. For an actor, to play the result is to concentrate on where a character may find himself at the end of the scene or play, instead of where he is at a given point in the drama. The journey or arc, and the dramatic possibilities of the present—where the future and one's path into it are, as in life, unknown—get short shrift. No matter the setting, a performance, like life itself, comes down to a series of choices, each one informing the next. However unexpected, whatever occurs along the way—a lost prop, a fellow actor inexplicably wandering off-script and improvising, or even the walls of the set crashing down onto the stage—must be incorporated. Otherwise, you might as well just drop the curtain, now.

I found myself doing the strangest and most wonderful things that spring. Like sitting at the dining room table, Sam perched on my lap playing with a plastic dinosaur, while a math tutor schooled me in the finer points of the Pythagorean theorem. For so long I'd affected a mock pride at having accomplished great things in life without ever graduating from high school, but in truth it had always bothered me. After talking this out with Joyce over a few sessions, I realized that although my dropout status may once have been a matter of circumstance, as the years passed it had become a matter of choice. If my failure to get a diploma bothered me—if it didn't fit with my idea of who I was today—then I could choose to do something about it. And so at the tender age of thirty-two, with my son registered to begin kindergarten the next fall, I applied to take the General Equivalency Diploma test.

After a few hours with the tutor (math was the only area where I felt vulnerable—those damn absolutes) spread out over a couple of weeks, I was ready. In the cafeteria of a lower Manhattan high school, sitting with a group of two hundred or so students of all ages, I breezed through the five-part G.E.D. exam. (I even managed to score sixty percent in math.) I had become one of the more unlikely members of the class of 1994. And, as it is for so many others, the summer after graduation was one of the best of my life.

Vermont–Martha's Vineyard–Summer 1994
We divided our time that June, July, and August between the two places we loved the most: the first half of the summer we spent at our farm in Vermont, and the second half on Martha's Vineyard. I had never been more happy in my life, and that particular summer stays with me like a treasured dream. In Vermont there are two old willow trees so close by the banks of the farm's pond that in summer the surface of the water resembles a speckled green impressionist painting. A rope swing is fixed to one of the higher limbs of the taller tree. With

Sam's arms around my neck and his long skinny legs wrapped around my waist, I'd grip the rope and together we'd leap from our picnic table launching pad, arcing out over the water. At the very top of the pendulum, I'd let go and we'd shatter the mirror full of leaves. Crawling onto shore, giggling hysterically, we'd shake cool water onto Tracy, sunning on a granite boulder, and swear up and down that we could actually see the trout scatter as we dropped.

Tracy had developed a passion for cycling. Hours were spent exploring the rocky trails and back-country lanes around the farm. Vermont's hills were hard work, at least for me, but the flat, paved up-island roads of the Vineyard, cooled by ocean breezes, proved to be more my speed. What I remember most about that August, though, was staring at Tracy on the beach. I've always enjoyed seeing my wife in a bathing suit, but now I was paying particular attention to one part of her anatomy—her belly. Just eight weeks into her pregnancy, only she and I could tell that she was beginning to show.

Manhattan — October 1994
The examination table was inclined, positioning Tracy so that even as the obstetrician glided the transducer over her gently rounded belly, they both had a clear view of the sonogram monitor. Or would have, had I not been in the way.

"Mike . . . you're hogging the TV."

"Sorry honey." I'd forgotten my glasses and was crowding the screen. This would be our first look at the new baby and I was nervous, but not for any specific reason. We both knew that there was virtually no chance of our child inheriting my disease. The doctors had also assured us before we even conceived that my P.D. meds posed no risk. I was just nervous because, hell, all dads are nervous at moments like this.

I'm pretty good at making sense of both satellite weather maps and sonograms, and basically there isn't much difference except for this: on a weather map, I look for coastline, and on a sonogram, I zero in on the spine.

And there it was. Perfect. But wait, something strange was happening. The spine was dividing, splitting in half clean down the center, and now it was opening like a pair of scissors. *What the hell?*

"Look at that," I sputtered. "Does that mean . . . ?" But I could already hear Tracy laughing.

"Twins," the obstetrician said.

I turned to look at Tracy just in time to see and hear her repeat the same word. "Twins."

"Oh my god," I said to Tracy, my face breaking into a smile. "There's *two* of them."

Later that month, Sam and I went on a road trip, just us guys. With the twins coming (Sam still had no idea how dramatically *his* world was about to change), I knew it would be a while before we'd have a chance to be alone together on an excursion like this. (Two years later, we'd spend sixteen days driving across America, from Manhattan to Malibu, but that's its own book.)

"If you could go any place you wanted for a weekend," I asked my five-year-old, "what would you want to see?" I was all ready to make arrangements to fly down to Orlando, but Sam surprised me, something he does a lot.

"Caves," he said.

And so we flew down to Washington, rented a car, and drove into Virginia's Shenandoah Valley where, according to the guidebooks, there are about all the mom-and-pop-operated natural cavern tours you'd ever want to see in one lifetime. Take it from me, there are. (Sam's favorite: the Luray Caverns, home of the "World's Only Stalagpipe Organ.")

Before we set out from D.C., though, we paid a visit to the White House to see George Stephanopoulos, who at the time was dating Tracy's best friend. George had offered to introduce us to President Clinton. As we sat in the Oval Office waiting for the Commander-in-Chief to make his entrance, Sam chided me for wearing a T-shirt and baseball cap on such an important occasion.

"I don't think it will be a problem with this president," I assured Sam, and was proven right when Clinton finally bounded in. Fresh, or maybe not so fresh, from a game of tag football on the Great Lawn with some college buddies, he was wearing a T-shirt and baseball cap, as well as a pair of too-snug nylon running shorts. Sam's a big fan of trinkets and souvenirs, what he calls *mojo*; he already possessed an

eclectic collection of old coins, Indian arrowheads, and similar trea-
sures. The President had an impressive *tchotchke* collection of his own
fanned out across his desk and he gave Sam a guided tour.

I remember being particularly fascinated watching George Stephanopoulos do his job, subtly briefing the President through the course of
our visit on commitments he had pending that Saturday morning. At
one point he suggested that, given a choice between tie or no tie for a
hastily arranged press conference on Saddam Hussein's latest violation
of the Iraqi No-Fly zone, his boss should not only sport a tie but something patriotic. This is the kind of voyeurism an actor lives for. It's a
measure of the good karma and synchronicity I was experiencing at
this point in my life that only a few weeks later, Rob Reiner offered
me the chance to play George, or at least a version of him, in *The American President.*

February 1995
At the end of the second week in February, I left the movie set in California and boarded a plane for New York. The babies weren't due
until March but, as Tracy's obstetrician told us, "It's easier to get two
Volkswagens out of a garage than two Buicks," so he recommended
inducing birth a month early. We still had no idea about the sex of the
babies, but we did know from the amnio that they were identical.
So, whatever they were, boys or girls, Tracy would be delivering a
matched set.

On February 15, 1995, we met our twin daughters. The first born
was tiny and as white as alabaster, and the second, eight minutes
younger, was a pound heavier and a lurid purple color. Something
called twin-to-twin transfusion had been happening *in utero*, whereby
one twin had been nearly monopolizing the blood supply. Happily, in
a matter of weeks after delivery, the two girls were equally healthy.

We named the smaller, older baby Aquinnah, the Wampenoag Indian name for the town in Martha's Vineyard where we'd spent many
summers. We wanted a colorful name for this pale, delicate little crea-
ture, and Aquinnah, according to one translation, literally means
"beautiful colors by the sea." The younger girl we called Schuyler, a
Dutch name meaning scholar, or teacher.

I had been learning something important about life over the course of this year of miracles, and the birth of the twins brought the teaching all the way home. During the long, agonizing period following my diagnosis, when Tracy, for reasons that are obvious to me now, was reluctant to consider adding to our family, I had grown bitter from regret. *That time is lost now*, I told myself, *and so is the child we might have had.*

Now we'd been given *two* beautiful infant daughters. This was the lesson: it wasn't for me to fret about time or loss but to appreciate each day, move forward, and have faith that something larger was at work, something with its own sense of timing and balance.

Tracy Pollan

CHAPTER SEVEN

Like a Hole in the Head

Boston—March 1998

"Can I get you something to drink?" Tracy asked the doctor.

It was Saturday evening, and we were in a suite at the Four Seasons in Boston. I was scheduled to have brain surgery in the morning. For security reasons—more specifically, for reasons of secrecy—I'd be staying in the hotel overnight and checking into the hospital only an hour or so before going under the knife—or in my case, the drill. Dr. Bruce Cook, who would be performing the surgery, had agreed to do the work on Sunday morning, when the surgery floor of the hospital would be virtually empty, in order to minimize the chances that word of the operation would get out. (The doctor later told me that Gavin De Becker's security operatives had made themselves "as inconspicuous as a group of very large people talking into their sleeves can be.") Dr. Cook had stopped by the hotel that evening to brief Tracy and me once more on the procedure, go over the benefits and potential risks.

"Diet cola, thanks, if you have any," the doctor said, taking a seat on the sofa.

"I'm surprised a neurosurgeon drinks diet soda," Tracy said as she placed his beverage on the coffee table. "I've heard it contains chemicals that might actually be harmful to the brain."

I rolled my eyes. I was addicted to the stuff myself and I'd been hearing this lecture from Tracy for years.

"Could be," the doctor said. "All I know is if I don't drink it, I get edgy."

Dr. Cook began to review the methods and objectives of the next morning's procedure. I was familiar with the drill, so to speak, but much of it was new to Tracy. My mom had flown down from Canada to be with me for the operation, and had joined us for the doctor's briefing. She hadn't heard any of it before and was visibly nervous. I knew that Bruce's calm, matter-of-fact confidence would do a lot to reassure them both.

"You know, of course," he began, "that this procedure does not address the Parkinson's disease itself. It is not a cure. It will not alleviate rigidity, balance issues, or many of the condition's other symptoms. What it *will* do, if successful, is eliminate that tremor on your left side."

That tremor on my left side, once an annoying twitch in my pinkie back in Gainesville (a lifetime ago), and only four years earlier the "wiggly hand" that I'd tutored Sam how to wrangle, had by now developed into something much bigger and more debilitating. Indeed, I could no longer characterize the tremor as a feature of my left hand, or even my left arm; it had become a domineering presence in the whole of my left side.

Every time my most recent dose of Sinemet would wear off, the disease presented me with a concise history of my symptoms—first the tapping of the pinkie, then the dancing hand, and within fifteen minutes or so, the whole of my left arm would be tremoring. Tremoring, actually, is too subtle a word—the tremor would start my whole arm bouncing. Flapping like the wing of an injured bird, it would generate a seismic energy that, although originating on one side, was forceful enough to shake my entire body. Sometimes while I waited for a pill to start working, I'd have to place all of my weight on top of my arm to hide the effects of the tremor. I don't mean I was just sitting on my hand, but actually *on* my arm—my left butt cheek wedged into the crook of my elbow. I'd sit like that for minutes at this ridiculously awkward cant, a human leaning tower of Parkinson's.

Tremor, of course, isn't the only symptom of P.D., but in my own version of the disease the left side tremor was so dominant, so overwhelming compared to any other symptom, that treating it with Sinemet had become problematic. Subduing the tremor meant taking an amount of L-dopa that exceeded my needs in other areas. For my other symptoms—such as rigidity and balance—this Sinemet assault was like shooting a mosquito with an elephant gun. The results were discomfort and dyskinesias. Over the four years I had been seeing Dr. Ropper, we had discussed ways to deal with this inequity. We experimented with a number of different pharmaceutical therapies, but increasingly, the option of surgery entered into our dialogue.

Should I choose to go that route, there was one operation in particular, the thalamotomy, that Ropper felt might help. He told me about a neurosurgeon in Boston, Dr. Bruce Cook, who was having particularly good results with the procedure. Promising to pay extra close attention to Dr. Cook's patients and their outcomes, my neurologist said that when the time was right, he'd arrange for the three of us to meet. That day came in January of 1998.

I flew up to Boston, where I met with Dr. Ropper and together we drove out to meet Dr. Cook at his clinic in North Andover, Massachusetts. I'd purposefully abstained from medicating myself that morning, so both doctors could see the tremor at its worst. Once again I submitted to the standard battery of tests, only this time with an added wrinkle. Dr. Cook videotaped me at my worst, then told me to medicate. He kept the tape rolling as the artificial dopamine did its work and the quaking eventually subsided. Then the three of us moved into his adjoining office.

Bruce Cook, a slim, personable, slightly balding grown-up version of the brainiest kid you ever knew in high school, provided a contrast to Allan Ropper, with his more athletic bearing, stoic square-jawed countenance, and full head of graying hair. In one way, however, they were unmistakably similar: these guys were smart. The more Dr. Cook described the procedure and the relief it might offer, the more committed I became to the idea of having this operation and having him perform it. Since my symptoms were still limited to my left, less dominant side (I'm right-handed), a cessation of tremor there would be as good as a return to normal.

Finally, I thought, my insides would match my outsides. Before P.D., at a time when outwardly I was the picture of confidence and physical agility, happiness, and success, inwardly I harbored self-doubt, was out of balance, and relied on alcohol to tip the scales. Now, having faced my fears, and reached a level of personal responsibility and peace, outwardly I gave the exact opposite impression. Could it be that this operation would at last bring both sides into alignment?

That, at least, was the dream. Getting Dr. Cook to sign on, though, was another matter.

"As Parkinson's tremors go," Dr. Cook told me recently, "yours was very severe; most don't get to be so bad. I try to talk people out of surgery if it doesn't make sense for them. Their goal in having the operation has to be a reasonable one." I hadn't been interviewing him, I realize now; he had been interviewing me.

"I do remember when I asked you how the tremor disrupted your life, what problems or disabilities did it present in what you did from day-to-day, you told me that you had a television show, and the tremor was difficult to hide because all these people were watching you. I have to tell you the truth, that didn't resonate with me. I thought, 'So what?' It's a TV show. Maybe next year a different one comes on."

The TV show was, of course, *Spin City*, by now nearing the end of its second season. In many ways, the sitcom was the return to television I'd dreamed about down in New Zealand. Soon after I'd returned home, I heard from two old friends in the business who knew of my interest in returning to TV. One of them was Jeffrey Katzenberg, the dynamic and hugely successful former Paramount and Disney executive who had recently formed DreamWorks along with Steven Spielberg and David Geffen. Jeffrey called to say that he'd heard a fantastic pitch for a sitcom that sounded perfect for me, from someone I knew well—Gary Goldberg.

I was hesitant. Naturally, Gary had been one of the first people I considered talking to, but we'd had such success together with *Family Ties* that to try to repeat it seemed risky. For one thing, it had been seven years since we had worked together and I had changed so much since then that I knew it would be impossible—and unwise—to fall back into our old relationship, which was virtually like father and son. I didn't want to be anything less than a full partner in this venture—could Gary live with that? For another, I was determined not to repeat myself by doing another family genre comedy, but to try something more sophisticated and adult, with an element of the comedic daring that I had admired in shows like *Seinfeld*.

Jeffrey was characteristically relentless, though, and flew Gary, along with a young writer-producer he was working with named Bill Lawrence, out to New York on the DreamWorks jet. The two checked into the Four Seasons in Manhattan and I met them there. It was great to see Gary again. As soon as he started to talk, I was reminded, as if I'd ever forgotten, just how good this guy was. Bill, hyper, hysterical, and whip-smart, was in his early twenties. His youthful energy seemed the perfect complement to Gary's time-tested experience. They pitched an idea about a deputy mayor of New York, reminiscent of the character I'd played in *The American President*, but a little more slippery and overtly comic. A week later, they faxed me a script, which I read even as it was spitting out of my machine. I'd read one page, laugh, then pass it to Tracy, who'd be laughing as I read the next. When the pages finally stopped coming, and the two of us finally stopped laughing, she and I were in total agreement—this was the show.

After assembling a fantastic cast and a top-notch staff of very funny young writers, we debuted in September 1996. The reviews were terrific, and while our ratings, spectacular at first, did level off after a few weeks, they settled into a range that suggested long-term success.

My instincts had served me well. Here I was, living in New York with my family, getting laughs from a studio audience in a show I could be proud of. Acting in as well as producing a weekly network television series does, however, involve a great deal of stress no matter how perfect the circumstances. And the situation was near perfect, with one caveat: my partnership with Gary was, as I'd feared, proving to be somewhat fractious. Our mutual respect and storied history notwithstanding, each of us was far too opinionated and perfectionist to have anything but the last word on creative issues. Gary had been in the producing business far longer than me, and was even more resistant than I was to the idea of ever having to explain himself. While the first two seasons had been a success, the stress of our creative conflict, added to all the other pressures involved in doing a weekly show, was taking its toll, and without question, exacerbating my symptoms.

So it was that, nearing the end of my sophomore season on *Spin City*, I met with Drs. Ropper and Cook to discuss the possibility of surgical relief. But as Dr. Cook now says, the demands of a weekly television show were not sufficient reason in his estimation to commit to so drastic a procedure. I recently asked him what was it that finally convinced him to accept me as a patient.

"It was something else you said to me," he said. "You talked about Sam. About how difficult it had become to do something as simple as read a book to him. That you couldn't keep the book steady or turn the pages by yourself, and he would have to hold it for you. You also mentioned how difficult it was to go to his student-teacher confer-

ences because you couldn't count on being able to time your medication correctly."

Dr. Cook summed it up this way: "A lot of people can be on TV,
but only one person can be your kid's father. When you described it
to me in those terms, it made sense. I was ready to go ahead with the
procedure."

I informed my business partners of my plans, grateful that I had
been honest with them about my P.D. from the outset. Though Gary
and I were more at odds creatively than ever, he was warmly support-
ive. He and Jeffrey understood the physical difficulties I'd been dealing with and were hopeful for a positive outcome. I then invited each
of the cast members into my office and hit them with a double
whammy. I told them, for the first time, about my diagnosis and the
fact that I'd be undergoing brain surgery at season's end.

Aquinnah and Schuyler were too young to comprehend what I
was about to do, but I held them the night before I left for Boston and
felt good about the fact that soon they wouldn't have to turn the
pages of their favorite storybooks while I read to them.

For Sam, there was one last book to hold, one Dr. Cook had sent
in the weeks before the operation: *The Big Book of the Brain*. Referring
to its simple but clever illustrations, I was able to explain to my eight-
year-old what the doctor was planning to do. Basically, a surgical version of our old squeeze-the-thumb game; though, now, if it all worked
out as planned, we'd be able to count a lot higher than five.

BRAIN SURGEONS AND ROCKET SCIENTISTS

Now, not quite three months after I'd first met him, Dr. Cook was in
our Boston hotel suite, and I was coveting his soda. I had entered the
twelve-hour presurgery no-liquids zone. For that matter, I wasn't allowed any Sinemet, either—the symptoms had to be fully present
during the procedure. Thirsty, symptomatic, and a little edgy myself, I
was eager to get down to business.

"Can you explain again what you're going to do and why it

works? I know Tracy and my mom are a bit nervous about the lesion part—how injuring a small part of my brain can actually help me."

Dr. Cook nodded and leaned forward over the coffee table. "The goal of the operation is to disable the brain cells responsible for the tremor. The target is deep in a part of the brain called the thalamus— an area about the size of a walnut that controls body movement. We're looking for a particular structure within the thalamus which is responsible for the tremor—the VIM nucleus, a group of cells approximately two millimeters in diameter.

"You'll be brought into the O.R. and a metal frame, or halo, will be fastened to your head with small screws. During the procedure, the frame itself will be bolted to the operating table so you won't be able to move your head around. Just as important, the frame helps us guide our instruments.

"You'll be sedated while this happens, with liquid valium, so you won't remember much, but you'll be awake. In fact, we need you to be conscious throughout the whole surgery, to answer our questions; that's an integral part of the operation, helping us confirm that we're where, in your brain, we want to be.

"Once the frame's on, but before it's bolted to the table, we wheel you out of the O.R. to the Magnetic Resonance Imaging machine."

"Let me ask a question," Tracy interjected. "You do the MRI *after* the frame is on? I thought you couldn't bring metal anywhere near one of those machines."

"That's true, but the frame we use is aluminum," Dr. Cook answered. "It's nonferrous, which means it doesn't respond to the magnets."

Tra, I was impressed, *good catch*.

"We do the MRI scan to find the VIM nucleus. We also see the areas we want to avoid—the internal capsule containing all of the information responsible for movement that goes from your brain down the spinal cord. If this internal capsule is damaged, there's a risk of paralysis.

"Next we go back to the operating room, fasten the frame to the table, and raise you on an incline, almost as if you're sitting in a La-Z-

Boy. Now we drill the hole in your skull and use a microelectrode—
a long tube with a narrow tip encasing a filament—to explore the
area. The electrode allows us to pick up the electrical signals that the
brain cells make and see them on a computer screen. The signals are
incredibly small and weak—this is the electrical output of just one or
two cells. The least little signal from any electrical equipment causes a
huge interference, so we have to turn off everything else in the room,
even the lights."

"I'm sorry," I interrupted. "But I don't remember hearing this
part before. You're going to operate on my brain with the *lights out?*"
I pictured a cadre of medieval barbers trepanning my skull by candle-
light.

Dr. Cook smiled reassuringly. "Conveniently, there's a large wall
of windows in this operating room."

Low tech meets high tech, I thought. Ever since, I have been scrupu-
lous about turning off my cell phone in hospitals.

The doctor continued. "We pass the electrode down through the
thalamus and look for the characteristic signals. As we listen to the
cells and do things like touch your finger, for example, we look for re-
sponses on the computer screen. What we're looking for is a spot
where we get a response only when we touch the thumb and index
finger because that is the area directly behind our target area.

"The next step is to run an electrical current through the electrode and ask you if you experience any feeling, tingling, or numbness
in your thumb and index finger. This is why you have to be conscious. When we get that response, we're directly behind the spot we
want to be.

"We like to find that spot as quickly as possible, because each time
you probe a new track with the electrode, you add a new risk."

"Exactly what are those risks?"—Mom, this time. But I could tell
from Tracy's body English that she was only a millisecond behind with
her own version of the same question.

"The biggest risk is bleeding in the brain from the various probes.
Overall, the national estimate is a one in one hundred risk of causing
any degree of bleeding, but with the microelectrodes we'll use, it's

very very rare. The rest of the risks are paralysis, as I've already mentioned, numbness, garbled speech, and an inability to swallow and
control secretions."

There was a brief pause in which I could feel all the eyes in the
room turn to me. I smiled, radiating, I'm sure, a genuine and heartfelt
confidence. I was well aware of the risks, and while I didn't take them
lightly, I felt they were far outweighed by the potential benefits.

"It's okay, Doc, you can keep going."

"Now we move forward three millimeters from the spot where
we get that good response. We put some current into the electrode; if
we've hit the right spot, this will temporarily stop the tremor. That's a
very good sign. The only thing left to do then is to put in a slightly
larger electrode, with enough power to make the lesion—to kill the
target cells. When we turn up this macroelectrode, it may cause your
speech to temporarily garble, because the current spreads beyond the
target area. But first we perform a test by heating up the probe a couple of degrees, enough to stop the activity but not enough to cause a
lesion. We examine you to make sure you still have all those functions
we don't want to impair—that you can swallow, speak, and whatnot.
This is the patient-participation part of the program. Now we go up
to a stronger current until we've heated the target area to the temper-
ature needed to kill the cells. Then, we take the electrode out and
you're done."

Tricky stuff. Everyone fell silent. It was a serious moment, but a
phrase I'd tossed off a million times before kept popping into my
head: *This isn't brain surgery.* Yet of course this time, it was.

Which got me to wondering:

"Why do *you* think it is . . . ," I asked Dr. Cook, partly to break the
tension, but also because I really wanted to know, "that brain surgery,
above all else—even rocket science—gets singled out as the most
challenging of human feats, the one demanding the utmost of human
intelligence?"

To my surprise, Dr. Cook actually considered my question for
a beat, took a swallow of diet soda, and then offered an answer:

"No margin for error."

Jesus, he's right, I realized. *That's it.* I mean, when you think about

it, that's probably what gives brain surgeons the edge over rocket scientists. We've all seen *Apollo 13*. Those NASA guys always have the old
"plastic bag, cardboard tubing, and duct tape" option to fall back on
when the shit hits the fan. Neurosurgeons have no such leeway. What
it comes down to is this: if a brain surgeon screws up, it means a
multimillion-dollar malpractice suit, but if a rocket scientist screws up,
it means a multimillion-dollar hit movie starring Tom Hanks.

No margin for error. I was still marveling at the perfection of that
answer. *He's absolutely right, one little hiccup and . . . So why am I smiling?*

Holy Family Hospital, Methuen, Mass.—Sunday Morning, March 15
Valium or no valium, I remember things. I remember my head being
shaved and asking them to leave some bangs in front so, post-op, I
could let them hang out from under my baseball cap and people
would think I still had a full head of hair. I remember the stinging
pinch of the screws and mumbling something about Torquemada
when the aluminum frame was fastened to my skull. I remember a
slight vibration, some pressure but no pain, when the tiny hole was
drilled through the top of my head.

I remember—this must have been a couple hours into the operation—Dr. Cook asking me to count to ten out loud. Somewhere between two and four, though, the voice I heard counting sounded as
though it was coming from somebody else. A slow baritone warble at
first, it suddenly modulated up and down, changing pitches, changing
speeds, as if it were a record and some drunk at the party was leaning
on the turntable. At eight, I stopped counting.

"*Heyyyy . . .*" I growled in my new *Incredible Hulk*, slow-mo voice,
"*You guys are messsssing with my brrrrain.*" I remember them laughing.

And then I remember someone (Dr. Cook?) asking me to put my
hand in a position that would cause it to tremor. He wanted me to
make my hand tremor, to see it shake. I tried, but my hand wouldn't
cooperate. So I moved it again, and it still wouldn't tremor. Now I was
getting mad at myself; I felt like I was being a bad patient.

"I'm sorry," I remember saying (my regular voice back now). "But
it won't. I can't make it shake. It just won't do it."

"Great. That's it," the doctor said. "We're done."

I remember lifting my left hand up in front of my face, turning it over and over, splaying out my fingers, obedient and smiling. *That's it. They're done.*

Anguilla, the Caribbean — April 1998
Another day in paradise.

Dr. Cook cleared me to fly down to the Caribbean with my family just two days after the surgery; it was Sam's spring break. During my two weeks of rest and recuperation, I'd been getting up early every morning, around 6:00 A.M., before Tracy, before Sam and the girls, and this day was no exception. I rose from bed quietly without waking Tracy, threw on a pair of shorts and a T-shirt, wrapped my stubbly head (with its comical tufted forelock) in a blue bandana, slipped out the back door of the hotel villa, and made my way down the cliff stairs and onto the beach.

After walking for a quarter mile or so I sat down on the soft white sand and rested my forearms across my knees. Pelicans were fishing about ten feet offshore, wheeling and diving spectacularly, but they weren't the object of my attention. I was focused on my hand. I stared at it, and waited. Inside of five minutes my fingers began to flutter. It was subtle, no one else would ever have noticed, but it was there.

It was just like at the beginning, just like before, with one very big difference: this wasn't my left hand I was looking at. There was no question that the operation had been a success; my left side was as still as the sheltered blue bay in front of me. The problem now was with my right—the tremor had moved into the right side of my body. I wasn't surprised. This wasn't altogether new, and had nothing to do with the surgery. In fact, nothing the doctor did that day could have caused this most recent development in my symptoms. The lesion was created in the right hemisphere of my brain and therefore would only have an effect on the left side of my body. I'd actually begun to notice it back in February, after my first meeting with Dr. Cook. Probably the subsiding of the tremor on my left had just made the deterioration on my right side more noticeable.

I was sad, but I wasn't angry. I'd known for years that this was an inevitability. I have Parkinson's disease; it's a progressive disorder. It's just doing what it's supposed to do. *So, what was I supposed to do now?* I rose, brushed the sand off the back of my legs, and started to make my way back toward my wife and sleeping children. The answer was clear. After all that I'd been through, after all that I'd learned and all that I'd been given, I was going to do what I had been doing every day for the last few years now: just show up and do the best that I could with whatever lay in front of me.

I picked up some shells for the kids and stuffed them into the pockets of my shorts, and somewhere along the way, as I had almost every day since I'd stopped drinking six years earlier, I said this prayer:

> *God grant me the serenity to accept the things I cannot change*
> *Courage to change the things I can*
> *And the wisdom to know the difference.*

Mr. Fox

CHAPTER EIGHT

Unwrapping the Gift

I need to explain the "on-off" phenomenon. This Jekyll-and-Hyde melodrama is a constant vexation for the P.D. patient, especially one as determined as I was to remain closeted. "On" refers to the time when the medication is telling my brain everything it wants to hear. I'm relatively loose and fluid, my mind clear and movements under control. Only a trained observer could detect my Parkinson's. During one of my "off" periods, even the most myopic layperson, while perhaps not able to diagnose P.D. specifically, can recognize that I am in serious trouble.

When I'm "off," the disease has complete authority over my physical being. I'm utterly in its possession. Sometimes there are flashes of function, and I can be effective at performing basic physical tasks, certainly feeding and dressing myself (though I'll lean toward loafers and pullover sweaters), as well as any chore calling for more brute force than manual dexterity. In my very worst "off" times I experience the full panoply of classic Parkinsonian symptoms: rigidity, shuffling, tremors, lack of balance, diminished small motor control, and the insidious cluster of symptoms that makes communication—written as well as spoken—difficult and sometimes impossible.

Hypophonia, hypomimia, and "cluttering" can all get in the way of verbally expressing feelings and ideas. Hypophonia weakens the voice so badly that for some, like Muhammad Ali, simply making yourself audible demands a tremendous effort. So far I've been spared that particular challenge. When I'm "off," my struggle is with "cluttered speech" combined with hypomimia, the medical term for the "mask effect" often observed in the faces of P.D. patients. My ability to form thoughts and ideas into words and sentences is not impaired; the problem is translating those words and sentences into articulate speech. My lips, tongue, and jaw muscles simply won't cooperate. What words I do smuggle through the blockade can be heard, though not always comprehended. Try as I might, I can't inflect my speech to reflect my state of mind. And it's not like I can liven up my halting monotone with a raised eyebrow; my face, utterly expressionless, simply won't respond. Like Emmett Kelly, but without the greasepaint, I often appear sad on the outside while actually smiling, or at least smirking, on the inside.

Micrographia is precisely what it sounds like—tiny writing. I have a stockbroker friend, a fellow Young Onset patient (amazingly, the friendship predates our diagnoses) whose secretary was the first to recommend he consult a neurologist. Over the course of a year or so, she had found it increasingly difficult to decipher his memos, and finally confronted him with the evidence of his incredible shrinking handwriting. Without drugs, my own penmanship becomes similarly microscopic. Combined with the stubborn refusal of my "off" arm to move in a smooth, lateral, left-to-right direction, the result is a fractured column of miniature scribbles.

This:

When I'm "on", this is what my handwriting looks like.

Becomes this:

This is what my handwriting is like when my meds are off and micrographia kicks in,

These impediments to self-expression are not the most painful or debilitating features of Parkinson's disease, yet they madden me more than even the most teeth-rattling full body tremor. When the meds are "off" and P.D. has already rendered me a prisoner in my own body, the suspension of my telephone and letter-writing privileges seems excessive.

Then there's the sensation of not being able to settle, or land in any one spot for more than a second or two. When I'm "off," I feel like I'm dangling from a coat hanger that has been surgically implanted under my skin in the muscles of my back, wedged between my shoulder blades. The sensation is not quite one of being suspended in the air; it's more like being jacked up, with my toes scraping and kicking at the ground, straining for purchase, so that, if only for a moment, both feet can plant firmly and bear the full weight of my body. During the years I spent promoting the fiction that none of this was actually happening to me, my only recourse was to isolate myself and grit it out.

Three to four times every day, I go through the transitions between the two poles, navigating the tricky passage from the land of "off" to "on." The most surreal aspect of this thrill ride is that during every "on" time, I delude myself into believing that that, and not the other, is my "normal" condition.

None of the pills I take gives me even a mild buzz, but the freedom of movement and the interlude of physical grace they provide are intoxicating. I don't squander a nanosecond of this time contemplating the inconvenient truth that what I'm experiencing is not "real." I don't think about that when I'm splashing in the surf with Aquinnah and Schuyler, fishing for bass with Sam, or huffing to keep up with Tracy on the bike rides she loves so much. I truly do forget and, lost in this sublime ordinariness, it's easy to miss the subtle twitches, creeping rigidity, and vibrating sensations urging me to crack open the vial and toss back another little blue pill.

Every P.D. patient's experience is unique. Mine is this: If I miss or ignore those early-warning signs, there's no second chance. I am down for the full sixty to ninety minutes. It's no good upping the dosage, either—that only results in exaggerated dyskinesias (random, spastic, hyperextended movements of the extremities) when the L-dopa finally does take effect. As with the "on" period, it is hard to believe that the "off" is ever going to end, and it doesn't help to remind myself that it always does.

Arranging life in order to be "on" in public, and "off" for as little time as possible, is a balancing act for any P.D.er. In my case, the gut-wrenching prospect of losing my balance, figuratively or literally, on *The Late Show,* say, or at a public event where there was no way to avoid close scrutiny, loomed ever larger the longer I remained in the closet.

Learning to titrate medication so that it kicked in before an appearance or performance, sometimes within minutes of my cue, be-

came a process of continuous tweaking and refining—lots of trial
with little room for error. Timing a punchline was a joke if I hadn't
timed my meds accurately. I became a virtuoso at manipulating drug
intake, so that I'd peak at exactly the right time and place.

When the L-dopa begins to work, and the current "off" segues
into a fresh "on," the sheer relief of the transformation is its own special high. The people close to me are attuned to the physical ceremony that marks my latest transition back into the world of the fully
functioning—the subtle sigh, accompanied by a sudden spastic thrust
or two of my left leg, immediately followed by the outstretching of
my arms and rolling of my head. The leg thrusts are involuntary but
entirely welcome, because they signal the beginning of the end. As
the tension leaves my body, it always travels down and through that
particular limb, and then into my foot, which rotates three or four
times. Finally, as if being pulled by the force of a vacuum, the tension
disappears, departing through the sole of my left shoe. The extension
of my arms, and rolling of my head, are simply my body's way of celebrating the reunion of mind and motion.

This ritual ending of an "off" period is immediately followed by
another personal rite, this one marking the return to "on" status. If
you ask Tracy or anyone else who spends a lot of time with me, they
will tell you that I do, and say, the same thing every single time: I
smile, close my eyes, and then, like Barry White on helium, croon, "oh
baby . . . I love it when the drugs kick in."

"ON," "OFF"—AND "OUT"

Spin City *Season Three—1998*
Presenting an accurate snapshot of my symptoms at any one point in
time is never easy, but what I've just outlined describes fairly well the
body I had to work with at the beginning of *Spin City*'s third season.
In the months following the thalamotomy, the success of the procedure in taming my left side was a happy and obvious matter of fact.
Just as obvious, though, was the rapid escalation of the new tremor

on my right side—worsening at a rate I could track almost on a daily
basis. I wonder if the disappearance of the furious flapping in my left
arm had also served to throw the other symptoms (rigidity, hypomimia, and the rest) into sharper relief. Whatever the reason, there
was no doubt that after a sweet but all-too-brief post-op plateau, my
disease was confronting me with a whole new set of challenges, personally as well as professionally. It was also hastening a decision, long
postponed, to bring the private and public sides of my life into closer
alignment. Keeping my disease secret was rapidly becoming unten-
able—and destructive.

Most P.D. patients will tell you that stress exacerbates their symptoms, and during the summer of 1998 my job suddenly got a whole
lot more stressful. In response to our persistent creative conflicts, Gary
Goldberg decided he would not return to the show for the third season, remaining instead in L.A. to be with his family and pursue other
projects. Though at the time the split was grueling emotionally, I'm
convinced it ultimately preserved our friendship—in many ways
stronger today than ever before—and set the stage for a professional
reconciliation two years later that would ensure the series' future after
my retirement. In the short term, though, I now found myself with
the creative authority I'd craved for the first two seasons: a vast in-
crease in my responsibilities. *Be careful what you wish for*—I was now in
charge of the show.

It's not that I didn't have tremendous help. Bill Lawrence returned
to the show, as well as writer-producer David Rosenthal, and most of
our talented, if eccentric, writers, technical crew, and administrative
staff. Andy Cadiff, who had served brilliantly as director during the
previous season, was given the added title of *Spin City* producer, and
proved an invaluable partner in running the set. Danelle Black, the
president of my production company, became a consulting producer,
and as the executive closest to me, was inundated with requests for my
time and attention. Danelle's skill at running interference for me tran-
scended mere professional responsibility—this was loyalty and friendship of the highest order.

Still, I now had countless production issues to oversee and decisions to sign off on during each twelve-to-fourteen-hour day: rewrites for that week's episode, outlines and story arcs for scripts weeks in advance, casting and crew hirings, wardrobe and set consultations, music and editing oversight, and the continued tending of diplomatic relationships with the network and studio. All of this I enjoyed. Well, *almost* all of it: my least favorite duty, as a lifelong hater of mathematical absolutes, was establishing and then sticking to a weekly production budget.

As demanding as all this was for me, I was beginning to appreciate how truly difficult I was making life for the people I worked with—the majority of whom didn't know about my health issues. I'm thinking of all the times my symptoms forced me to reschedule appointments at the last minute with various department heads, only to have to reschedule again and again, and sometimes ultimately cancel with no explanation. My behavior must have seemed flaky at best, and at worst arrogant and disrespectful. The many last-minute production delays, running anywhere from a few minutes to a half an hour or more, that I usually blamed on some vague injury or "important phone call from the West Coast," must have been a source of mystery and annoyance. Not that it was any easier for those who knew what was really going on. Danelle, Bill, Andy, the cast, and the handful of others I had let in on my secret were under constant pressure to cover for me, to come up with fresh excuses and, if they didn't have time to check their stories against mine, worry they were going to betray my confidence by being caught in the whitest of lies.

There were already rumors, of this I was well aware. Some of them originated, I suspect, in Boston. My frequent visits to that city for medical treatment and consultation had somehow been brought to the attention of a pair of local newspaper gossip columnists.

They were the first, I believe, to link me to some vague and undefined "mystery" illness—as far back as 1997. To their great indignation, I basically ignored them, and because their speculation was so unspecific, these mentions gained little wider attention. It wasn't until 1998 that the national tabloids cautiously picked up on the story. They printed a few items, at first blind, and then some that referred to me directly as having been stricken by an unknown illness and currently undergoing treatment.

The first time I heard the word "Parkinson's" from any of the Florida-based national scandal sheets was a very up-close-and-personal event. One morning early in 1998, shortly before my operation, Jimmy Nugent, my *Spin City* driver and a long-time friend, arrived to pick up Sam and me at our Upper East Side apartment. As on many weekdays, Jimmy would first drop Sam at school and then take me to the set. We were walking the few short steps from the front door of our building to Jimmy's idling SUV when a particularly harried woman, who seemed to appear out of thin air, jumped in front of me, disregarding Sam and flustering Jimmy. Identifying herself as a reporter from *The Star*, she started peppering me with questions about my health. Without saying a word I smiled, shepherded Sam into the car, and climbed in after him. We started to pull away and to my amazement the woman stepped into the street behind us as we pulled away, waving her arms and screaming after us at the top of her lungs, "Parkinson's disease!" What was she thinking? That hearing those words would get me to halt the car, step out, and say, "Well, yes, as a matter of fact"?

People who worked for me continued to receive calls from the tabloids, particularly *The Enquirer*, throughout 1998. They were now freely using the word "Parkinson's," at least in their private conversations with us, though still shying away from making such a declaration in print. Our response was, as it would be with any enquiry of this sort, "No comment," adding only this: "Print whatever you want to print, but make good and sure you believe it, because if you get it wrong, you know you'll hear from us." I felt no sense of dishonesty in taking this position. I am not a politician or an elected official, so it's not as if the public interest would somehow be served by publicizing intimate information about my health.

The Enquirer made the case that my fans have the "right" to know, an argument all too reminiscent of their protestations around the time of the wedding. My reaction was roughly the same. I'm sure that anyone who followed my career might be interested were I to tell them about my situation, but I'm equally sure they would not like the idea I'd been bullied into making such a disclosure, and further, would direct their ire toward the bully. The tabloids know this, and fear a backlash from their readers as much as they fear lawsuits. They held the story.

So who were the tipsters? In the case of the initial Boston items, a number of possibilities came to mind: airport workers, cab and radio-car drivers shuttling me to and from hospitals and clinics, maybe even fellow patients who'd noticed me slipping in and out of the side doors of my doctors' offices.

But really, what did any of it matter? I wasn't going to be consumed by this sort of guessing game. By now I had come too far, and wasn't about to surrender to a paranoia that I understood could be as destructive as any disease. And if *who* was talking didn't interest me, *why* they were talking seemed even less important. People do what they do for their own reasons—it's none of my business finally and wholly out of my control. I could only be concerned about myself and be responsible for my own actions.

In fact, it was that sense of responsibility, much more than the badgering of the checkout counter gossips, that was edging me toward "coming out." Life would undoubtedly be easier for all of my friends, family, and co-workers if I could be open about my health. And I had a responsibility to myself as well. Not only would my job as a producer be made easier if I didn't have to work so hard at secrecy, but the part of *Spin City* I loved best—acting—would be a lot less stressful.

As it was, each week's show presented a brand-new set of creative and physical challenges. Could I count on my body to respond in performance the same way it had in rehearsal? This gradually became a moot point, as rehearsal became a luxury I could less and less afford—yet another baffling behavior in the eyes of the uninformed, who easily could have interpreted it as arrogance or indifference.

By now I could see that the strain I put myself (and everybody else) through by trying to be funny without being upstaged by my invisible pet elephant was as absurd as it was exhausting. Whatever I appeared to be doing onstage, I was, in fact, doing something else: hiding symptoms with a repertoire of little tricks and distracting maneuvers—manipulating props, leaning against walls and furniture, and when all else failed, jamming my hands into my pockets. Many days I had to concentrate more on my physical relationship to the scene unfolding around me than to emotional, comedic, or dramatic content. All the while I was doing the math—how long since the last pill? . . . how long until it wears off? And at what point in the show will I have to take another? "Please . . . let it be during a scene I'm not in."

I mentioned how quickly I must react to the harbingers of an "off" cycle, and the consequences if I don't. If the warning came when I was in the middle of a four-to-five-minute scene, there wasn't a damn thing I could do to stave off the return of my symptoms. I had a name for this crisis of circumstance: "turning into a pumpkin."

"Turning into a pumpkin" live onstage would blow the whole thing. If a studio audience were to detect a tremoring of my arm, a slowing of my speech, or a rigidity of my movements, it would undoubtedly betray the fact that something was wrong, and that something, whatever it was, would be decidedly unfunny. This had become my greatest fear, just as making an audience laugh remained one of my greatest pleasures.

So I did everything I could to make sure the audience didn't know I was sick. This, as much as anything, had, by 1998, become my "acting." I have always thrived on my relationship to the audience, and feared taking any risk that would distract or detract from it. Coming out of the closet was just such a risk. Timing a joke depends on the audience being with me, wherever I choose to go, and if their attention is lost for even a second while they are watching my arm or a hitch in my gait, then I've lost them. I was beginning to realize that this, more than anything else, was what was keeping me from telling people that I had Parkinson's disease. If an audience didn't know what I was dealing with, they wouldn't know what to look for, so I still had a shot at making them laugh. But if they already knew before they even took their seats in the audience or turned on their televisions at home that I was battling an incurable neurological disease, would they still go along for the ride, or would they be watching for symptoms and feeling sorry? The bottom line was this: can sick people be funny, or—to put it more bluntly—can you laugh at a sick person without feeling like an asshole?

It was becoming abundantly clear, though, that to carry on as I had been for the first part of the 1998 season could only be destructive to my hard-won sense of who I was. Over the past seven years I had experienced so many highs and lows, and had finally set about facing my fears. I had come a long way toward decompartmentalizing my relationships and attitudes, bringing what I felt inside into a truer relationship to what I said and did. So much of the distance my disease had put between me and the people I cared about had been narrowed. But what about the audience? Until I felt ready to tell them my story, my life would never be fully integrated, and as happy as I was in every other area—my marriage to Tracy, my relationship with my kids, and all my other interactions with the outside world—this last fear, rooted in concern for my career, which is to say for my relationship to my audience, was keeping me from being truly free.

I can vividly remember all those nights when the studio audience, unknowingly, had to wait for my symptoms to subside. I'd be backstage, lying on my dressing room rug, twisting and rolling around, trying to cajole my neuroreceptors into accepting and processing the L-dopa I had so graciously provided. When that approach failed, I'd spruce up the walls with fist-size holes, the graffiti of my frustration. How much longer could this go on?

Manhattan—November 1998

As soon as I entered Joyce's office, I collapsed on the couch. It was Friday morning. I had a show to do that night and was feeling the weight of the week's work pressing down on every part of my being.

"I've had this feeling lately," I began. "One I haven't had in years. That old feeling like I'm waiting for the other shoe to drop."

Joyce was quiet, considering me for a beat. Then, when she was sure she had my full attention, she gave a slight smile and said, softly and simply, "Michael, you have Parkinson's disease—the other shoe dropped a long time ago."

Almost as if I had walked into a hug, I immediately felt enveloped by a wave of emotion. My eyes welled up and tears spilled their warmth onto my cheeks; tears not of sadness or self-pity but relief, pride, and deep, deep gratitude. Joyce was right. The other shoe had already dropped, and I had survived. There was nothing left to fear. *You're only as sick as your secrets.*

It was time, I was ready.

ALADDIN SANE

New York — November 30, 1998
Phase one was complete. *People* magazine already had the story, and just as the issue was hitting the newsstands, I was embarking on phase two: telling my story again, this time in front of a TV camera.

It was a simple plan—two interviews, one print, one television, the news would be out and I could get on with my life. But I, of all people, should have known that nothing ever goes quite according to plan. *People* broke the story on their web site on Thanksgiving eve, nearly a week earlier than expected. The response had exceeded anything I could have imagined, life as I knew it would never be the same, and now, in yet another surreal twist, I found myself in the middle of an argument between my wife and Barbara Walters.

Argument might be too strong a word. It was more like a minor disagreement—over a leather coat. A week or so earlier, I'd met with Barbara (and her producer) in her East Side apartment to discuss the parameters of the interview I'd offered to do. As I was leaving, she noticed me struggling with my coat—I was dyskinetic and having trouble getting my arm into the sleeve. She asked me if that was a symptom of P.D. I said it was. Now, midway through the taping, during a pause while the cameramen changed reels, she asked if I'd be willing to take my jacket off and put it back on again in front of the camera to demonstrate my dyskinesias.

Tracy was adamantly opposed, and spoke up. To stage such a demonstration would come across like a play for sympathy, she felt, and she knew that was the last thing I wanted. Barbara countered that letting people see me struggle with my coat would give them a more complete picture of my symptoms. I stepped in and explained that it was a moot point anyway. The Sinemet was working right then, so I could get in and out of the coat with ease. I had no problem with describing that particular symptom on camera, as long as we skipped the floor show. Whatever tension there had been evaporated, and Barbara leaned forward to give Tracy a hug. "You're a lucky fellow, Michael. She loves you very much." Didn't I know it. *How about that Tra, sticking up for me even when it means going toe to toe with Barbara Walters.*

Once we had returned to the set, but before the cameras began to roll, Barbara tapped my knee. "You know this isn't just morbid curiosity," she said. "People care about you. This is a learning experience for everyone."

Los Angeles—November 19, 1998
Having finally made the decision to share my experience with Parkinson's, I had one goal in mind: to give an honest account of how, over the last seven years, I had integrated the disease into a rich and productive life. It was important for me to convey my optimism, gratitude, perspective, and even an ability to laugh about certain aspects of life with P.D., being a firm believer in the joke writer's axiom that comedy = tragedy + time. I viewed my disclosure as a way for me to move forward in my life and career, not as a summation compelled by catastrophe.

This was not a tale of woe, as Tracy would remind Barbara Walters; I sought no pity, or tears. Nor was I eager to cast myself in the role of reluctant hero, breaking out of his silent suffering to take his fight public, and serve as a poster boy for the Parkinson's "cause." (I'd done a little research on existing foundations and, frankly, had found the landscape too confusing to navigate.) I was simply tired of hiding the truth from people and felt ready, finally, to present it to them on my own terms, with the hope that they'd respond to my story in the spirit in which it was offered.

Ultimately, though, going public would be the truest test yet of a

philosophy I'd been growing into over the course of the past seven
years in the wilderness. *Take the action and let go of the results.* That
sounds good, and I could definitely talk the talk, but could I walk the
walk? From the moment Todd Gold, the *People* magazine reporter,
pulled out his notepad and checked his tape recorder's batteries, talking was suddenly the last thing I wanted to do, but walking was out of
the question—for one thing, I was so anxious I could feel my legs
turning to jelly; for another, I'd made up my mind to do this, and I was
going to see it through.

The interview took place in the Los Angeles office of Nanci
Ryder, my publicist. I'd come to L.A. to inform executives from
DreamWorks and ABC of my decision; they'd given me their full and
unflinching support. By the time the two-hour interview was over,
Todd's notepad and audiocassettes were full—the tapes held my
words, and his shorthand scribbling had captured my behavior, tics,
tremors, and facial expressions. The realization began to sink in: *Oh
my god, what have I done?* I hadn't *shared* my story, I had *given it away*. It
was no longer *mine*.

What Todd knew, and I was just beginning to grasp, was that my
own words would make up only a part of the article he was about to
write. However sincere my upbeat and philosophical approach to the
illness, in the press coverage the *subjective* reality of my experience
with Parkinson's would inevitably be juxtaposed with the *objective* reality of the disease, in all its destructive cruelty. The rules of good
journalism demanded as much. Doctors, scientists, and in all likelihood, other patients would present a grim picture of this crippler of
nearly one and a half million Americans—and in the process, force me
to take a fresh look at it myself. When Todd's article finally appeared
in the pages of *People* magazine, I'd learn that even my own neurologist, Dr. Ropper, who had spoken to the reporter with my permission,
didn't sugarcoat my situation:

> Ropper is hopeful that Fox will be functional for at least another
> 10 years and maybe well into old age. But he cannot rule out the
> worst, which is that Fox may well have to give up work—and it is

uncertain whether he will need further brain surgery. "This is a
very serious neurological disease," Ropper says. "In extreme cases
patients live a bedbound existence where they require total care."

I thought about my kids. Tracy and I had always been able to
frame the disease for them; we were the sole explainers of its potential impact on their lives. Now, they would also learn about Parkinson's through the reactions of their teachers, classmates, and countless
others, well away from the security of our reassurance. The genie was
out of the bottle, and not only had I no way of knowing how big it
would get, there was no way to gauge its disposition. Would it turn on
me in spite for having kept it captive for so long?

Thanksgiving Weekend, Connecticut—November 26–29, 1998
As soon as the story hit the *People* web site, all hell broke loose. We
were packing up to spend the four-day holiday weekend with Tracy's
family in the country, and I couldn't get out of town fast enough. The
phone rang incessantly. Too nervous to speak with anyone, I'd check
the voice mail periodically and hear the messages from friends and
family. Some, especially those left by business associates like Nanci
Ryder, contained long lists of further messages from newspaper and
magazine editors, radio reporters, and TV newsmagazine anchors. For
some reason, the mention of a call from Dan Rather hit me right in
the solar plexus. It would be disingenuous to suggest that I didn't expect some media attention, particularly in the entertainment press, but
in no way did I anticipate the magnitude of the reaction. They were
treating this like a big news story. *Dan Rather?*

It quickly became clear that I was *the* big news story over that holiday weekend. My revelation was the lead item on all of the network
newscasts, there were hourly updates on the cable channels, and
above-the-fold headlines in big city newspapers throughout the
United States and Canada.

Holed up in Connecticut, I did my best to avoid television and
the newspapers. To say I was having second thoughts would be a gross
understatement—the number was well up into the triple digits and

climbing. I was sure that I wouldn't be happy with any of the coverage. What I dreaded most was being cast as a tragic figure, a helpless victim. TV's erstwhile boy-next-door stricken by an incurable disease, transformed into a frail object of pity. *Poor bastard.* Just as excruciating was how long the story lasted. I could tell from the telephone calls I was receiving from friends, as well as the growing stack of messages from well-wishers and media outlets around the world, that my story, as we say in showbiz, had legs. The coverage spilled over into days two and three and even four; still front page and near the top of the broadcasts. I became convinced that whenever I showed my face again people would flee in terror. After all the nonstop eulogizing, they'd figure they were seeing a ghost.

Yet when I finally stuck my toe into the swirling torrent of coverage, I learned just how badly I'd misjudged the situation. While some in the media (the usual suspects) were stressing the maudlin and sensational angle, in the vast majority of the reports, the overall tone was surprised but respectful—and concerned. In man-on-the-street interviews, members of the public offered expressions not so much of sympathy, as I feared, but of genuine empathy, as well as heartfelt wishes for a positive outcome. Even better, much of the follow-up coverage centered less on me than on Parkinson's disease itself: there were long, detailed features describing the condition, interviews with doctors explaining the process of diagnosis, the prognosis, and the variety of treatments available. A recurring topic of discussion was the heretofore little-known phenomenon of Young Onset P.D. Local newspapers and TV affiliates across the country were interviewing P.D. patients of all ages, giving them an opportunity to talk about their experiences and document their struggles, fears, and hope for the future. Scientists and researchers discussed potential breakthroughs and possible cures not too far over the horizon.

Without intending to, I had sparked a national conversation about Parkinson's disease. This I discovered on our last night in Connecticut. At the time I still wasn't ready to turn on the TV, but naively thought it would be safe to check my e-mail. *Wrong*—as soon as the AOL home page appeared on my screen, there was my picture, anchored by a scrawling headline. I half expected to hear the robotic chirp of Elwood Edwards greeting me with, "Welcome! You've got Parkinson's!"

I put off reading my e-mail—there was too much of it—and instead began to surf a few of the P.D. web sites I'd been visiting over the last few months. One in particular caught my attention. It was an online chat room for P.D. patients. I lurked there for a while, eavesdropping on their conversations. To a person, these patients were heralding my announcement and enthusing over the welcome turn in coverage, away from the celebrity angle and toward the patient community. Some commented on the impact the attention was already having on their own lives.

I distinctly remember one person writing, "I went to the market this morning and the cashier asked me why my hand was shaking. I told her it was Parkinson's, and she was really interested. 'Oh, just like Michael J. Fox.' For the first time in years, I didn't feel embarrassed."

Emboldened, I finally turned on my television set, and sure enough, there I was. MSNBC had combed through its archives, pulled several television interviews spanning the length of my career, and compiled them into a slapdash biography. A lot of it was in slow motion, giving the piece a somber tone: *This is the Michael J. Fox that was.* As any public figure will tell you, you know you're in trouble—dead, sick, or under indictment—whenever they start running footage of you in slow motion. It was as close to watching my own obituary as I ever want to get.

Still, for the first time in several days, I had the unmistakable feeling that everything was going to be okay after all. There was no question that some people would view the news of my disease as an ending, but I was starting to sense that in a much more profound way, it was really a beginning. I was ready to return to New York. First thing in the morning was the interview with Barbara Walters. I'd tell my story one more time, referee a tiff over a leather coat, and nod in agreement when Barbara leaned over to say, "You know, this is a learning experience for everyone."

OUT OF THE CLOSET, INTO THE CLASSROOM

Well, Barbara, it was definitely a learning experience for me. As much of an education as the previous seven years had been—my private Parkinsonian tutorial—the lessons that came in the wake of that fateful Thanksgiving have been all the more powerful and humbling. While there's no doubt that I needed every minute of those seven years to make my own accommodation with Parkinson's, I'm grateful I didn't wait any longer to share my story. To do so would have been to deprive myself of what has been one of the most rewarding—and educational—experiences of my life.

My greatest teachers now came from within the P.D. community itself. My coming out had an impact on their lives, as it turned out, but even before that, their stories—gleaned from what I read on P.D. web sites suddenly lit up with conversation—had at least as profound an impact on mine. It was as if I was looking in a window, and to my comfort and relief, there were lights on and people inside—people just like me.

More like me, as a matter of fact, than I had ever realized—beyond our common diagnosis, beyond the matching collection of pill bottles in our medicine cabinets, and beyond our shared physical tribulations. Just as I had, many of the P.D. patients online were logging in to cyberspace from the well-guarded security of their own private "closets." I had always presumed that my impulse to keep my diagnosis a closely held secret was motivated purely by my celebrity status. I soon discovered that a great number of Parkinson's patients, particularly those in the Young Onset category, were also hiding their illness from others. Each had their own reasons, but there were a few recurring themes. These I picked up on in the many letters and e-mails I received after my disclosure.

Fear of being marginalized and misunderstood—stigmatized—is a concern that comes up time and again. Carl, a high school teacher in Texas, was forty years old when he watched me on his local news at noon on Thanksgiving day in 1998. Though he wouldn't be officially diagnosed with Parkinson's until two weeks later, he didn't doubt that the symptoms he'd been living with for the last couple of years were almost identical to the ones I was describing. He wrote to thank me for my "public witness," telling me that it had "made my metamorphosis a bit easier. You showed people that a good, intelligent, vigorous person can get P.D.; this reduced the stigma of freakishness that otherwise attaches itself to the chronically ill, particularly if they are young."

Carol, a young mother and P.D. patient from New Jersey who is now a Parkinson's advocate, says, "I must have, for about four years, pretended I didn't have anything [wrong with me]. I didn't have a tremor. And I could sort of do that. And I felt terrible having to deceive people. When [you] came out and made it an illness not to be ashamed of, it made me stop pretending, it made me not be embarrassed about the idea of going on a walk and raising money. Made my kids see it as—not *normal*—but not *bizarre*."

The prospect of being considered bizarre, a freak, or an object of pity is enough to keep someone in the closet. For many, however, there is an even more basic concern, having to do with their very survival and that of their families. Young adults, many just starting out or just hitting their stride in life, with children and mortgages, car payments and yet-to-be-realized career goals, are terrified that Parkinson's will cost them their jobs, often with very good reason.

"Some guys must break out in night sweats wondering if the next day at work is going to be their last," says Greg, an attorney I met online at a P.D. web site. Greg was employed as a writer/editor for a legal information provider when he was diagnosed with Young Onset Parkinson's in March of 1995. He was forty-three years old at the time; today he's on disability. "I used to advise people to tell their employers [about their diagnosis] because under the Americans with Disabilities Act you were protected if you were disabled, 'deprived of a basic life activity,' such as being able to work," Greg explained to me recently.

"Supposedly you're protected if you tell your employer and request accommodations. The magic words are 'I have it and I need this to do my job.' But if the employer runs out of reasonable accommodations, or has attempted to make accommodations and found it too difficult, or they're just savvy and want to cheat—then they can just find another reason to fire you. They're thinking, 'What's this going to do to my insurance rate?'

"ADA or no ADA," Greg says, "there's the *law* and then there's the *real world*."

As I well understood, if you're a Young Onset Parkinson's patient, worried that being open about your diagnosis will hurt or even destroy your career, it's all too tempting to get caught up in an elaborate web of obfuscation. In an insidious way, the disease itself is your accomplice in this deception. The progression is slow, the symptoms are not immediately obvious—and who'd be looking for them in a forty-year-old anyway? To all outward appearances, you seem fine and you carry on with your life. But you're *not* fine, and you're getting worse, and so you wait as long as you can to tell anyone, adding the terrible burden of secrecy to the already considerable weight of your disease.

As I made the acquaintance of other P.D. patients, I began to put together a picture of the community I was now a full-fledged member of. I learned that there are nearly one and a half million of us, altogether, but the community is split into two very different demographic groups. Roughly ninety percent of P.D. patients are older, in their late sixties or seventies and beyond; many are infirm and living on fixed incomes—and without a great deal of political influence. Young Onset patients make up the remaining ten percent. These patients might constitute a real political force, if not for the fact that so many of them are still closeted.

I was beginning to understand why Parkinson's disease has traditionally received so little public attention, and relatively few government research dollars. I learned that in the mid-1990s, the National Institutes of Health were spending an estimated $2,400 per victim each year on HIV/AIDS research, $200 on breast cancer, $100 on prostate cancer, $78 on Alzheimer's disease, $34 on Parkinson's, and only $20 each on diabetes and coronary heart disease.

In the case of Parkinson's, the lack of funding was especially tragic, because the research opportunities were so promising. By the

1990s, scientists were following a number of exciting leads that pointed to a cure in the not-so-distant future. One of the more important of these new breakthroughs came in San Francisco during the 1980s. A doctor named Bill Langston had discovered a chemical compound, MPTP, in synthetic heroin that created advanced P.D.-like symptoms in young Bay Area drug addicts. (He wrote a gripping book about the phenomenon called *The Case of the Frozen Addicts*.) The identification of an agent that actually produced Parkinsonian symptoms opened up several promising avenues of investigation and gave scientists the ability to induce Parkinsonian symptoms in laboratory animals. "It created a tremendous renaissance in Parkinson's research," Dr. Langston says today. "As well as generating interest in the possibility that there is an environmental trigger for the disease."

There was a larger reason many scientists viewed Parkinson's as an exciting area of neurological research. According to Dr. Jeffrey Kurdower, a professor of neurological sciences at Rush-Presbyterian-St. Luke's Medical Center in Chicago, "of the big three degenerative neurological diseases—Parkinson's, Alzheimer's, and ALS (Lou Gehrig's)—we think P.D. will be the first domino to fall.

"We know its pathology, that it is the result of a loss of dopamine cells, and unlike the other degenerative diseases, we can treat it quite effectively, in this case with synthetic dopamine. We know the precise anatomy of where it occurs and have terrific animal models. Those are the three major factors for successful research."

"With Parkinson's disease," Dr. Langston has said, "the science has been way ahead of the money."

I was learning that it really wasn't a question of *if* Parkinson's could be cured, but *when?* The answer was, only as soon as we could pay for the cost of scientific research.

Whenever people debate federal funding for medical research, there's an assumption it's a zero-sum game. Any number of "special interest" groups, be they AIDS, cancer, or Parkinson's advocates, are all competing for a bigger slice of the pie. What's really needed, of course, is simply a much bigger pie. So why do some patient groups get more than others? And why are others left out in the cold when the money's being doled out? The answer lies, in part, with the fervor and commitment of the lobbying effort, and that starts in the patient community.

It's illustrative to draw a comparison between Parkinson's and HIV/AIDS, the group that receives the most government research money. Perhaps the most successful and inspiring movement ever to demand federal action to cure a specific disease, AIDS activism found its strongest voice within the gay community. Because a large proportion of those at risk or infected were young, vital, creative, and affluent, they were able to mobilize quickly and strategically in support of their cause. While some in this movement were, like Young Onset P.D.ers, closeted, the urgency of the situation compelled many to come out, and a system of mutual support in the community eased that transition. Yet those affected by Young Onset Parkinson's, surely the segment of our community in the best position to make a sustained, energetic commitment to advocacy and activism, have, for the reasons I've mentioned, been reluctant to speak up, never mind *act* up.

Because Parkinson's disease progresses so slowly it also discourages involvement, at least in the early stages, when a patient would have the most to offer. Not substantially disabled yet, many people just can't see around the corner until they make the turn and hit the wall. (I know this from personal experience.) By comparison, an AIDS diagnosis was, at least until recently, a death sentence, leaving no time to waste. In fact, AIDS activists took the rapid course of the disease into consideration in their organization of the movement. They planned ahead for succession, so that when those in leadership got sick, a new spokesperson would be ready to grab the megaphone. It was a brilliant and effective response to a devastating crisis. Such a level of organization was in short supply among those affected by Parkinson's disease.

Greg is one of a small number of Young Onset patients involved in grassroots P.D. activism. He remembers when he heard the news that I had publicly announced my diagnosis. "This is sort of embarrassing to say, but I have to tell you that my reaction was 'Thank God.' Suddenly the disease that nobody was interested in had become the disease of the moment. It spurred a tremendous amount of interest in the scientific and public arenas."

He added this: "Though I knew it would only be good news if you used your time wisely and got involved."

That day was coming. I didn't want to overreact out of sheer emotion, but to consider all of this new information very carefully. I had adopted a vaguely Taoist way of looking at things: *if you're not quite sure what to do, don't do anything yet; more will be revealed.*

I'd been given a lot to think about, not least the fact that I wasn't the only one who had done my time in the closet. And the more I thought about it, the more it struck me just how plush, well-appointed, and secure my own closet had been. My career, my position in the world, and my financial situation gave me advantages in confronting the disease that most of my fellow P.D.ers could only dream about. And now, having publicly identified myself as a person living with Parkinson's disease, there was little to keep me from playing an active role. Indeed, I was ideally positioned to step into the void left by all those patients who had so much more to lose by going public. I had a lot to be grateful for, and now found myself with a unique opportunity to give something back. But still, *if you're not quite sure what to do . . .*

By the end of 1998, my desk was covered with correspondence bearing the letterhead of various Parkinson's organizations across the country. All of them wanted my help in one way or another. The names of some of these groups implied a national reach, but on closer inspection they turned out to be local organizations affiliated with universities or hospitals or even individual researchers. Some were not set up to address research at all; instead, they were dedicating their time and resources to more basic patient concerns—caregiver support groups, quality-of-life issues, and other worthwhile considerations.

It was a bewildering and daunting landscape, and I set out to study the various players, reading their literature and meeting with them when possible. I soon began to understand that one of the reasons that the Parkinson agenda had not been carried out with a sense of purpose and unity had a lot to do with the factional nature of many of these groups, which refused to work together. The director of one foundation seeking my help even went so far as to say to me, in so many words, "Well, if you don't help us, then, at least, don't help them."

I began to get the feeling I was at a casting call for the part of "poster boy" in a production not at all ready for prime time. If and when I did become involved, I knew myself well enough to know that I'd have to make more of a contribution than merely lending my name to an organization.

But I wasn't there quite yet. I still had this other job to get back to ...

ONE LAST SPIN

New York City—December 1998
Friday night. Seven o'clock, give or take a few minutes, depending on whether my alchemy has been timed correctly and pill and brain are playing together nicely. Show time. The studio audience are in their bleacher seats and the actors are backstage waiting for cast intros. One by one, as their names are called, they run through the center of what we call the *bullpen—Spin City's* main office set—until they reach the imaginary line where the fourth wall should be. They take in the audience's applause, wave, bow, or, in the case of the guys, curtsy, then make a sharp right and circle around backstage again. I'm the last one out and usually execute the ritual in an identical fashion, except that after my wave I make a brief stop to say good luck to the writers, who are clustered around the studio's floor monitor. By the time I've rejoined Barry Bostwick, Michael Boatman, Alan Ruck, Alexander Chaplin, Connie Britton, Victoria Dillard, Richard Kind, and director Andy Cadiff, they're already in the throes of a communal preperformance whoop-up, a high-fiving, shoulder-slapping parody of a varsity football team, complete with sloppy huddle and group cheer, though nothing so crisp and uniform as GO-FIGHT-WIN—just a short, loud burst of random profanity.

Halfway through our third season, we'd never started show night any other way. But this Friday night is unlike any other. It's my first time in front of a studio audience since I disclosed my diagnosis, and I know that what happens over the next three hours or so will be a litmus test for the rest of my career—however long that might be. My friends in the cast understand what I'm going through; I can feel their support. Though a little less raucous than normal, they're even more generous with the hugs—and this is a huggy group.

When my name is called, I run down the center of the bullpen, but this time I don't stop or wave, and I don't make the sharp right to return backstage. I keep going, right through the fourth wall to the edge of the bleachers. With a boost from one of the camera operators, I climb up over the railing. Now I'm with the audience, practically stepping on the toes of the folks in the first row. I need to be this close. I need them to see that I'm okay.

And this too: I feel I need to give them permission to laugh. So I say hello, tell a few jokes, and ask if there are any questions. One young woman puts hers very simply: "How are you feeling?" "Better than I look," I answer her quickly and with a smile. "And I don't know about you, but I find me pretty damn cute." There is a brief delay and then, mercifully, a wave of warm laughter. Maybe this is going to be all right.

Minutes later, the cameras are in place and we begin playing out the episode's opening scene. We generally do each scene twice for safety, and as a rule, the laughs are always bigger the first take; by take two, the audience already knows what and where the jokes are.

Tonight is an exception. The reaction is much bigger the second time around, even though the performance is virtually identical. The first take had confirmed my worst fears. The audience *was* tentative, unsure what to expect, watching *me* rather than *my performance*. But thankfully, take two laid those fears to rest. After an initial hesitation, the laughter made it clear the audience could separate my reality from my work. As long as what I was doing was funny, they told me, they were ready to laugh.

What greeted me in the studio that first night was in keeping with the general reaction to my news, which without exception was generous, empathetic, and caring. I hadn't really known what to expect, and in fact the outpouring of support I received—there were times when it felt like an embrace—would have been impossible to predict or prepare for. My fear that I would now and forever be defined by my disease melted away. This was all *giving* and no taking. I felt as though I was being enriched by the gift of people's love and prayers, without being asked to pay for it with my identity or dignity. I was still me, people recognized, just me *plus* Parkinson's. It was the most humbling gift I've ever received.

After all the years on *Family Ties* and my many film roles, particularly the *Back to the Future* trilogy, I was used to people approaching me with variations on the theme *I feel like I've grown up with you.* I've always felt a sense of appreciation, and gratitude, to these people, who were, after all, my audience. So many of the good things in my life had come to me because of their support. The way I always thought about it, the audience and I were parties to a sort of mutually beneficial and respectful transaction. But this tsunami of goodwill washing over me now put the lie to the notion of such a clean or businesslike exchange. There is a deeper connection here, I understood, a profound relationship. *I'd grown up with them too,* and they were letting me know that they intended to stand by me.

I heard from other people too, including public figures who had been diagnosed with Parkinson's. Billy Graham and Janet Reno both sent letters and eventually a telephone message came from Muhammad Ali. For some reason, I returned his call from the phone in my bathroom. In the mirror I could see my eyes welling up as he said, in his eloquent whisper, "I'm sorry you have this, but with both of us in this fight, we're going to win now."

Then there were the people I met on the street in New York City, while out running errands or taking my kids to school. In the weeks after my disclosure, I had dozens of encounters with strangers, some of which took the most curious turns. Many people would approach me in a spirit of sympathy, or even pity, that, at least until I understood it, made me uncomfortable. These people were grieving for me, perhaps because, to them, the news of my diagnosis was fresh. Having lived with this "news" for seven years already, I was done with grief and had no patience for it. Yet after a while my understanding of these encounters deepened. When these people came up to me, I could sense them searching my eyes for some trace of fear. Finding none there, my consolers would, I'm convinced, see their own fear reflected back at them, and sometimes they would cry. Illness is a scary business, and somewhere deep inside, or maybe not so deep inside, we're all wondering if it could happen to us, and how we would cope if it did. Many times I ended up giving comfort and hugs to people who had intended to comfort me, and before saying good-bye, could hear myself reassuring *them* that they were going to be okay.

At one time or another, during times of personal struggle or loss, we've all heard people tell us they would "pray for us." Just an expression, I'd always thought, until I felt the power of that sentiment when it is offered, and *meant*, by tens of thousands of people. The feeling is overwhelming; I have no doubt that being on the receiving end of so much spiritual energy has gone a long way to sustain me over the last couple of years. I no longer underestimate the power of prayer.

Nor, it seems, do some scientists. I recently read about an experiment in which researchers at Columbia University tested the power of prayer to help women with fertility problems to conceive. A group of strangers, members of several different religious faiths in America, was asked to pray for a group of women in a Korean fertility clinic who had no knowledge of the experiment. At the same time, a separate control group at the same clinic received no prayers. At the end of the study, fifty percent of the women who'd been prayed for got pregnant, while only twenty-six percent of the control group conceived. This is exactly the opposite of what the researchers had expected—their stated intention had been to *dis*prove the efficacy of prayer.

The reaction to my announcement allowed me to return to my regular routine with a new sense of freedom. Though I still struggled to appear smooth while at work—Mike Flaherty, after all, didn't have P.D.—I no longer felt pressure to hide my symptoms the rest of the time. Now I could choose where and when to medicate, and to do it for comfort rather than camouflage.

Without my even realizing it, my whole system of symptom management changed. I began to see that being "off" in a public situation was really only a problem if *I* found it troublesome—if it kept me from doing something I wanted to do. If not, then being "off" was downgraded to the status of mere inconvenience. My tremoring, shuffling, and dyskinesias might earn me second looks from people, but what the hell, I was *that guy from TV*. I was used to getting second looks. So what if the second look now might mean, *oh, that's right, I heard he has Parkinson's.*

One evening a few months after I revealed my diagnosis, Tracy and I attended a benefit fund-raiser in New York City, one of those glitzy galas with speeches, a charity auction, and for a grand finale, a big-name musical act—in this case, the Who. All through the early part of the evening, during the speechifying and fund-raising, the lights in the banquet hall were ablaze, and there at table number six sat shaky me, extravagantly symptomatic. Maybe it had something to do with the salmon appetizers—sometimes eating too much protein interferes with the Sinemet. Rigid almost to the point of being frozen, except for a persistent flapping in my right arm, I was aware that many of the diners at the surrounding tables couldn't keep their eyes off me. It didn't bother me a bit, although I did try to be extra careful during the auction part of the proceedings—having Parkinson's at an auction can be an expensive proposition.

"I just hope my pills kick in by the time the Who comes on," I told Tracy. "Because I want to be able to relax and enjoy the music." That's all I was thinking about. I realized this represented a 180-degree change in outlook, a change made possible by my willingness to let others in on my disease. A year earlier, I would have looked at the same situation the other way around. *If I can just hold it together now so nobody notices*, I'd have told myself, *I don't care how I feel when the lights go down and the show starts.* Disclosure had allowed me to rearrange life so that I could get more from it. Sure enough, the lights went down, Pete Townshend windmilled, Roger Daltrey screamed, and I felt that welcome, quick couple of spasms in my left leg—*oh baby, I love it when the drugs kick in.*

With my P.D. out in the open, negotiating my responsibilities while finishing out the 1998–99 *Spin City* season was significantly easier than it would have been had I remained closeted. Whether people knew or didn't know, however, made no difference to the disease, and my symptoms continued steadily to worsen. Even without the burden of maintaining a false front, the stress of the job was still considerable, and by the beginning of April, when the show wrapped and we all went off on hiatus, it was clear that I was in worse shape than when we had begun production the previous August.

In preparation for the next season, we made some changes, hoping to lighten my load. One of them was Gary's idea. He and I had reconciled our differences—Gary had called to show support soon after the events of Thanksgiving, and I consulted him often on various production questions. "You know, there's no law that says you have to do the show on Friday nights," Gary said. "Why don't you film on Tuesdays instead? That way you get a nice two-day rest in the middle of your workweek."

In June, as usual, we assembled the producers and writing staff to hash out story ideas for the next season. The writers would develop these over the summer months and have them in script form by the time we returned to work in August. It was at one of these meetings that I suggested introducing a new cast member, someone with a certain amount of notoriety, who could take some of the pressure off me. My partner Danelle Black mentioned Heather Locklear, erstwhile femme fatale from both *Dynasty* and *Melrose Place*. Tracy and I had shared a table with Heather and her husband, Bon Jovi guitarist Richie Sambora, at the Golden Globes a few years back, and I remembered them as funny and relaxed dinner companions. We spent a lot of the night kidding one another about being at the "loser" table because, while Heather and I had both been nominated, neither of us took home the statue that year.

"She'd be a home run for us," I told the *Spin City* writing staff. True, she hadn't done a sitcom before, but I didn't think she'd have any problem with the comedy. After all, *Melrose* and *Dynasty* had been so campy, they were just a laugh track away from being sitcoms anyway. So the offer went out, and we were thrilled when she accepted. The move paid off, and in the end, I believe, it secured the future of the show.

Still, even with Heather on board to carry many of the story lines and handle much of the publicity work that had previously fallen to me, I realized early that autumn that my days as an actor on a weekly television series were nearing an end. It seemed that no matter how many concessions I made to my illness—fewer workdays, less rehearsal time, delegating more and more of the peripheral duties—it was never enough. The disease continued to take its toll. I could still get the job done, but I found that most of my time off the set was now spent resting, girding myself for the hurdle of the next episode. More than ever, the energy it took to perform my job well robbed me of the opportunity to devote time to the other interests in my life. There just wasn't much left for my family and for what was becoming a growing involvement in Parkinson's advocacy work.

U.S. Virgin Islands—December 31, 1999
After reading this far, you might conclude that all of my epiphanies come to me at or near a beach. Well, here's another one. Tracy and I were snorkeling with Sam, while Aquinnah and Schuyler were playing with friends at the shoreline. It was late in the afternoon, the best time, we were told, to spot sea turtles. I was dubious. We'd been coming to this resort for the last three winter vacations and I hadn't seen one yet. But now, directly ahead of me in the blue-green water, Sam was pointing excitedly. Then his head disappeared above the surface. T and I popped up to join him. "Did you see it?" he sputtered. "It's a big one."

The three of us submerged again just in time to see a sea turtle push off the sandy bottom where he had been resting, trailing a billowing cloud of fine white sand. Keeping a respectful distance, we swam along behind him as he grazed the strands of sea grass just inside the coral reef. Satisfied they'd finally gotten a good look at one of these elusive creatures, Tracy and Sam made their way back to dry land, but I was mesmerized.

As the turtle and I swam on together in disjointed tandem, the turtle trying to ignore me and me trying to pose no threat, I thought of all those documentaries I had watched as a kid: thousands of hatchling baby sea turtles making their way toward the safety of the ocean while seabirds dive-bomb, picking them off one by one. Only a handful will survive. And that's just the beginning of a turtle's ordeal. I noticed that this one was missing a sizable chunk of the rear flipper on his left side. How old was this guy? I wondered. An adult, obviously. What wars had he been through?

Leave him be, I thought, he's earned his peace. And I turned back toward shore. When I got back to the beach, Tracy was lying on a towel reading her book. I gently took it from her, puckering the pages with my wet, salty fingers.

"I'm done," I said.

"That's nice, honey," she replied. "Why don't you dry off while I read a few more pages, and then we'll get the kids ready for dinner."

"With the show, I mean. I'm done with the show. I'm going to retire at the end of the season."

The 52nd Annual Emmy Awards—Shrine Auditorium,
Los Angeles—September 10, 2000

After four seasons and one hundred episodes playing Mike Flaherty on *Spin City*, this was my fourth Emmy nomination for the role. The three previous years I had gone home empty-handed, but Tracy and I never failed to have a good time at the Emmys. It gave us an excuse for a rare romantic weekend getaway; we'd check into our favorite L.A. hotel, spend our days lounging by the rooftop pool, and enjoy a nice meal or two out. It was also a chance to catch up with old friends we'd left behind when we moved to New York.

Win or no win, the Emmys was always a celebration, and that was especially true this year. My final *Spin* episode aired May 23, 2000, though I'd announced my pending retirement back in January, shortly after we got back from the Caribbean. Unsure what my leaving would mean for the show's future, I wanted to give the cast and crew plenty of warning, in case they had to find work or relocate their families. When the farewell episode was broadcast, I was overwhelmed once again by the public reaction. A third of the television audience that night tuned in for my last episode.

Even better was this: It turned out the show would be able to carry on after all. Gary Goldberg agreed to return as executive producer, provided the show moved operations to the West Coast. Heather and most of the cast would come back as well, and Charlie Sheen would join the show as the new deputy mayor. I felt bad for the New York crew who would have to find new jobs, but I was thrilled for the cast and for Charlie, who, besides being a talented actor, was an old friend. The survival of the show was good news for me too, since I owned a stake in it. I'd get to watch Charlie do my old job and still receive a paycheck. God bless America.

What made this Emmy weekend really special, though, had more to do with Tracy than me. Earlier in the year she had turned in a masterful, heart-wrenching performance as a rape victim on *Law and Order: SVU*. The guest role earned her a richly deserved Emmy nomination, her first. The awards in the guest performance categories had actually been given out the previous week and unfortunately Tracy hadn't won, but during the ceremonies a clip of her work was shown, along with that of her fellow nominees. It felt perfect that we should share the evening in this way. Throughout our marriage, the circumstances of my career and then my illness had put tremendous pressure on Tracy's aspirations as an actor, and this recognition from her peers was overdue.

When Gillian Anderson called my name to collect my award for Lead Actor in a Comedy Series, it would be disingenuous to suggest that I was surprised. While I was proud of my work that season, I would have to be in deep denial not to recognize that I was the sentimental favorite. But honestly, it was Tracy who I was thinking about when I bounded up to the stage. We make a point of not being one of those gushy Hollywood couples; we treasure the intimacy of our relationship and hold it close, but this time I couldn't help but gush. Most of my acceptance speech was dedicated to expressions of admiration, gratitude, and love for my wife.

It was a great moment, and I was fully in it. If I'd had a second to think about it, I might have reflected on what a different person I was now, compared to the young man—the boy—who stood before this audience accepting this award fifteen years earlier. Overwhelmed and completely unsure of myself, the joke I offered that evening—"I feel four feet tall"—betrayed a lot more about who I was than I realized at the time. And though this time I didn't say the words, there would have been no better way to mark my progress since that long ago evening than to have said, very simply, "I feel five foot five."

Nothing more, nothing less, just exactly who I am.

BACK TO THE FUTURE

This is the true joy in life, the being used for a purpose recognized by yourself as a mighty one; the being thoroughly worn out before you are thrown on the scrap heap; the being a force of nature instead of a feverish selfish little clod of ailments and grievances complaining that the world will not devote itself to making you happy.
—George Bernard Shaw

Senate Appropriations Subcommittee Hearing, Washington, D.C.—
September 28, 1999
The setting is as intimidating as it gets: one of those Senate hearing rooms you've seen so many times on TV, where the person giving testimony at some point invariably covers his microphone and leans over to hear the whispered cautions of his lawyer. Now I am that witness, preparing to speak before a Senate subcommittee. Dozens of flashbulbs pop in front of me, blinding me momentarily. I'm not here because I'm in trouble. Or rather I *am*—along with nearly one and a half million other Parkinson's patients on whose behalf I appear—*in serious trouble*, but of a kind far graver than any group of senators could ever cause. These senators can, however, help to get us out of this trouble, and that's why I've come to Washington.

At issue is federal funding for Parkinson's research, which, as I told the committee, is inadequate and disproportionate to the amounts devoted to other areas of medical research. The underfunding of P.D. research, I tell these senators, represents a serious missed opportunity, given the current state of the science and the very real prospect of a cure. Scientists testifying after me stressed that a cure could come within ten years, but only if sufficient financial commitment is made to the effort.

My presence at these hearings marks a momentous personal step. While it's been almost a year since I first revealed I have P.D., this is the first time I've ever taken a public position of advocacy. *If you're not quite sure what to do, don't do anything yet; more will be revealed.* Well, now more *had* been revealed, like the fact that my presence at this hearing might make a difference. That, at least, is what Joan Samuelson, founder and director of the Parkinson's Action Network (PAN), told me when she called to recruit me for this trip to Washington. She was putting together a panel of people, including scientists and patients, to implore Congress to direct more money to the National Institute of Neurological Disorders and Stroke.

Joan is an attorney from northern California who was diagnosed with Parkinson's in the late 1980s at the age of thirty-seven. She continued in her legal career until 1991, when there was a push by Democrats in Congress to lift the Bush administration's ban on federal funding of fetal tissue research. (Scientists wanted to learn if healthy brain cells from discarded fetuses could be transplanted into the brains of people with P.D.; antiabortion activists had persuaded the Bush administration to ban the work.) Frustrated by the inaction of various national Parkinson's foundations, Joan moved to Washington and became a lobbyist. Her efforts, along with those of Anne Udall, daughter of the late Congressman Mo Udall (himself a P.D. patient), played an important part in getting the ban lifted in 1992. Since then Joan has continued in her role as a leading Parkinson's advocate, founding PAN and emerging as a true hero of the Parkinson's movement.

After the hearing, our little group of patients and scientists embarked on a tour of the offices of several senators and congressmen. We met with Representative Bill Young, chairman of the House appropriations committee, Representative Jerry Lewis, chairman of the defense appropriations subcommittee, and on the Senate side, (then) Majority Leader Trent Lott (along with a dozen or so Republican senators he'd assembled in his office), and Senator Arlen Specter, chairman of the Senate appropriations subcommittee overseeing NIH. Everyone gave us plenty of time and a respectful hearing. And while the senators didn't come through with any extra appropriations, both chairmen on the House side did end up making specific directives that increased funding for P.D. research.

As Joan and I left the corridors of power we must have looked like a pair of drunken sailors; the day's hectic events had brought our symptoms to full boil, and both of us were a little wobbly. But something else was going on with Joan—I noticed that she was fighting back tears. "Am I missing something?" I said, baffled. "I thought we did pretty well back there."

"Oh, it was fantastic," she said. "It's just that it's always been so hard to get anyone to even *listen* to us, never mind invite us *into their offices.*" She flashed me a smile. "It's a whole new world."

Snippets of my testimony were featured on several of the nightly news broadcasts. One line in particular from my prepared statement got a lot of play: "In my forties, I can expect challenges most people wouldn't face until their seventies and eighties, if ever. But with your help, if we all do everything we can to eradicate this disease, when I'm in my fifties I'll be dancing at my children's weddings." I had made a deliberate choice to appear before the subcommittee without medication. It seemed to me that this occasion demanded that my testimony about the effects of the disease, and the urgency we as a community were feeling, be *seen* as well as heard. For people who had never observed me in this kind of shape, the transformation must have been startling.

Later that day, when I finally got a chance to see the hearing broadcast in its entirety on C-SPAN, I was struck too, but by a transformation of a completely different kind. Sure, the symptoms were severe—I looked as though an invisible bully were harassing me while I read my statement. My head jerked, skewing my reading glasses as if the back of my skull were being slapped. I was fighting to control the pages of my speech, my arms bouncing as if someone were trying to knock the paper out of my hands. But through it all, I never wavered. I saw in my eyes an even, controlled sense of purpose I had never seen in myself before. There was, ironically enough, a steadiness in me, even as I was shaking like a leaf. *I couldn't be this still until I could no longer keep still.* The bully attacked from every angle, even from within my own body, but I wasn't about to give in, or be distracted from what I had come there to do.

Instead, I issued a challenge that took the form of a promise: "The time for quietly soldiering on is through. The war against Parkinson's is a winnable war, and I have resolved to play a role in that victory."

WORKING MYSELF OUT OF A JOB

In the last couple of years, I've gone from talking to my agent on a cellular phone to discussing cellular biology with some of the world's leading scientists. It's a whole different world. If I'm with my peers in the entertainment business, I can at least fake being one of the smarter people in the room. In a group of neuroscientists, I just try to listen carefully and take a lot of notes.

People often refer to my role as an advocate and the work I do with the foundation I formed after leaving *Spin City* as my new *job*. I suppose it is, although that's not the term that most readily comes to mind. These days I have a lot of jobs; many of them aren't exclusive, and few if any fit into the 9-to-5 routine. My *job* is whatever I happen to be doing at the moment—whether it's giving a speech, changing a diaper, writing a book, or recording the voice of a computer-generated mouse. The work of the foundation has, however, become my *passion*, and I bring to it every resource, both internal and external, available to me.

During her interview for the position of the executive director for the Michael J. Fox Foundation for Parkinson's Research, I explained to Debi Brooks that our goal as an institution was nothing less than planned obsolescence. What I had in mind was an organization built for speed, eschewing bureaucracy and taking an entrepreneurial approach toward helping researchers do what they say can be done: find a cure for Parkinson's within the decade. Our optimism on this score was matched only by our impatience.

"I remember you warning me," recalls Debi, forty-two, a former vice president at Goldman Sachs, "that if I ever found myself making plans for a Tenth Annual Fund-Raising Dinner, I should consider my-self fired."

There was no existing blueprint for accomplishing what we wanted to do. Debi and the board (an extraordinary group of individ-uals drawn not only from my world, the entertainment business, but also from Debi's, the New York financial community) were faced with the challenge of inventing a system that could identify the researchers doing the best work and then get money into their hands as quickly as possible.

The work of medical researchers and the funding of their research has historically proceeded at a snail's pace. It takes nearly a year, for example, from the time the National Institutes of Health receive grant applications to the time their money is awarded. For our foundation's own grant-making procedure we set about speeding that system up. Working with a scientific advisory board led by Dr. William Langston, we devised a way to streamline the process by simplifying the applica-tion form and assembling a scientific review board that would iden-tify the most meritorious proposals within three months.

We knew we were really onto something when the NIH ap-proached the foundation to ask if they could funnel a portion of their own funds through our fast-track process. By the end of our first year we'd already achieved two major goals that even in my most opti-mistic moments I'd thought would take years to reach. In quest of a cure for Parkinson's disease, we had identified some of the most promising research. And we'd influenced the federal government to adopt our methodology and sense of urgency in funding that research.

Since my first testimony in Washington, I have often been called upon to represent the P.D. community in the media, most notably during the national debate about embryonic stem cell research that monopolized the news during much of the summer of 2001.

Embryonic stem cells are taken from ten-day-old embryos left over from in vitro fertilization and discarded by fertility clinics. Thousands of these unwanted cell clusters, smaller than the head of a pin, are frozen and then, after a time, routinely destroyed every year. Most cell biologists believe that because these cells are too young to have dedicated themselves to any one physiological function—brain cell, kidney cell, bone marrow cell—they are "pluripotent." That is, they have the potential to become any type of human cell. Introduced, for example, into the substantia nigra of a Parkinson's patient, they could evolve into dopamine-producing cells.

The implications are staggering. If the potential of stem cell research is realized, it would mean an end to the suffering of millions of people—a rescue, a cure. But the potential benefits are not limited to P.D. Stem cells could lead to breakthroughs in developing treatments and cures for almost any terminal or catastrophic disease you can think of. This is one of the reasons that support for this work has galvanized a coalition of advocates from just about every patient community in the nation. If stem cell research succeeds, there isn't a person in the country who won't benefit, or know somebody who will.

There is controversy, however. Even though the embryos from which these cells are derived are developed outside the womb and routinely discarded, antiabortion activists adamantly oppose using them for research no matter how many people stand to benefit.

During the 2000 presidential campaign, it was well known within the world of medical advocacy, if not to the general public, that George W. Bush opposed the use of stem cells, even though several key conservative, and even right-to-life Republican legislators, supported the research. The issue cut across the usual political lines, probably because disease is itself nonpartisan. In the weeks before the election, I wrote an Op-Ed piece for the *New York Times* suggesting to the then governor of Texas that to allow for federal funding of this area of study—one with the potential to save the lives of millions of present and future Americans—represented exactly the kind of compassionate conservatism he espoused. What could possibly be more "pro-life"?

As important as the issue was to us in the patient community, we were surprised and gratified when stem cell research received so much media attention the following summer. I found myself in the middle of a national political debate, giving interview after interview and personally lobbying administration officials. In the end, the newly elected President Bush was forced to take a position, and he ultimately allowed some federal funding of this work to go forward, albeit in a limited fashion. It was not everything we were hoping for, but it was more than the president's initial position would have led anyone to expect.

I had spoken out regarding stem cells as a patient, not as the president of a foundation. The foundation itself is not in any way political—our sole concern is to identify the best research and then to raise money and distribute it to the scientists conducting that research as quickly as possible. Because of our entrepreneurial approach, however, we can react to political currents promptly and, sometimes, creatively. Shortly after President Bush strictly limited the number of stem cell lines available for study, we offered a $2.5 million grant to any researcher or scientific institution that develops a line of dopaminergic cells—cells capable of producing dopamine. We won't allow ourselves to be deterred, distracted, or hampered in our mission.

When I engage in public debate on these and other issues, I do so as a patient first, but there's no question my notoriety helps. One of the reasons I can raise funds and attract attention to the cause is because I am a celebrity. And yet I am wary of being regarded merely as a "poster boy." In fact, when we first launched the foundation, I didn't want it to bear my name. At one point I thought I had come up with a terrific name: PDCure. Before I brought it to the board, however, I thought I'd try it out on Tracy. I wrote the name down on a piece of paper, put it in front of her, and said, "What do you think?"

After a beat, she looked up at me and said flatly, "Pedicure?"

My name attracts attention, provides access, and therefore helps us achieve our goals somewhat faster than we otherwise might. Is this fair? Is it right? Well, that's a complicated question, but the fact remains: *I have this disease.* This is not a *role* I'm playing. Like any other patient, my participation is uniquely informed by my experience. I know the issues, I'm compelled to understand the science, and I share my community's sense of urgency. Quite apart from all that, I happen to possess this most rare and useful currency—celebrity—and I've discovered a wonderful way to spend it.

Washington, D.C.—September 14, 2000
Not long ago I spoke once again in front of a Senate subcommittee, this time about the urgent importance of federal funding for embryonic stem cell research. I devoted a portion of my testimony that day to the issue of celebrity advocacy, to exactly why it was that I had been invited to speak and why I accepted the invitation. This is what I told the senators:

> By now, many of you have heard my story. But you haven't heard this story, about a thirty-eight-year-old book editor, Anne, whose P.D. caused her to lose her job at a publishing house, plunging her from New York's middle class into poverty. She's now forced to live on Medicare and SSDI benefits, which are nearly consumed by her monthly medication costs alone. Nor have you heard about Greg, a former lawyer, now living on disability, who corresponds with me regularly. Two weeks ago, his friends and family watched in horror as he disappeared into stony immobility while waiting for a prescription delivery that had been delayed. Nothing demonstrates more dramatically just how tenuous "normalcy" is for someone afflicted with Parkinson's. And you've never heard about Brenda, a fifty-three-year-old former computer specialist. Recently, her drugs failed to kick in and she found herself frozen in the bathtub with no one to help her. She remained there for hours until enough medication reached her brain to allow her to crawl out of the tub. By this time she was suffering a panic attack and couldn't speak. She finally reached her computer, and used that to contact friends for help.
>
> None of these people mind that I get more attention than

they do. What they tell me, over and over, is that if I get a shot in front of a microphone—I should start talking.

So here I am.

A TREE GROWS IN BURNABY

Middlegate Apartments, Burnaby, British Columbia — 1971

When I was ten years old and living in that three-story walk-up with the unheated swimming pool and the strip mall across the street, we had a mouse in our apartment. It wasn't a pest, at least not to me anyway, but a pet; a tiny white rodent with pink ears, eyes, and nose. I kept him in an aquarium with one of those little go-nowhere-fast exercise wheels, a water bottle, and a section of window screen laid on top and weighted down with a book to secure it in place.

As it turned out, the book wasn't quite weighty enough. I probably should have gone with *War and Peace*, because the mouse escaped. The timing of the breakout couldn't have been worse. Nana was staying with us for a couple of nights while her new apartment in the neighborhood was being readied for her to move in. Terrified of mice, she also had a bad heart, and everyone, but especially me, was worried that at some point, perhaps while she was asleep, the mouse might skitter across her bed, or maybe her forehead, and send her into cardiac arrest.

Fortunately, that didn't happen. Nana moved into her new place, and the mouse was never seen again. I was forbidden to buy another one. Dad confiscated the aquarium and filled it with potting soil and a couple of old houseplants. The newly converted terrarium was relegated to our apartment's narrow balcony, but that was the last attention that those philodendrons or spider plants or whatever they were ever received. Within weeks the plants were dead. The next summer Nana too would be gone, her heart finally giving out.

The following Christmas my mother placed a dish of unshelled walnuts on the coffee table. I didn't eat walnuts, but I picked one up and carried it around with me for a while. At some point I wandered out on the balcony, dropped the walnut into the aquarium, and pushed it down with my thumb into the earth. And I forgot all about it until the next spring, when to my amazement, a tiny green shoot pushed out of the soil. The walnut had taken root. Perhaps because my nonlinear kid logic connected the aquarium to the mouse escape to my grandmother, I always regarded this tiny miracle as a message from Nana, a sign that she was still with me. I don't remember telling anyone else about it, though I do remember tending the seedling for a while, making sure to water it and occasionally move it into the sunlight. But springtime also means spring cleaning, and I came home from school one day to find that my baby walnut tree was gone.

Los Angeles — March 1995
The filming of *American President* was winding down. Sam, Tracy, and our two new baby daughters, Aquinnah and Schuyler, were waiting for me at home in New York. I was just beginning to entertain the notion of a return to television so that in the future I wouldn't have to be away from them like this any more than necessary. This was a time of tremendous optimism and renewal in my life, and I owed a large part of my happiness to my work with Joyce. She too was back in New York, of course, but I kept my regularly scheduled 9:00 A.M. appointments and would wake up early to call her on the telephone at 6:00 A.M., West Coast time. One morning I preceded my phone call with a fax. I had woken up with a dream, scribbled it down on hotel stationery and sent it ahead to Joyce.

> *I'm on our farm in Vermont. I'm helping a young boy, about ten years old (Sam? Me?) to cross a pasture where horses are grazing. On the other side is the caretaker's house. Once we get there, he leads me into a large country kitchen and I'm amazed at what I see. On every surface—the table, countertop, and fireplace mantel—are jars and planters filled with budding plants and saplings. It's a home nursery and it's flourishing. We walk across the room, and in the corner is a built-in cabinet. The boy says to me with a smile, "Wait till you see this," and then swings the cupboard door wide open.*

It's hard to process what I'm seeing. It can't be possible—but inside this tight, dark, airless space, a tree has been growing. Growing isn't even the word for it, really—it's absolutely thriving. In response to the tight quarters it's taken on the appearance of a bonsai tree. The trunk and branches are thick, and now, with the door flung open, the tree continues to grow right before my eyes, as if in time-lapse, new branches reaching out into the airy light of the kitchen and bursting into leaf.

I know instantly what kind of tree it is. It's the walnut tree. And it's been growing all this time.

Tracy Pollan

Acknowledgments

Aquinnah and Schuyler, now that Shaky Dad's book is done, I'll be taking you to school more often. Sam, thanks for making the extra effort with your homework so I'd have more time to do my own. Tracy Pollan, my wife, my best friend, I love you. It was one thing for you to go through this journey with me, but to then also allow me to share so many intimate details with others is characteristically generous. I'm still amazed that in far less time than it took for me to conceive, create, and deliver this book you managed to do the same with our fourth child, Esmé Annabelle. (Okay, I did help with the conception.) She's a miracle—and there's one more wedding I look forward to dancing at. We have so many more happy chapters to write together. This family, this life, this love make me a lucky man indeed.

My mother, Phyllis Fox, deserves much of the credit for this book—and I am not only referring to the hours she spent on the phone, walking me through our family's fascinating history. (I wish I could have included more of it.) She and my father, William Fox, were also responsible for supplying me with the resilience and strength I needed to get through this book and this life. In preparing to write, I also spoke at length with my big brother, Steve, about many things, but particularly that difficult episode around the time of Dad's passing. He understood why I had to include it here, and perhaps because it was merely a passing shadow across an otherwise deep and lasting friendship, he gave me his blessing. I'd like to say to my sisters, Karen, Jackie, and Kelli, that I have learned so much from being a part of this family and I love you all more than I could ever express here. Perhaps another book.

Joyce, thank you for everything. Working on this project required spending more hours alone than I ever had before and you helped make it possible for me to actually enjoy the company.

I knew from the outset that I would have to write this book myself. The story was too personal for it to be told in anyone's words but my own (100,000 of them give or take, at least 40,000 of them personal pronouns). Still, I've never done this before. I'm not a professional writer. I understood that I would need a mentor in this process, an experienced and talented editor, preferably someone I was close to, to show me the ropes, to be honest with me about what worked and what did not. Luckily, my brother-in-law Michael ("Keep Going") Pollan agreed to serve in this role. Only with so wise and patient a teacher could I have met this seemingly impossible challenge. Over the last twelve months, Mike slogged with me through the events of my life when he might have preferred to concentrate on the events of his own, particularly the recent success of his own book, the brilliant

and best-selling *The Botany of Desire.* My gratitude extends to his wife
Judith Belzer and son Isaac for allowing me to intrude on so much of
their family time. Michael's insight, friendship, humor, and passion for
the possibilities of the written word were not all that he shared with
me. He was also kind enough to introduce me to his agent, Amanda
"Binky" Urban at ICM. Thanks, Binky, for your support, enthusiasm,
and expertise in guiding me through the labyrinthine world of pub-
lishing. And I thought show business was a fun house.

In December of 2000, just as I was beginning to write about
Gainesville, Florida, and the irrepressible dancing pinkie, I began to
look for a writer's assistant. Basically, I needed someone to type for
me. I can't operate a keyboard. I wish I could blame it on Parkinson's,
but I never could type. Heidi Pollock showed up at my office door
and stayed on the job a full year. Not only can she type faster than I
can think, she provided a method to my madness, helping me to organize, research, and when I was really stuck, find the *mot juste.* Heidi
proved to be a supremely intelligent, funny, and invaluable partner, and
I would not have survived the experience without her.

The belief and confidence that everyone at Hyperion has shown
in this project, even as I missed deadline after deadline, has been tremendous. President Bob Miller, thanks again for your wonderful letters;
the generous compliments wrapped in sports metaphors always provided a lift just when I most needed one. And Leslie Wells, I couldn't
have asked for a smarter or more understanding editor. Thanks too to
her assistant, Carrie Covert, and to Martha Levin who helped get the
ball rolling. Bob Iger, you were right—there's no place like home.

This book would never had been written were it not for the support and encouragement of the P.D. community. Ever since I went
public with my diagnosis, my fellow patients have been my greatest
teachers. They've helped me to see that my story is not only my story,
that a great many of the 40,000 first-person pronouns here are
plural—because we *are* a we, in the boat together, and awaiting the
same rescue. Don't lose hope, because it's coming.

Not all of them realize it, but all of the following people helped
make this book possible, and they have my love and gratitude:

Dr. Allan Ropper, Dr. Bernard Kruger, Dr. Bruce Cook, Corky and Stephen Pollan, Lori Pollan and Allan Bahn, Dana Pollan and Mitchell Stern, Danelle Black, Joan Samuelson, Debi Brooks, Michael Claeys, Mindy Miller, Greg Mann, the staff of The Michael J. Fox Foundation for Parkinson's Research, Lonnie and Muhammad Ali, Dr. Mitchell Blutt, Joyce and Barry Cohen, Steve Cohen, Glenn Dubin, David Golub, John Griffin, Irwin Helford, Jeffrey Katzenberg, Kathleen Kennedy, Milly and Mort Kondracke, Fredric Mack, Nora McAniff, Michael Price, Lily Safra, Jeffrey Kiel, Carolyn and Curtis Schenker, Donna Shalala, Fred Weiss, Dr. J. William Langston, Jeffrey Kordower, Jackie Hamada, Miyoko Love, Natasha Klibansky, Kim Kimbro, Iwa Goldstein, Amuna Ali, Bridgette Roux-Lough, Nanci Ryder, Leslie Sloane Zelnik, Cliff Gilbert-Lurie, Skip Brittenham, Marian Toy, Raquel Tinio, Glenn Koetzner, Chris Coady, Greg Wasson, Peter Benedek, Mark Seliger, Michael Rosen, Sally Fanjoy, Gavin De Becker, Gary David Goldberg, Bill Lawrence, Andy Cadiff, Justin Sternberg, Bryan Lourd, Kevin Huvane, Bob Philpott, Cam Neely, Jimmy Nugent, Pat O'Brien, the cast, crew, and writers of *Spin City* (Tom Hertz and Tim Hobert, thanks for the joke), Bob Gersh, Todd Gold, Barbara Walters, Jennifer Grey and Clark Gregg, Denis Leary, Chris Rock, Jon Stewart, Amanda and Ted Demme, Emma Tillinger, James Taylor, Arlene and Alan Alda, Phoebe Cates and Kevin Kline (love that Shaw quote), the people at DreamWorks, ABC-TV, and so many more . . .